"Dynamic, Dazzling and Awesome are synonymous with Florence Littauer—the person, the author, the speaker. Florence is one of God's gifts—*Dare to Dream* is her gift to you . . . and a perfect gift for those you care for. Buy it!"

Judith Briles
Author of *When God Says No,*
The Christian Woman's Guide to Money,
The Confidence Factor

"Florence was the keynote speaker at our Leadership Conference, where over 1,000 businessmen and women sat spellbound as she delivered the speech, *Dare to Dream*, from her forthcoming book. It was challenging, touching, and hit home with a message of great impact on all of our lives. Our business will never be the same."

Craig and Carole Holiday
Owners
Holiday Consulting International

The following are a few of the comments taken from evaluation forms regarding Florence's presentation at FHP's Senior Plan Annual Regional Sales Meeting:

"Superb! Florence has added a great joy to my life. She really brought excitement to this session, providing each individual with her special touch of success. What a close!" "Exciting! Let's have her again." "My public speaking role model!" "Best part of this whole event." "Fabulous!" "A truly grand finale." "She is the best speaker I've ever heard." "Humorous and educational. you saved the best for last." "What an eye opener, Great!"

Frances L. Bertini
Training Manager
FHP, Inc.

"Since the vast majority of people go to their grave with their dreams unfulfilled, this practical book, written in an entertaining way, can facilitate not only encouragement and dreams, but will show how to continue the process, to transform God's inspiration into a consistent daily reality. I can't wait!"

Gwen Sherman
Executive Senior Director
Mary Kay Cosmetics

"Few people on earth can move an audience like Florence Littauer. She's insightful, humorous, and practical. She was instrumental in helping me discover the importance of personality differences. But what I've appreciated about her most of all is the influence she's had on my oldest son; who grew in his skill as an encouraging discipler to a group of high school kids he ministers to."

Gary Smalley
Bestselling author and family expert

"Florence Littauer has actually lived the title to her book *Dare to Dream*. She is the message herself. Don't miss this phenomenal opportunity."

Cavette Robert
Founder and Chairman Emeritus
National Speakers Association.

"What great news to hear that Florence Littauer is coming again to share with more New Zealanders, her unique blend of life experience, perception of human nature and warm understanding—and she makes it such fun to listen to her!

An experience not to be missed!"

Dame Cath Tizard
Governor General
New Zealand

"Florence Littauer has the wonderful ability to inspire others through her teachings. I have found her material valuable not only in my personal life, but in my business life as well. *Dare to Dream* promises to be her best effort yet."

Tom Hopkins
Nationally known author, sales trainer, motivator

DARE TO DREAM

DARE TO DREAM

Florence Littauer

WORD PUBLISHING

Dallas · London · Vancouver · Melbourne

Library of Congress Cataloging-in-Publication Data

Littauer, Florence, 1928–
    Dare to dream : beat the odds and win personal success / by
Florence Littauer.
        p. cm.
      ISBN 0-8499-0736-5
      1. Success—Religious aspects—Christianity.   I. Title.
    BV4598.3.L57 1991
    158—dc20   91-15147
                                                                              CIP

1 2 3 4 5 9 AGF 5 4 3 2

Printed in the United States of America

Table of Contents

FLORENCE LITTAUER

"The only thing that stands between a woman and what she
wants in life is often only the will to try and
the faith to believe that it is possible."

Thank you for sharing your talents with us.
With Appreciation and Respect
Dexter and Birdie Yager
Yager Free Enterprise Day
August 31–September 2, 1990
Charlotte, N.C.–Rock Hill, S. C.

DEDICATION

In April of 1986 I was presenting a leadership seminar in Ohio encouraging the participants to realize their potential. CLASS trains people to think logically and creatively, to be alert to everything in their surroundings, and to prepare a simple message based on their own experience and knowledge. Throughout the three days, the staff and I use different types of simple outlines to reinforce the importance of thinking in some sense of order. We need to see outlines so that we can think outlines, so that we can write outlines before we can speak in outline form. For practice I give a magazine ad to staff members and ask them to outline it and give an impromptu talk.

My brother Jim, an outstanding orator, was attending this CLASS. For fun, I asked him to create an instant outline and give us all a mini-message. He came up to the front of the class, drew himself up to his full height, and began to speak in a deep voice. He got instant attention when he said, "Today as we sit here in Ohio, my wife Katie and daughter Cindy are backpacking through mainland China." He then explained that he and Katie had always loved to dream, not impossible dreams, but dreams that were beyond the ordinary. They had taught their six children to think big, to expect to study abroad, and to learn foreign languages. (Cindy speaks both Chinese and Hebrew.) They also encouraged them to appreciate art and music, and to never be content with the status quo. In encouraging their children, they had done the same themselves.

Katie had a dream to go to China, spend time with the people in the villages and learn a whole new culture, all without any official tour guide. Jim explained in his message that Katie had to dare to dream that she might one day do this. She had to prepare the dream intellectually and physically so that she could wear the dream, as she was at that moment doing. "She called this morning," Jim added, "and last night she slept in a seedy youth hostel in Canton." We all shuddered at the thought, but Jim went on to conclude, "When she comes home, she will share the dream with our church and with the Chinese friends she has in Ohio!"

We were all impressed with Jim's impromptu presentation and with Katie's pluck and fortitude, but I was also delighted with his outline:

- Dare to Dream
- Prepare the Dream
- Wear the Dream
- Share the Dream

As I repeated Jim's outline with future classes, I was aware of their excited and approving response. What a simple way to express the good life. We must take the risk and *dare to dream*. We can't sit around and wait for good fortune to drop in our laps, but we must *prepare the dream*. When the time is right, we must move out and *wear the dream*, put it on as a garment. And when we have achieved some measure of success or learning or creativity, we should *share the dream* and what we have learned with others to help them and cut down on their time of preparation.

From Jim's instant outline came the framework for this book. As I thought about the four steps, I realized that some of us need to *repair the dream*, so I inserted that note of hope.

I thank Jim for giving me his outline and Katie for living it.

I dedicate this book to my two brothers who have been an inspiration to me from the time of their birth, who have followed this outline for life, and who have kept me laughing even in difficult times:

Rev. James Walter Chapman   (Bath, Ohio)
"Ron" Ralph Frederick Chapman   (Dallas, Texas)

All three of us had to stretch to even *dare to dream*. We did everything we could to *prepare our dream* so that we could now in mid-life *wear the dream*. We've each had moments when we had to *repair the dream* and we are all eager to *share our dream* with others so long as we shall live.

Florence Chapman Littauer
Lake San Marcos, California

THANKS TO SHARE

My thanks to Marilyn Heavilin, the author of *Roses in December* and *When Your Dreams Die*, for her willingness to set aside the time to help me prepare this manuscript, and to Pam Stevens, who researched, validated, and annotated the individual stories we have used.

Both Marilyn and Pam are staff members of CLASS, Inc., and Marilyn edits the manuscripts sent to us by CLASS graduates. Each one is a writer and speaker, and I'm so grateful they were willing to spend their time and energies that we might share this book with others.

"Every adventure starts with a moment.
Every journey starts with a step.
Every dream starts with a dreamer.
Anything is possible if you dare."

INTRODUCTION

Dreams sometimes pick up a bad name. They seem to hang around with people who appear lazy and unmotivated, people who sit on the porch swing and wish on a star, people who visit fortune tellers in hopes of good news about the future, people who sleep a lot and spend their waking hours analyzing what they just slept through, people who buy lottery tickets and wait for the big day when the right numbers will be read on the late night news. Dreams associate with poets, artists, and musicians who live in lofts over tailor shops, have only a thin pallet on the floor, and eschew amenities. Some wear smocks and berets and some don gossamer wings to dance lightly over rooftops in the moonlight. Many lie down in green pastures, while others run through meadows picking daisies.

As a whole, dreams don't seem to be our friends or live in our neighborhoods. They seem to line up with Wishful Thinking and Lady Luck, and they don't relate to those of us in the real world who work for a living, those of us who don't swing on a star or catch moonbeams in a jar, those of us who don't have time to tiptoe through the tulips or leap tall buildings in a single bound, those of us who don't live in ivory towers somewhere over the rainbow but dwell in houses with mortgages and leaky roofs, those of us who have to mow our meadows and are allergic to pollen and petunias. So should those of us in the real world even *dare to dream*?

> "The best way to make a dream
> is to wake up first.
> In dreams begins responsibility."
> —Delmore Schwartz

What is the difference between a goal and a dream? In the last decade, books on goal setting have proliferated and at least one is on the coffee table of every successful person. All of the upwardly mobile seekers have attended seminars where planning out their day to perfection is considered an essential to the good life. Get up at the crack of dawn, read five minutes' worth of positive literature, jog through the spacious park outside the front door, eat a breakfast of grapefruit and oat bran, and you're set to take on the dragons of the day.

Goals are clear and specific. They can be regulated and evaluated. They can be counted, charted, and checked off. We all need goals in life, but do we really need dreams? Dreams add that touch of imagination to our goals, that vision to our plans, that hope to our future. To *dare to dream* brings excitement into the ordinary. It shows us life can be better. Yes, there is more to life than this. There's little risk in setting realistic goals, but you have to *dare to dream* !

> "You and you alone can
> determine your dreams."
> —Robert Schuller
> in his first radio broadcast to Russia

The Dreamer

On March 31, 1988, Ron Chapman went on the air at 6:00 A.M. as usual. As the most prominent disc jockey in Dallas, he spends four hours each morning giving cheer and encouragement to his loyal listeners as they head out to face another day. For twenty years they've depended on him to keep them laughing when their life is no fun, to make them feel good about themselves when they're insecure, and to help those stalled in the rush-hour traffic to *dare to dream*. In return they've been faithful. They turned up when he gave out bananas from the drive-through window of a bank, they filled the Cotton Bowl to be extras for the movie "Semi-Tough," and they came out by the thousands at the crack of dawn to hear the Dallas Wind Symphony play at a Labor Day Sunrise Party he sponsored.

Ron Chapman's fans don't dare miss a morning of KVIL for fear they'll miss the chance of a lifetime. They never know what he'll come up with next: a new car a year for life, a weekend trip to London, or a camel race in Egypt.

March 31 was different. Ron asked something of his listeners. "Send me twenty dollars. That's all I want." No promises. No explanations. Nothing in return. He knew some of them would do it, but even he was amazed when the next morning four thousand checks arrived in the mail, and another five thousand came in on Monday. He went on the air

Monday afternoon and said, "That's enough! Don't send any more. We don't even know what we're going to do with all this money." In spite of this announcement, people kept sending money. Some slipped checks under the door at night or begged the janitor to take their money after hours. There was a stampede to give away twenty dollars for no reason at all.

No worthy cause—no feeding of orphans, no relief for earthquake victims—but in their hearts, the donors all knew that if Ron Chapman asked for the money, they wanted to be part of whatever he had up his sleeve. They didn't want to miss out. They listened each morning as Ron counted up the money and totalled the 12,156 checks amounting to more than $240,000, almost a quarter of a million! Not bad for three days' work! "It was like deadline time at the IRS," Ron Chapman said with excitement.

Newspapers picked up the story and some asked, "Is this legal?" One listener called the Federal Communications Commission in Washington and talked to the supervisor of investigations in the mass media division. After hearing the simplicity of the request he replied, "As long as they don't make any promises or say they'll spend the money one way and then spend it on something else, there doesn't seem to be anything fraudulent about that. There's nothing wrong with saying, 'Send us your money.'"

In fact, after he thought about it for awhile, the investigator added, "That's unbelievable. I may have to move to Dallas!"

Newspapers and radio stations from all over the country began to call and ask questions. "Where did you get the idea? How did you dare to ask for money for no good cause?"

Ron explained that he had been at a staff meeting with the new owners of the radio station and had told them how successful his contests and promotions had been in the past. "We get better response to these than anyone in the business. I even believe if KVIL were to go on the air and say, 'Send us twenty dollars,' people would do it." The group laughed at this possibility and that was all Ron needed to hear. That challenged him to try it. "I'll show them," he said to himself.

He spent no time planning what to do with the money and spent no money on the promotion. He just made the request and the checks poured in. "I thought maybe I'd mail them back their checks with two dollars interest and a T-shirt," he said, "but that was before I saw the response. We can have fun on the air for weeks deciding what to do with the money." And they did have fun, taking in suggestions ranging from building a museum for Lawrence Welk in South Dakota to sending a Dallas group of cheerleaders to a contest in Australia.

Headlines all over the country captioned "KVIL DJ gets big bucks after appeal to listeners." "DJ leaves listeners red-faced, in the red."

Star sent a photographer who had Chapman lie on the floor covered with checks with his head peering out from the piles of money. *People* published his picture holding handfuls of checks and with more heaped up on the desk before him. Their headline stated, "Ask and Ye Shall Receive, Believes Dallas Deejay Ron Chapman—Which Is How He Made $244,240." They went on to say,

> Without so much as *hinting* at salvation, suicide, or the last days, Ron Chapman, a deejay at Dallas radio station KVIL, triggered a flood of donations from his audiophilic flock. On March 31, as a whimsical test of his medium's power, he made a simple on-air request: "Go to your checkbooks," quoth he. "Write a check payable to KVIL. Fun and Games. Make it in the amount of $20 and mail it to this address." That's all he said. He never stated why he wanted the money or what he'd do with it. "I thought I might get three or four hundred checks." says Chapman, 51, who'd planned to return the money to each donor with a bag of sponsor goodies. But it quickly became obvious that many goodies would be needed. Four thousand checks came in the next day's mail; 5,000 arrived the day after. Recently KVIL announced that a total of 12,212 checks—worth $244,240—had been received. And according to the FCC, since no promises were made, there's no fraud. But KVIL won't keep the loot. Instead, it will be donated to charities and civic projects. "We've done some crazy stunts," says Chapman, "but this is the biggest."[1]

Interviewers asked, "Do people want their money back? Is anyone angry?"

"Nobody is angry," Chapman said. "The only anger we have had has been from people who could not send their check to us once we put the deadline on it. That's when they were angry. They were angry because they could no longer send us their money for a reason they did not know."

As the ratings of KVIL were climbing by the minute, competitors stood by in amazement. How could a promotion that cost nothing produce so much publicity?

"If it was planned as a promotion, it shows signs of genius," said the station manager for a rival station. "I ask myself, would I send somebody twenty dollars just because they asked for it? It's unfathomable. In all my years of broadcasting I've never seen anything like it."

Newspapers and magazines as different as the *Baptist Journal* and *USA Today* wrote lead articles about the incident. Tom Brokaw on

NBC and Peter Jennings on ABC interviewed Ron Chapman on their news programs, and "Entertainment Tonight" made him a special feature. *Newsweek* did a column on him, and papers in Australia, New Zealand, Great Britain, and Germany told the tale of the disc jockey who tuned in to $240,000 for no reason, no strings attached.

Inquiring minds want to know, who is this man? Who is this person that's called by the *Dallas Times Herald* "incessantly cheerful . . . Number One disc jockey in Texas . . . a legend in his industry . . . King of the morning rush hour?"

Where did he come from? How did he achieve his dream?

Well, I'm the one to tell the tale, for I'm his sister and I've been with him from the beginning.

I was there when he was born in the depths of the Great Depression, and even I didn't *dare to dream* that either one of us could ever succeed.

As I remember my mother crying, "Here's one more mouth to feed," I didn't know that mouth would one day be entertaining thousands of people each morning and making more money than Mother could have ever dreamed.

Ron Chapman's photograph as it appeared in *People* magazine.
Courtesy of the *Dallas Times-Herald*.

When I helped him with his homework and dated his teachers to get him out of high school, I didn't *dare to dream* that one day I'd spot his picture on the cover of *D*, the magazine of Dallas, and read, "The real Ron Chapman—cheerful and chirping—the Emperor is in his tower—the magic is about to happen!"[2]

> "Learn the sweet magic of
> a cheerful face."
> —Oliver Wendell Holmes

PART ONE

Dare
to
Dream

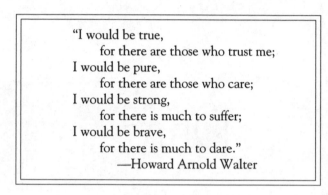

> "I would be true,
>   for there are those who trust me;
> I would be pure,
>   for there are those who care;
> I would be strong,
>   for there is much to suffer;
> I would be brave,
>   for there is much to dare."
>   —Howard Arnold Walter

Dare to Dream

There was much to dare in 1935 in Newton, Massachusetts, and the dream was over for our family. The business my father had worked for over thirty years had closed down in the Depression, leaving him with no employment and no retirement. There were few positions available and none for a man fifty-seven years old who had not graduated from high school. Walter Chapman found himself with no job, no money, and no dream. What he did have was little me, seven years old, and brother James at four, plus a pregnant, depressed wife twenty years his junior.

I knew my mother was going to get me a new baby, but I had no idea where babies came from. I remember one evening around Christmas when I was already in bed and the doorbell rang. We never had company in our tiny tenement, so I sat up and strained to hear who was at the door.

"Oh Dorothy!" my mother exclaimed. "Come right in, dear."

I peeked out to see who Dorothy was and recognized the lady from church who drove a big black Packard. I knew she must be rich.

"Katie, I don't know how to put this," the lady said, "but I have never been able to have children. My husband and I have always wanted a baby, and we have enough money to give a child everything he could possibly want. I know you and Chappie can hardly feed the two you've got, and I wondered if you'd let me adopt your new one."

I gasped through the crack in the bedroom door. Give my baby away?

"You could come and see him. . . ."

21

Come and see him? We already had the crib set up next to my bed. Why couldn't *she* come and see him? I cried as I looked at the empty crib and saw the silhouette of the bars reflected from the streetlight outside my room. I'd had so much fun playing with little James, combing his blond curls, putting him in my old dresses and pretending he was a girl. I was ready for a new live doll and this lady wanted to take him away before I even had him in my arms.

"It's true," I heard my mother say, "we can't afford a new baby. But if God has sent me this baby, He must have something special in mind for him."

The two chatted for a while and then Dorothy got up to leave. She put on her black coat and then clipped on over it what looked like a whole fox. It had a head with beady eyes and a tail hanging down. When the lady pressed a button, the mouth opened and she clipped it onto the other side. The animal seemed to be biting off its own tail. As I watched this scene with fascination, Dorothy said, "If you change your mind, Katie, let me know. I'll take the baby off your hands any time of the day or night."

"Any time, day or night," I thought. "I'd better keep a close watch over this one."

On the morning of January 25, 1936, my mother calmly announced she was going to get the new baby. We had no car so a friend was going to take her to the hospital. I remember kissing her goodbye and promising to be a good girl, a pledge I was forced to make at each farewell throughout my childhood. We had no phone, so I went up the hill to Natalie's house and kept calling the hospital until I received the news. I had wanted a baby girl since I already had a brother, but the nurse said, "Mrs. Chapman has a new little boy."

I wondered if she'd give him away because I knew she wanted a girl, too. I ran down the street to tell James he had a new brother. I determined I'd take good care of my new baby and if that lady in the Packard ever drove up I'd hide him.

When he came home from the hospital and I looked at him, I fell in love with my baby. I sat by his crib for hours on end and read stories to him that he couldn't understand. One day I wrote a poem and then mailed it in to the *Wee Wisdom* magazine. My first published work came out in April 1936.

My Baby
by Florence Chapman (7 years)

I have a little baby
As sweet as sweet can be;

His great big eyes are just as blue
As the waters of the sea.

His smile is so very cute
And chubby is his nose;
He has a lovely dimpled hand,
And funny little toes.

This poem may not seem impressive today, but recently *Wee Wisdom* did a fiftieth anniversary issue and "My Baby" was resurrected and republished.

We all discussed what to name my baby. I'd been named after my two grandmothers, Florence and Marcia. James was from my mother's father and his middle name, Walter, was the same as Daddy's. Evidently my mother had contrived all these because my father said, "I'd like to name this one, if none of you mind. I want to name him after my two best friends, Ralph and Fred."

So he was christened Ralph Frederick Chapman at the Newton Highlands Congregational Church. When asked his name as a toddler he'd often answer "RalphFred," which would bring the response, "Oh, Alfred, what a nice name."

Ralph and Fred, who were both childless, were thrilled to have a little namesake, and within a few months they each agreed to lend my father a thousand dollars apiece to buy the Riverside Variety Store in Haverhill, Massachusetts.

We moved into the shabby brown building with yellow trim, a Gulf gas tank out front, and two repair garages filling the backyard. Inside was the store, full of penny candy and Hostess cupcakes. That became our living, dining, and playroom, and little Ralph took great pleasure in riding his red train out from behind a counter into the feet of a startled customer. Behind the store was a kitchen with a black slate sink where we took our baths and washed the dishes, a tiny den with room for a couch and our upright piano, and a bedroom where all five of us slept in layers.

The whole place was so small that if we talked in the den the customers could hear us clearly in the store. We all had loud voices right from the start, and Daddy had a signal that if we were talking about someone and that person entered the front door, Dad would start singing "Holy, Holy, Holy" at the top of his lungs.

We were so well trained that if I hear that hymn anywhere today, I instantly shut my mouth.

Life in the store was fun for Ralph because it gave him a captive audience everyday. From the moment he could complete a sentence, he had a natural sense of humor and a precocious sense of timing. People were fascinated by this little child who could repeat every singing commercial in perfect pitch and who could recite "People who live in transparent domiciles should refrain from hurling geological specimens promiscuously" when he was only four. I soon found that he could learn anything I took the time to teach him, and more exciting was the fact that people would pay money to hear him. I had a walking gold mine on my youthful hands.

Customers gave me five cents every time he recited a piece and when the store was empty I'd take him down to the garages, stand him on the hood of a car in for repairs, and charge the mechanics to listen to him. As demand increased I raised my rates.

Today he says, "I liked applause early on. And so I've always wanted to be Ya-Ha! Give me a spotlight and let me go!"

Ralph looked upon school as an audience waiting for an event. He said to his first grade teacher, Miss Horton, "Are you a lemon?" When she said no, he quipped, "Don't you like to be squeezed?" Not all teachers appreciated his constant humor, and few of them could get him to study. Some would say in despair, "Why aren't you smart like your brother and sister?"

My mother was afraid to go to PTA meetings and hear bad news, so I would go in her place. I'd defend him to the teachers and then water down their comments for my mother. When he got to high school and was too busy to read *Silas Marner*, Mother would read his assignments and give him capsule commentaries each night.

Even though he didn't care much about Silas, he spent hours each day listening to the radio and memorizing the words to popular songs. He saved up money from his paper route and bought Spike Jones records. Soon he could lip-synch everything Spike sang, and he became a favorite act at local talent shows. Together we bought a record player that could cut music into a blank record, and Ralph began making discs with his own voice.

He recalls with excitement the day that Haverhill's first radio station began transmitting. "I was eight or nine and my hometown newspaper said they were going to put a radio station on the air—our first one—and would be running test tones at 3:00 in the morning. I set the alarm for a quarter to 3:00 and couldn't believe it when I heard these sounds coming from a radio station in my own town."

Ralph, accompanied by a friend on the piano, recorded "Mule Train" and took it to WHAV in hopes they'd play it. No average person would dare to dream that the station would take a homemade record of "Mule

Train" and make a hit of it, but Ralph had high expectations and the station fulfilled them.

By the time he was a freshman in high school, he had hung around WHAV so long that they allowed him to do announcements and some live commercials. They even gave him a fifteen-minute show of his own twice a week.

Each morning he'd turn on Carl de Suez of Boston's WBZ-AM. Carl had the biggest following in New England, and Ralph would breathe right along with him and sing every song he played.

"He inspired me to be a morning man. He never seemed to have a bad morning."

De Suez featured a "Boys in the Back Room" segment, a round table free-for-all on politics, sports, and whatever else might come up. Ralph remembers, "It was very infectious, communal and family-like. It felt good and it felt like fun. I learned from that show that if you get up in the morning exposed to people having fun, it's hard to stay down."

Young Ralph stayed up all the time as long as he could play at the radio station. He had boundless energy, exceptional musical ability, a mind that raced ahead of everyone, and an innate sense of humor that put the last laugh onto anyone else's story.

He stayed down, however, when he was in school. It all seemed to be so pointless, all that Latin and algebra that he knew he'd never use. I remember the day when he was trying to do some "mixture problems." The question asked about the proportion of tons of Colombian and Brazilian coffee beans. He looked up at my mother, who was, as she called it, at her "wit's end," and said, "The only way I can do this is if you order a couple tons of these beans, have them dumped in front of the store, and we go out with a big spoon and mix them up."

Mother burst into tears. She never quite caught on to his sense of humor, and the few times he did "tickle her funny bone" she'd cover her mouth and try to choke her laugh down. "The last thing I want to do is encourage him in this foolishness."

I was a teacher at Ralph's high school, and we went back and forth each day together. I was still watching over him to make sure that no one stole him away. I was a combination sister-mother-teacher, and everything I learned I shared with him. We were invited to parties as a team because people knew when we were around there would never be a dull moment. We kept up-to-date on world affairs and politics and we would develop some good lines on current topics. Then we waited for someone to bring up the subject. This "rehearsed spontaneity" made us the life of any party.

Ralph was always better at parties and radio than he was on his school subjects. The only thing he really liked was band and chorus. He had taken trumpet and voice lessons, and with his natural talent he excelled at both without having to practice. When the band was not marching, the instruments were locked up in a chainlink fenced space called the Band Cage. It was near the room where I taught and Ralph had a key to it. When no one was around he would adjust the mouthpiece of the tuba so that it stuck through a hole in the fencing. Once classes started, he would walk by the cage and give a big blow on the tuba. Teachers would come running and head for the cage. He would be gone, and they would find the door locked. No one could figure out how the horn could make this blast by itself in a locked cage. We had teachers' meetings where they discussed the Phantom of the Band Cage, and finally they assigned a teacher to guard the door full-time. Imagine his surprise when, dutiful as he was, the blast was heard loud and clear from the rear of the cage. He unlocked the door and tripped over trumpets and drums trying to reach the culprit in the corner. But no one was there. The Phantom had struck again. As the teacher-guard refused to go back to the haunted cage, Ralph and I decided he'd better call it quits.

Ralph next turned to making the typing class into a rhythm band. Before class he'd tell the eager typists the name of the song for the day. When the teacher walked in and assigned the page they were to type, all eyes would turn to Ralph. As he nodded, they would all type to the beat of the selected song. "Alexander's Ragtime Band" was a favorite to type to as it paced out right for the bell to ring at the end of each line. "Jingle Bells" was a real hit at Christmas. To make him pass, I finally had to promise his teacher that Ralph would stop musical typing and that I'd never let him take typing from any poor unsuspecting teacher ever again.

In his last two years of high school, Ralph took my speech courses and I gave him the only A's he ever got. The A's looked so odd on his report card that I had the principal come in and observe Ralph's extemporaneous speaking. Ralph pulled a topic out of a box and gave a hilarious five-minute message on "Why are sponges full of holes?" The principal was impressed and agreed that Ralph deserved an A.

During Ralph's time in high school, patriotic people were still planting post-war Victory gardens, and we had a left-over teacher who offered gardening for a quarter of a credit each summer. The pupil had to plant a garden, keep notes on when he planted the seed and when he harvested his crop, and turn in a report in September along with a sample of his produce. Since Ralph needed every point he could get, he signed up for gardening and went to the orientation meeting each June. In three summers he never planted a seed or harvested a squash. The day before school started again, he and I would go to Lil's Fruit and Vegetable Stand and buy whatever she had on hand. I would then write a glowing report on the emergence and maturity of his produce and attach it to the basket of samples he presented to the teacher. When he graduated in 1953, Ralph had a quarter of a credit more than the bare minimum. Without the three quarters of a credit he got from gardening and without Lil's diligence in the summer sun, Ralph Chapman would not have made it through "Pomp and Circumstance." As Mother and I sat in the audience that night, she leaned over and whispered, "You and I should be getting the diploma. We're the ones who did the work."

Yes, we did much of the work, but Ralph had the charm to get us to do it.

Did either one of us *dare to dream* at that time that Ralph would ever be a success? Or would he be as Mother feared, "If he doesn't get serious and get down to business, he'll never amount to a row of pins."

> "I dare do all that may become a man;
> who dares do more is none."
> —William Shakespeare

Porch-Swing People

Some of us, amused by my brother's antics, may say, "I wish I had a sense of humor. I can't sing or act or think up clever things. If you're not an up-front personality, is there any hope?"

Some of us may have had parents who thought we didn't amount to "a row of pins." Some of us may have little education or a feeling that we're not smart enough to become anything.

A few of us may have achieved great goals or made a lot of money, but we still feel insecure inside. Perhaps we've asked ourselves, "Who am I?" and not heard a clear answer.

No matter where we are in our self-evaluation today, we can move on. We can *dare to dream.*

After all, as poet Robert Browning asserted, "A man's reach should exceed his grasp, or what's a heaven for?"

It's always easier to relax than reach, to give up than grasp, but we want to stretch rather than just settle into the status quo. If we rested until the perfect path to success opened before us, we would all be sitting on the porch swing of life waiting for directions. Let's pretend that's where we are today, all of us lined up on that glider on the veranda looking out to blue skies and sunshine forever. We can smell the sweet flowers of success, but if we're going to pick them we'll have to get up. We can see ideas flitting around like hummingbirds, but to use one we'll have to get a net and capture it. Some of us would prefer to rock where we are than to get up and move on. Some prefer to accept what's good rather than to aim for the best. Some would rather sit on a safe sofa than to *dare to dream*.

We've all heard the statement, "Without a vision the people perish," and yet many of us are without a vision taking the fatalistic approach that "if God wanted me to have a better job He'd send a personnel manager to my front porch."

"If only it was that easy," writes motivational author William Davis in an article titled "Let Me Through; I Have an Idea." Having an idea is a positive start, but will wishful thinking be rewarded? Davis goes on to say:

> It is a popular myth that the essence of innovation is having ideas. If only it were that simple. An idea is merely the starting point; innovation is about making things happen, which is a great deal more difficult.
>
> Intrinsically, ideas have little value. It is only when they are implemented by determined people that they become influential.

This book is not to chart an all-purpose course to financial success, but to give you the momentum to move off the porch swing of life and *dare to dream*.

Whatever your personality, background, or desire, you will find stories in this book of people that are just like you.

Don't be a porch-swing person any longer. Don't stuff your laurels into a pillow and rest upon them. Don't rock in indecision and inertia.

I'm calling you off the porch. Come on, let's head for the starting gate.

Three Minutes to the Starting Gate

Many of us depend upon other people to lead us through life and make our decisions for us even when we have the ability to map out our own route. We need to move from where we are to the starting gate and *dare to dream.*

Dreams are not dull reality or they wouldn't be called dreams. They are beyond the norm and they give excitement and creativity to life. So much of what we read today consists of practical steps to an immediate goal. "How to" books have flooded the market and I am personally grateful that everyone who buys these wants to learn how to do something better. Without that desire to improve and get on with a better life, those of us who write would have no market. In teaching leadership seminars, I find people eager to do whatever we say. Give them a pencil and a three-point plan and they are ready to move. Where I find the problem is that many of the seminar attendees haven't tried to think up three points of their own. Their minds are so conditioned to depend upon someone else for direction that when the seminar leader says, "Get up early and walk briskly around the block," they write it down avidly and consider it a new thought.

When I am speaking and have occasional bursts of creative brilliance, people respond, nod, smile, possibly even applaud. But the moment I say, "Here are three steps to help you get along with difficult people," they all reach instantly for a pen. They'll write on the backs of envelopes, on church bulletins, and even on the cash register receipts from the supermarket. They want the three steps to happiness, and if possible they want it in sixty seconds or less. That's why those one minute manager books are so popular. They give us the answers to life and they give them to us now. Instant success in a box, like instant potatoes or minute rice.

I'm glad we're all open to new ideas and quick suggestions, but I'd like to move our minds beyond the quick fix from someone else into the realm of dreaming up these steps for ourselves, into believing that we could tailor-make our own steps to success if we would just sit down and try.

Some people wake up one day with a fire in their heart and they instantly know their mission in life. Dr. Spock always had a passion for babies and childcare, Bette Davis knew she would become the best actress possible as she always "kept her eyes on the prize," and Arsenio Hall longed to be on television since childhood when he idolized and imitated Johnny Carson. Each of these well-known names seemed destined for success, set for stardom.

What about you? Do you have a burning in your bosom? Does your blood race when you think about your dreams?

While many are gifted with an innate gumption, some of us seem to be void of a vision that propels us. If you are missing your momentum or your direction is dormant, it is time you discovered your dream!

But where is the starting gate? Where can we discover a dream?

Look at Other People's Lives

In my personal growth, I have been continually inspired by the lives of other people. Whether I was reading about them or talking with them, I have found there are basic principles we can learn from other people's experiences even if they are in a totally different line of work. We can profit by asking them questions and listening to what they say.

Be Open to Challenge

When I first met John Smart, national sales director of an Australian food company, I could tell that he could sell just about anything. He has an engaging Popular Personality and his eyes sparkle as he talks so fast I can hardly keep up with him. As I asked about his life, he told me that he had grown up with the opinion that he would never be a success. After one business failure when he was at a particularly low point, he met a woman who challenged him to sell encyclopedias. Under her tutelage, he became the top salesman in Australia and was flown to London to receive a plaque.

Not only did he achieve his goals, but in the process he began to feel better about himself. Naturally, I wondered who this woman was and what kind of magic she had that could take a defeated man and lift him to the top.

John was thrilled to tell me about Rosemary Moore and provide me with more information about a woman who learned not to take no for an answer.

Don't Take No for an Answer

Rosemary is a sixth-generation Australian who had ancestors with pioneering spirits on each side of her family. Samuel Pratt Winter, on her father's side, left Ireland at the age of fourteen for Australia, cutting through twenty miles of forest between Portland and the Wannon River in Victoria and settling in the valley nearby. Samuel Winter-Cooke, nephew of this first settler, became a member of the first Australian Federal Parliament. Rosemary's mother's ancestors were Scots who migrated to New South Wales and one of them, Sir John Robertson, became the first premier of New South Wales. One of Rosemary's favorite ancestors was her mother's father, John Geddes, an adventurous man who first brought refrigeration to Australia. Rosemary descends from a long line of achievers and dreamers who no doubt heard a few folks say, "It can't be done." Rosemary comes by this trait quite naturally.

At the age of forty, Rosemary felt unfulfilled and decided she wanted to do something different with her life. She answered an ad reading, "Teachers or women ambitious to teach." When she learned that it was a job selling encyclopedias, she wasn't interested. That is until her husband Michael told her she couldn't do it and definitely should not try. That was all Rosemary with her choleric personality needed to hear. She felt challenged and said, "I will do it." As all beginners do, Rosemary started on her friends, who bought the encyclopedias from her without listening to her sales pitch. That is, until one friend stopped her and said, "Unless you persuade me it is good, I'm not buying it." This made her get to work and the sale built her confidence. She felt she had contributed excellent reasons and actually deserved the sale. However, the critical environment from people who were not her friends became too strong, and for her first year she fulfilled her husband's prophecy and hardly sold at all.

Knock on Doors

Rosemary went back to her supervisor and asked how she could improve her sales. "You could knock on a door," was the reply, "but I don't think you could do that." Rosemary agreed that she probably couldn't do that and left. By the time she got out to her car, her feisty pioneering spirit rose up and she decided that if her supervisor thought she couldn't do it, she had to prove her wrong. Rosemary ran the seventy stairs back to the front door and said to her supervisor, "What do you mean I couldn't do that?" At this time the supervisor challenged her to master the art of door-to-door sales.

When she asked her father's advice, he answered, "There are only two worthwhile considerations, your God and then your own opinion. Don't be directed by anyone else's opinion. Your ancestors knocked on the door of this continent. I don't see any reason why you shouldn't knock on doors." And that she did; she shattered national and international sales records for *World Book Encyclopedias*. Rosemary believes, "Everyone who is going to achieve anything must learn not to listen to the don't-doers. If you want a give-up decision made for you, they'll make it. Like flies, the don't-doers are everywhere. When Walt Disney had a new idea, he'd ask his friends whether or not he should go ahead with it. If enough of them said, 'For goodness sake, don't do that,' he concluded he was onto a winner and did it. I always thought that was inspiring. Besides, Jesus Christ was a direct salesman, and look how He influenced the world!"

Rosemary has gone on to be a part of the Zondervan Corporation with the Book of Life division in Australia. And because of her success, she has also been granted distribution rights for New Zealand and Canada.

Forget Yourself and Help Others

Rosemary says that in a sales environment, success depends on "forgetting yourself and helping the other person achieve his goals." She is convinced that in terms of human nature, people make the mistake of concentrating on personal ambition. "Forget yourself, and work for the things you believe in: your product, your company, your manager, your family, or your country. Then, and only then, can other things come through you. Too many of us want to take more and more and give less and less. We must work, plan our work, and work our plan. Stamina is important, too, both physically and stamina of character. Character is the resolve to keep going long after the desire to do so has passed."

Discipline Yourself

Self-discipline is another quality needed to be successful. It is the one single quality common to all achievers. Achievement also takes goal-setting. Rosemary looks at a goal and says, "Why can't I?" In 1974 she surpassed the American record and won the New World Sales Record for the Book of Life. But Rosemary believes winning isn't everything and it isn't to be accomplished at the cost of things of permanent value, such as personal relationships, our own reputation, and the reputation of the institutions and organizations to which we are attached.

"Damage to either of these lasts longer than the taste of victory."

Find Balance

"The secret of success is finding the balance. Success starts, is maintained and ends with attitude—a creative and activity-producing attitude—and an acknowledgment that life does not owe us anything. Life was here first! To be successful you need to have a dream, make it a goal, then chase that goal for all you're worth. Keep your eyes on that goal at all times, because obstacles are the things you see when you take your eyes off your goal. Then, when you have achieved it, take stock of how best you can share it."[3]

Rosemary practices what she preaches and has been instrumental in inspiring many John Smarts to pick themselves up from defeat and go knock on a few doors. She has taken her sales skills and shared them freely with others so that they, too, might achieve.

Do you have people in your life that have said, "You couldn't do that!" Why not take their negative words as a challenge to see if you really could dare to dream? You will never really know the answer unless you try!

Be like Rosemary and be willing to knock on a few doors. Rosemary has done well financially, but her goal in life was not to get rich. Rather, she wanted to share what she had with others. She was willing at midlife to reevaluate her position and to make a fresh start.

Many of us equate money with success, but being rich isn't a dream. What you do with your life is what is important. Will your dream make a difference?

The December 11, 1989, issue of *Time* magazine featured an article on lawyers that are leaving the practice. While they seemed to make plenty of money, the hours are long, leaving little time for their families or anything else that may be important to them. Greg Howard, known as the creator of the "Sally Forth" comic strip, left law to practice something more fulfilling. He, too, had concluded that the goal of riches isn't a dream.

Check Your Current Position

Should you look to your job? Maybe. Do you love it? Does it excite you to go to work each day? If it does, maybe you have already discovered your dream. Many people choose a career path based on the advice of a parent or teacher. They head off to be a typist or a technician because "you'll always be able to get a job in that field" and they hate every day of it. I know of very few people who love their lives and are happy in their jobs who are doing what they set out to do straight out of high school. It is unfair to think that at eighteen every person will know how they want to spend the rest of their lives.

Rod started delivering mail, and after a few years he moved up to postmaster. But every day he dreaded getting up and going to work. Rod's whole personality changed when he discovered his dream. After twelve years of building a career he didn't enjoy, he left the post office to join a design organization. Today, as vice president of this company, he has found a creative side that had lain dormant and he thrives on the challenge of meeting new clients' demands. Perhaps it is time for you to make a change, too.

Start Young

Rosemary found her dream at mid-life, but there are some people who found their desires at a young age. Although she is still a teenager, Marla knows she wants to be a teacher. She came to our leadership CLASS and was a most avid listener. When it was her turn to stand up and demonstrate what she'd learned, she expressed herself so well that the adults were awe-struck. Marla could outline her thoughts with ease and she could see the value of being alert to the life around her. When she returned home she wrote:

> As a future advanced placement English teacher I want to say a humongous thank you for laying the foundation for the rest of my life in three short action-packed days. You have edified and affirmed me so completely that I haven't had time to feel helpless because I'm so young. My head swarms with vivid possibilities of how to apply what I have learned, now!
>
> You have spent time just on me and that quality time is stored in my reservoir of info, that will be used for a lifetime. You're hope for the hopeless.

Robert C. Davis also began planning his career in high school. He was working with his father selling mobile homes in Brunswick, Maine, when his dad suggested he take a Dale Carnegie course. Neither one of them knew much about it, but they did know that in sales it was important to be able to win friends and influence peple. As a seventeen year old who was trying to sell mobile homes to adults, Robert wanted to learn all he could to increase his credibility. "It was very beneficial to me in dealing with adults to overcome my lack of confidence about my age. After I took the class my sales doubled, my income tripled, and I said, 'This is really neat!'"

While attending Bates College, Robert, who has an outgoing optimistic personality, kept telling people about the Dale Carnegie course and signing them up. What started as a volunteer activity turned into a sales position promoting classes. As Robert said to me the day I met him, "I didn't know enough to know I couldn't do what I was already doing."

At the age of twenty-one, Robert became the youngest Dale Carnegie instructor in the world, even though he was still in college. By this time the whole Carnegie organization had their eyes on this young man who had done in a short time what many mature men had taken years to accomplish. Robert's single-minded determination to be the best and achieve the most kept him moving into the position of area manager, and when he was twenty-two he was awarded the Dale Carnegie license for the state of Maine and later the territory of Vermont and part of New Hampshire and Massachusetts.

Keep in Touch with the People

On the day when I was taken to meet Robert, he was heading out to teach a class in Massachusetts. Part of his success is due to the fact that he keeps teaching, keeps in touch with the needs of the people, and keeps a close eye on his instructors. He makes sales calls on big corporations himself and he personally trains his new staff. He is taking no chance of losing what he has so quickly achieved.

As thirty-five-year-old Robert gave me a proud tour of his new lavish suite of offices and classrooms, I saw framed documents that showed he was a member of the Chairman of the Board Club because his franchise produced business in excess of 150 percent of quota, that he was the recipient of the President's Award for program quality and graduation percentage, and that his franchise had received the Outstanding Production Award for 1984. In five years, Robert's business went from four employees to fifty-five instructors, twenty-two full-time representatives, and three administrators.

Work Hard

When I asked him the secret of his success, Robert replied, "There's no secret. I just work hard and have a positive attitude. Each morning I say to myself, 'This is going to be a tremendous day,' and then I list the reasons why."

That made me stop and think. What do I dwell on the most each day? You can't stop long to ponder when you're with Robert Davis, for at a flicker of disinterest, he's off to Massachusetts. As we said goodbye I asked, "Has your Dale Carnegie training changed you personally?"

"Oh yes," he replied. "I used to be very abrasive and hard on people who didn't do things right, but I got over that." There was an instant raising of the staff eyebrows as if in a quiet chorus of surprise, and one muffled chuckle broke out in the corner. But Robert didn't notice.

He was already giving a seminar to the new instructor he was training. "I'll tell him all the way down what I'm going to do in the class; then he'll watch me do it, and on the way home we'll review how I did it."

There's no secret to his success; he just works hard and has a very positive attitude.

Look to Your Creativity

I meet many people who tell me sadly that they have no creativity. By that they mean they're not artists or opera singers. Few of us are, and yet we are all born with an ability to think creatively. Pulitzer-Prize-winning author and psychiatrist Dr. Robert Coles has made much of his living by investigating the minds of children. In his book *The Spiritual Life of Children*, he shows pictures children have drawn of their concept of God. He states, "Many children are unwilling to accept the fact that God looks the way he does in church windows or in particular books." Coles is far more interested in children's creative concepts than in their artistic ability.

Dreams Are Like Bubbles

All of us are born with natural creativity and with inquisitive minds. Each little child pictures his own brand of Santa Claus, Guardian Angels, and the Tooth Fairy. When asked to draw their view of God, each one came up with his own personal creation. If we all started out wide-eyed and inventive, when did it stop? Who cut it off? Who put our ideas into a little box and said, "This is the norm. This is the way we think around here."

I remember when my daughter Marita's teacher called me in to discuss why Marita drew a picture of me with purple hair. The teacher, searching for some psychological truth, had told Marita to make my hair a "normal color." When I asked Marita why she'd given me purple hair, she said simply, "They didn't have any blonde crayons."

We've all heard the expression, "He burst my bubble." It's sometimes used to excuse why we didn't pursue a certain dream or why we lost our initial enthusiasm for some project. But often our bubble is burst because our type of creativity wasn't "acceptable" and someone wiped out our desire.

When Daryl was in the sixth grade, he wrote a poem for his English class. He enjoyed doing it and was surprised at how creative he'd become. He passed it in proudly and could hardly wait for his teacher's reaction.

When his paper came back with a failing grade, he was devastated. He dared ask why and the teacher told him it was obvious he had copied it from somewhere. Daryl told me, "I never copied from anyone or anything in my life—either before or after—because I never thought anyone else could do it as well as I could. However, I did not challenge her, and now I realize that since I did not, perhaps she saw that as an admission of guilt. But I never did like that teacher and I did not write anything again for years."

By the time Daryl got to high school, he dared to try again. He was assigned to write a story on his greatest handicap. Feeling he didn't have one and remembering how the truth had done him no good, he made up a creative story about how he got a wooden leg and how this trauma had affected his life. He meant it to be funny, but the teacher found out he didn't have a wooden leg and flunked him. He couldn't win whether he was honest or not!

That did it for Daryl. He never wrote anything again. His teachers had burst his bubbles.

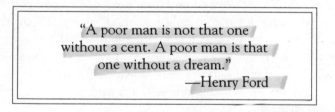

"A poor man is not that one without a cent. A poor man is that one without a dream."
—Henry Ford

Picture for a moment a bathtub. It's empty, cold, and hard. Now turn on the faucet and balance it to the perfect temperature for you. Something cold is warming up. Now pour in some bubble bath, and suddenly the ordinary becomes exciting. The aroma is pleasant, but the best part is watching the bubbles grow. Out of one tablespoon of liquid comes a mountain of bubbles. So little becomes so much. The stronger the force of the water, the bigger the bubbles become. Is there anyone of us who can resist the temptation of jumping into such pleasure? Some of you may want to go right now and start running the water, throw in some magic bath beads, hop in, and continue to read.

But what happens if you get called to the phone before you get in the tub? You shut off the faucet and leave the warm bubbles that may have mounded even higher than the tub itself, intending to come right back.

However, the cares of the world detain you, and when you return, the fluff and the fun have gone out of the bubbles. They've died down a bit, and many have disappeared forever. But all is not lost. You turn on the water again full force, and with the new encouragement fresh bubbles appear. The water gets warm again. You've revived what seemed to be dying.

Now consider our childhood minds. We've each been given at least a capful of creativity. Left in the bottle it doesn't produce any new ideas, but poured out into a warm environment it begins to bubble. The stronger the encouragement, the more full the force, the more bubbles appear. So many little children are just bubbling over with enthusiasm and excitement, their minds overflowing with creative thoughts. But what happens if we get left alone with no one stirring up the waters, no one keeping the bubbles alive? After a while the enthusiasm cools down. The bubbles burst and we're left with just a tub of cold water and perhaps the remnant of a few tiny bubbles here and there. But don't despair. We can turn on the tap again. We can bring some of the bubbles back to life. They won't be as big or as lively, but they can be stirred up one more time.

Think about your creativity as a child. Was it heated up and encouraged? When you poured yourself out, were you allowed to bubble to the surface? Or were you left alone with no one fluffing up your bubbles until one by one they popped and disappeared? Did you perhaps have someone who beat down your bubbles, who took a paddle to them and pushed them under until there were none left alive? One would pop up here or there and they'd say, "Don't try that. What a dumb idea. It'll never work." And your bubbles went down the drain.

I want to help you put the bubbles back into your life, to encourage you to *dare to dream*.

Look to Your Family Background

Many of us, in an effort to be our own people, don't take the time to look for any hereditary tendencies or talents that may give us some direction. Did any of your ancestors dare to dream? Was there an adventurous spirit in hard times that you haven't needed in easy times? I see the difference in my eagerness to get an education in the forties and my children's blasé attitude toward schooling. They weren't hurting; there wasn't the same desperate desire to "pull yourself up by the bootstraps" because they were already up.

For years I have used my family as examples, but it was only recently that I went back to England to my father's birthplace and looked up some records. At the same time my brother Jim went to Exeter, New Hampshire, and researched the history of our father's family when they first arrived in the United States. Together we got a view of a pioneer spirit we had not thought about before.

In 1883, Thomas Chapman and Maria Broadley Chapman dared to dream. As they packed up their meager belongings and bade farewell to their families, they prepared for the long voyage from England to the New World. With their two little sons in hand, they walked the familiar streets of Rochdale, Lancashire, passing the harness shop where Tom worked, the old spired church where the babies had been baptized, and the soot-soiled brick row-houses where they had lived among their friends for several years. It was hard to say goodbye, but even harder to stay. Life was predictable in Rochdale, but Tom had a dream beyond the coal mines and the factories.

Once settled in Exeter, New Hampshire, Thomas started his own business as an itinerant harness maker going from town to town each week looking for work. Maria watched over her two boys, Walter and Arthur, and in 1892 she gave birth to the first girl in the Chapman family for several generations. Thomas was proud that he had broken the male chain, but little Maria was sickly from the start, and when she was barely six months old, she died of meningitis. Maria, lonely and homesick for her family in England, had counted on this little girl to become her companion. When she lost her baby, she went into a deep grief which led to her own death four months later at the age of thirty-six. Thomas told his sons, "She died of a broken heart." Because Tom was on the road so much, the burden of household responsibilities fell upon Walter.

After their father's death, the two boys moved into a rooming house on High Street, and Walter earned their living as a delivery boy for Carlyles' Dry Goods Store. Arthur married Agnes, the daughter of Irish immigrants in Boston, and they had two sons, Walter and Arthur. Walter continued to live in rooming houses and worked hard to become the manager of an S. K. Ames Butter and Egg Store. His father had dared to dream and had brought the family to the new country. Walter had continued the promise of a new life by working his way up in the grocery business from errand boy to manager. In 1925, Walter was wearing the dream. He had money in the bank, he was manager of a store in Newton Highlands, Massachusetts, and he was a confirmed bachelor. That is, until he took his two-week summer vacation at Hampton Beach. It was there that he fell in love for the first time with a shy, slim violin teacher who was waitressing for the summer at the same hotel.

Katie Florence MacDougall and Walter Chapman were married the next June in the living room of her family home in Merrimac, Massachusetts. After a honeymoon in the White Mountains, they moved into a little white cottage in the Highlands to live happily ever after.

The dream from immigrant to American success was fulfilled when I was born into this family. On April 27, 1928, finally there was a Chapman daughter! I was born to a father who was fifty and a mother of thirty. Surely they were mature and settled for life, but within the space of the next few years my father was in an accident followed by a lawsuit and lost all of his savings. My little brother Arthur died shortly after birth, and then S. K. Ames closed its doors, leaving my father jobless and without his expected pension.

The Great Depression took the country by surprise, and by the time my father was sixty he had three young children and a disheartened wife to support. The family was living in a small tenement and he was a time-keeper on a road gang working for Roosevelt's Works Progress Administration, the WPA.

The dream had died. The great American success story was over. I remember my mother weeping as she packed a lunch for my father to take out into the cold Massachusetts winters where he had to stand all day by the side of a road and check the construction workers in and out. Mother taught a few violin lessons to earn some necessary money, and I became a junior mother with a deep sense of responsibility to my little brothers James and Ralph.

It was in December of 1935 that I was invited to a charity Christmas party. I didn't know the words "disadvantaged" or "deprived." Those labels hadn't been invented yet. But I did sense that I was there because I was poor. Wearing a pale WPA dress, I sat next to the lady who had been assigned to chaperone me. When my name was called, I walked up the aisle in the American Legion Hall to receive my gift. I looked up into the face of the lady doling out the presents. She looked like an angel to me as she smiled and announced, "Florence asked Santa to bring her Shirley Temple paper dolls and here they are." I stared at her beaded gown and satin slippers and it was at that moment that I dared to dream, "Someday, Florence, you're going to be that elegant lady in a gown standing on a stage giving presents to others." Even at that young age I knew I was on the wrong side of the stage. I wanted to be the giver and not the receiver. I dared to dream that someday I would be that lady on the stage.

That sparse Christmas was made happy by a visit to Grandma MacDougall's. It was during that vacation in Merrimac that my mother found a little store for sale for two thousand dollars. By borrowing money from his two best friends, my father bought the Riverside Variety Store and we moved into the three tiny rooms behind it. If our tenement in Newton seemed small, the back rooms of the store were like closets. The one bedroom had wallpaper that looked so much like a jungle that my father would wake up in the morning and say, "Every time I open my eyes I expect to see a monkey jumping off the wall."

We tried to make fun out of our dreary circumstances, but for Mother this was no laughing matter. Her honeymoon cottage was but a memory, and her hopes for even an adequate house had fled forever. Some people talk about how to make a house into a home—Mother had to make a store into a living room.

How do you make a house out of a store? How do you repair the dream? Where other people had a front porch, we had a public sidewalk adjoining the three cement steps that led up to the door. Where others had a lawn, we had weeds and a gas pump with customers honking for attention. Where other people had regular windows with curtains, we had store windows with Coca-Cola signs. Where others had white houses with black shutters, we had old brown clapboards with peeling paint and dingy yellow trim.

Where others had a living room, we had a store. Where they had furniture, we had a rack of newspapers, a table with cakes, jelly rolls, and whoppie pies, a long glass case full of penny candy and sticks of gum, two big ice tanks with bottles of milk and Canada Dry ginger ale moving anxiously against each other as the ice melted and the water level rose. Behind the table where we ate and played Monopoly was an ice cream freezer stocked with fudgesicles, popsicles, and creamsicles. Wait a minute, perhaps our differences weren't so bad after all. In fact, my friends thought coming to my store was fun.

Where they had dull wallpaper, we had bright signs of bathing beauties drinking Coca-Cola. Where others had a mere candy dish on the coffee table, we had a whole *case* full of peppermint patties and jelly beans. Where others had an occasional ice cream cone, we had a freezer full of fudgesicles. Where my friends spent lonely evenings at home, we had a perpetual party with surprise guests shifting by the minute.

As Dickens wrote, "These were the best of times and the worst of times." They were the best in that we had a father and mother home with us twenty-four hours a day. We were loved and supported emotionally, we were taught music by my violinist mother and piano by

Aunt Sadie. We were encouraged to read and memorize poetry by my
father. We spent evenings in the store playing board games with the
customers and Sunday evening in the little den where I played hymns
on the piano while Mother accompanied on the violin, Ralph played
the trumpet, and Jim sang. Sometimes people in the store would be
touched by a favorite hymn and come in and sing along. Yes, these
were the best of times, warm, friendly, and never alone.

These were also the worst of times in that we were poor, had no car, no
phone, no washing machine, no hot water, no bathtub, and no hope. I
remember the lady who looked at the three of us standing in the store and
said, "It's a shame there's no hope for those children, for they appear so
bright." All three of us heard that comment and even though we'd read no
books on motivation, we all determined we'd show her. We dared to dream.

As I went back over our family history, I saw people who were willing to
take a risk, I saw parents who thought they had prepared well for their
dream, only to see it all fall apart. But I also saw they were able to make
the tough times count. They didn't give up. They gave us intellectual
stimulation, musical knowledge, and a love for the English language.

The noted columnist Russell Baker was a young man who, according to his mother, had "no more gumption than a bump on a log." In
his book *The Good Times*, Russell traces his gift with words back to his
mother and her family. He says, "There seemed to be a word gene that
passed down from her maternal grandfather. He was a school teacher,
his daughter Lulie wrote poetry, and his son Charlie became New York
correspondent for the *Baltimore Herald*."

Russell didn't wake up one morning knowing he would be a Pulitzer-
Prize-winning writer, but he looked to his home, his family for direction.
His mother bought him volumes of *The World's Greatest Literature* and
kept encouraging him to achieve more.

I looked back on my maternal side and found that my grandfather
MacDougall had written poetry. My mother gave me samples of it in
his own handwriting. There were love poems to my grandmother, a
soulful ode to the dead collie Noble, and a tearjerker to the family called
"If I Go First, I'll Wait for You."

My musical mother never mentioned she had poetic talent, but she could
sit down and quickly dash off a birthday poem for a friend. I've always loved
to write humorous verses, Ron can think in rhyme as he's talking at a fast
pace on the radio, and Jim writes all his holiday sermons in poetry.

As Russell Baker, we inherited word genes from both sides of our
family. How about your family? Are there some traits or talents that
may be lying dormant in you? Some of us never look to see.

Bob is a minister in Bradenton, Florida. He traces the roots of his dream to his paternal grandfather. His grandfather was an outstanding member of the farm town in Texas where he lived. He was a respected member of the local church, but he had grown dissatisfied with the teaching he was receiving.

One day a group came by and asked if they could put a tent on the corner of his property and hold church meetings there. Bob's grandfather agreed and began attending. That little tent church offered what he'd been looking for. Bob's father later became a minister in that little church, and today both Bob and his brother are ministers with that same denomination. Bob echoes what Robert Dale says in *Keeping the Dream Alive:* "Our dreams provide a core message that we pass along from generation to generation. They are stories to tell about our heritage. Our dreams provide us with the continuity and content for an ongoing conversation with tomorrow's leaders."

What about you? Is there a common thread in your family that you could look to for direction?

Look to Your Own Desires

There is a big difference between looking to your family for a challenging dream and accepting their idea of what you should become in life. To fulfill a dream it has to be *your* dream, not someone else's.

Is there something bubbling inside you that you've always wanted to do but assumed it was impractical or wouldn't fit your family's expectation? Since I wrote my book *Silver Boxes: The Gift of Encouragement*, the one comment I hear the most is "I could have been something if only I'd heard an encouraging word." I try to give each one hope by saying, "It's never too late to dare to dream. I didn't write my first book until I was almost fifty. Get moving!" I'm convinced from the overwhelming response I've received from *Silver Boxes* that almost everyone has a latent desire within them that has not been fulfilled.

Why Not?

Carolyne told me that from the time she was a little child she loved to draw pictures and she wanted to be an artist. Her family felt she couldn't make a living that way and encouraged her to get a college education. Before she finished, her father died and she felt she was studying to please someone who had left her. For two years she mourned her father's death and took care of her sick mother while putting her own life on hold. Toward the end of that time she realized she was not out looking for a job because she had no enthusiasm for routine work. At that point, she started going to church to find meaning in life and the Sunday school superintendent found out she could draw. He asked her to do some art work for the preschool department, and she was suddenly excited. This experience led her to become a kindergarten teacher, and in her words, "I've been teaching now for eleven years and loving it. I'm using all my talents for the children and I've also gone back and earned a master's degree in the illustration of children's books."

Carolyne was sidetracked for a while because she was trying to fulfill family expectations instead of following her own desires.

On the plane home from South Carolina I sat next to Sylvia, a doctor of podiatric medicine. As she observed me writing, she asked what I was doing and I excitedly told her about this book. She wanted to know how I got into writing and what the book was about. After I had given her a summary of *Dare to Dream*, she said, "I'm the result of a dream."

At the close of World War II, Sylvia's father fled his native Latvia as the Russians were tightening their grip on his country. He hid away on a boat that went from Latvia to Germany, and pedaled off into the country on a bike, not knowing where he was going but fleeing troops each time he saw them. At one point he climbed up the side of a waiting train with his bike, lay on top of the bike, and held on to a vent as the train sped through the countryside. Sylvia said wide-eyed, "If you've seen those movies with people hanging on to the top of a speeding train, you can picture what my father went through."

When he got off the train weak and exhausted, he found himself in Germany and he was picked up and put into a displaced persons camp. Ultimately released and in poor health, he worked his way to the Netherlands and later checked into a hospital. A nurse took a special interest in him and they later married. They both wanted to get away from the bitter memories of the war, and they applied for entrance to both the United States and New Zealand. "Whichever comes first will be the right choice," they determined. "By the flip of a coin," Sylvia said, "I'm an American and not a New Zealander."

Her parents started a new life in Grand Rapids, Michigan, where many of Dutch descent have congregated. They learned a new language and worked hard to scratch out a living. As Sylvia grew up, her parents told her that she was going to have a better life. They put aside a little money every week and helped her get through Calvin College. She worked her way through medical school, completed her internship, and set up practice in Albemarle, North Carolina. Sylvia is the success her parents wanted her to be. She is the result of their dream.

As we talked she reflected, "Now that I've made my goal, I've relaxed. There's no excitement in my life. You've made me realize that what I've achieved is *their* dream, and that now I need to find a new dream, a dream of my own."

Perhaps some of us have been busy fulfilling other peoples dreams. Could it be time to find one of our own?

Heroes, captains, and kings; things dreams are made of, right? But a professor as a hero? George Will once said that a "good teacher is a benevolent contagion, an infectious spirit, an emulable stance toward life. That is why it is said good teachers enjoy a kind of immortality: their influence never stops radiating." Many teachers have encouraged their students by giving uplifting and inspiring words of hope for their futures when no one else had taken the time to do so.

Professor Keating, played by Robin Williams in the film "Dead Poets Society," was definitely a hero. He felt and lived as though his vocation was his calling. In the film Keating so inspires, excites, and motivates seven of his students in poetry that they resurrect a secret society, the Dead Poets. They are given to calling Professor Keating "O Captain, my Captain," from Walt Whitman's poem about Lincoln's death, "Ode." And they often are heard repeating the phrase *carpe diem*, better understood in English as "seize the day." They meet at a clandestine cave and read and recite classic poems, which made me go home and get out my volume on *America's Best Loved Poems!* These seven prep school lads from the Ivy League, who are being taught by other professors much less interestingly, experience from this poetry a real bonding and a delight for life itself. You can almost hear Arthur William Edgar O'Shaughnessy say:

> We are the music makers,
> And we are the dreamers of dreams,
> Wandering by lone sea breakers,
> And sitting by desolate streams;
> World-losers and world-forsakers,
> On whom the pale moon gleams,
> Yet we are the movers and shakers
> Of the world forever, it seems.[4]

In a world that demands practicality and professionalism, Professor Keating refreshed the boys from a free-flowing spring of words and dripped the honey of poetry on their tongues until they craved more and more. Yes, Professor Keating was a hero!

However, where heroes walk there always lurks a villain. Unfortunately in the movie, as in real life, there are also those who discourage individuality—they want to clone you to their likeness—and demand minute perfections. In "Dead Poets Society," the villain is the father of one of the boys, who isn't satisfied with his son's performance and vocational choice. He was an overly strict, militaristic, tight-lipped man, bordering on fascism, who insisted and then demanded his son go to Harvard Medical School. The sad result was that the son chose to commit suicide by shooting himself, rather than give up on his own dream and give in to a father he could never please anyway.

I wanted to say to myself at this point, "Oh, it's only a movie," but then I realized that the reason this movie touched me with its wonderful moments of humor, inspiration, and adolescent awakening to the awesomeness of life was that it also reflected the very disheartening fact that many, many people have had their hearts shattered, and their dreams blown to pieces by those who never really believed in them. Oh, they had been told they were on their side, but only if they made the right choices, went to the right colleges, married the right mate, and carried out the parent's dream. What a terribly sad commentary for such usually very intelligent people.

In Proverbs 22:6 Solomon, the wisest man who ever lived, says: "Train up a child in his way and when he is old he will not depart from it." We often train them up in the way *we* think they should go instead of taking into account their *own* needs, desires, and personality types.

The tongue is a powerful thing! It can curse or it can bless. With it we can discourage or encourage. It can make us a villain or it can make us a hero in the eyes of those we speak to day in and day out. We can be dream breakers or dream makers. The choice is ours. Which will it be?

When my brother Jim was the chaplain at the Air Force Academy, he had a situation so similar to the one portrayed in "Dead Poets Society" that you would think they were both fiction from the same author. A cadet came to him expressing a desire to leave the academy. He wanted to go to a liberal arts college, and he didn't know how to withdraw. As Jim talked with him, he found the boy's father was an Air Force colonel who had decided when his son was young that he would go to the academy. He had prepared the boy to fulfill not his own dream but his father's. When the cadet went home for his Christmas break, the boy told his father of his desire to leave school. The father was irate, blamed Jim for putting these ideas in the boy's head, and sent him back to the academy. He called him a wimp and a failure and asked, "What would my friends think if they knew my son couldn't make it at the academy?"

The boy reported back, told Jim the results, went to rifle team practice, and shot himself. I assume the father rationalized to his friends, "The boy was weak from the start—I did my best—if he'd only listened to me and stayed away from the chaplain."

In life, as in fiction, many people don't realize their dreams because they have been hitching their wagon to someone else's star.

Tom Hopkins is one of the outstanding sales trainers and motivational speakers in the United States today, but if he had gone along with his parents' plan for his life, he might not have achieved such a goal.

When I first attended the National Speakers Association convention and met Tom Hopkins, I was impressed with his reputation and his speaking ability. I also found he was willing to share his dream with others. As I got to know Tom he told me: "All my life, my dad's burning desire for me was to have me become a famous attorney. My mom and dad saved enough money to send me, their eldest son, to college. After just ninety days I knew college wasn't for me. I had tremendous difficulty dealing with the required courses. So I quit college and returned home.

"My dad was very depressed about my decision. After all, it was his dream for me for fifteen years. After a while, he came to my room to talk with me and said, 'Tommy, your mother and I sacrificed and saved for fifteen years to send you to college. I want you to know now, that we'll always love you, even though you'll never amount to anything.'"

Oh, how many discouraged adults have told me similar stories. "My parents never believed in me. They said I'd never amount to 'a row of pins.'" Tom felt guilty for his decision, but he knew in his heart that college wasn't for him.

Tom said, "My father was heartbroken and I hated knowing that I had put him and my mother through that grief. These days I consider my explanation to my parents to have been my first motivational talk because I decided right then and there to build my own dream—to do something wonderful, to make something of myself to make my parents proud of me again.

"Once I had achieved my dream of success and made a name for myself in the field of sales, I decided to help others do the same. I don't try to give other people my dream. I do try to help them decide what their dreams are and show them ways to turn them into reality. I have been fortunate to have helped hundreds of thousands of people achieve some sort of success in their lives simply by daring them to dream their own dreams, too."

I'm more impressed with Tom today than when I first met him because I've seen firsthand his willingness to help others. I also saw his teachable spirit when he brought his wife and family to hear me teach a leadership seminar. Few people on top of their profession think there's anything left for them to learn, but Tom is always open to a new burst of growth.

Tom has truly "amounted to something" by daring to dream in the direction of his own desires.

Look to Your Own Talent and Experiences

What do you do well? Is there some interest you have that could become an occupation? Where have you been successful? Do you have a special talent?

When I needed to go back to work because of some financial reverses in our business, I thought of teaching school again. I had the education and it seemed the logical choice, but I was forty-five and I didn't have the spirit to tackle the teenagers of the day. I had already been doing some volunteer speaking on people's personalities and Fred and I had also been teaching marriage classes in our home. I wondered if I could possibly make a living if I began to charge for my speaking. I remember how daring I was to put a hundred-dollar price tag on each message. Within a few months the requests for my speaking had doubled. I remember one lady saying to me, "Well, if you charge, I guess you must be good."

From that time on, I continued to build my speaking business. I worked on my skills and polished my messages. I began to write books and expanded my subject matter. In 1985, my husband realized that what I was doing was better than his business and so he sold it and became my business manager, director of our offices and warehouse, travel agent, companion, encourager, and best friend. He is also now a speaker, popular television and radio interviewee, and the author of two books of his own. This new mid-life career began when I looked at my life experiences and moved in the direction of my skills and talents.

Is your dream hidden in your interests and successes? What have you done that has excited you, that has really worked?

Twenty years ago Sybil Ferguson had a personal success—she lost fifty-six pounds. The ladies in her neighborhood wanted to learn her secrets.

They gathered together each morning to discuss their diets and lend support. More and more wanted to join. Sybil latched on to something that interested her, something that she had been a success at, and today the support group that met in her kitchen is repeated in thousands of locations throughout the United States and Canada. Sybil's diet success of twenty years ago is today's Diet Center with over forty-five million dollars in annual revenues. Sybil's weight loss was more than just a diet—it became a dream![1]

As a teenager, Pam was a local beauty queen and a candidate for Miss California. But the week before she went to the state contest, she found out she was pregnant. She had to give up her big chance, marry the young man, and forsake all hopes of an education. The marriage was tumultuous. Neither one wanted to be in it, but they tried to do the right thing. Pam recalls that if her husband didn't like what she had cooked, he would throw it at her. This marriage produced two daughters and a bundle of bad memories, eventually ending in divorce.

What does a single mom with no education do for a job? She worked in a department store, dabbled in day care, baked cookies at a grocery store, and became a dental assistant. No matter what she tried, it was never more than a temporary job.

When she met and married Bill, she found the first stable person she had ever known. He had put himself through college by working in parking lots and had gone on to get a degree in political science. Bill says he "stalled off getting a real job by working as a probation officer after graduation." A few years later, the parking company he worked for in college came to him and offered him a position with their company managing parking lots. Later Bill bought the company and has done well financially. But as he says, "How excited can you get over a parking lot?"

Both Pam and Bill hoped for something they could do together and really enjoy. Because of the problems they had raising her two daughters with a step-father, they realized they needed some help. So they enrolled in a parenting class, and the material they learned made such a difference in their life that others began asking them to teach a class themselves. They got the leaders' guide, added some of their own stories, and invited a few couples into their home. They loved teaching the class, and helping other people with their problems was so rewarding. When the first nine-week class was over, so many others wanted to attend that a second parenting class was started. Their church heard about the success of their class and asked Bill and Pam to teach at the church. The first class was filled up immediately and several couples had to be turned away. Pam and Bill found their dream in helping others from their own experiences.

I met Pam at my speakers seminar, where she had come to polish up her skills before teaching the class at church. She plans to write a book that will combine the story of her life, the parenting skills she and Bill have learned, and some successful steps. She is now working in my office dealing with authors and speakers every day and is putting together a talk for mother/daughter banquets. She hopes to slowly change over to a full-time speaking career and is now back in school getting a degree in counseling.

Bill had never thought of being a speaker, but now he, too, has something to say that many people need to hear. Together, they are training parents at a counseling center and in the elementary school system in their town.

My first memory of Ron Howard was when he was the lisping little boy in "The Music Man" waiting for the Wells Fargo wagon. Many of us recall how adorable he was as Opie on the "Andy Griffith Show." We watched him for years as he grew up in Mayberry and then moved into his teenage role as Richie on the popular "Happy Days" series.

Ron was in show business from the time he was two in a Baltimore production of "The Seven Year Itch," and he was already an established star by his teens. Besides acting, Ron also studied film making in high school, where he took second place in an Eastman Kodak national competition. After high school, he was accepted at the USC Film School, but when he took a part in "American Graffiti" it pre-empted his graduation from USC. Ron hasn't allowed that to keep him from accomplishing his goal or to put a damper on his dream.

Many of us would have been excited to be a successful movie star, but Ron wanted to go beyond acting and use his creative talents in directing and inspiring others.

Films such as "Grand Theft Auto," "Splash," "Cocoon," "Willow," and "Parenthood" have been chalked up on his credits. Ron had an interest in show business which became the first step in the accomplishment of his later goals. The television sitcoms and his study in film making have all been steps in the process of his dream of becoming a director in the industry. Yes, Opie and Richie have grown up and Ron Howard is still growing up himself, still learning and still stretching.

> "There is nothing like a dream
> to create the future."
> —Victor Hugo

Popular recording artist Billy Joel was a poor student and didn't think he needed education to write songs. Billy loved music right from the start, and he was banging out tunes on the piano when he was only four. His mother dragged him to lessons until he quit at eleven because "I didn't like practicing from a printed page. I still think teachers should allow more individual creativity."

During high school he often played in a band until 4:00 A.M. and was too tired to go to school. His mother considered him a failure because he didn't graduate, and others said, "You'll never make a living in music." By the time he was twenty he was beginning to think they were right and he attempted suicide. Three weeks in a mental hospital surrounded by seriously ill cases challenged him to never feel self-pity again.

Billy Joel played in a piano bar for a living, and wrote the autobiographical song "Piano Man" from his experiences. His recording rose quickly to the top twenty, and suddenly he was on his way to fulfilling his dream. Even though he finally made it to the top in the music industry, Billy had an inner longing to know what had happened in history and he found himself learning more after he'd left school than before because he could choose his own subject. When he reached forty, he said of himself, "I'm a history nut who is pretty much self-taught, since I didn't graduate from high school. At one point in my life I even thought I wanted to be a history teacher."

Billy Joel found that his own life and his love of history gave him material to use that would touch the hearts of people and teach a lesson at the same time. He wrote down "sound bites" of experience and they became songs. Even without education, he combined his talents and his interests into a career that has brought him to the top and has since become quite philosophical. "At forty," he says, "you may have to take a little more inventory, but you tend to deal with things a little more calmly. And you know that you don't have the corner on wisdom at any age." With his marriage to Christie Brinkley, Billy feels he is finally growing up. He's wearing his dream and he's willing to share his philosophy with others.

"I'm living proof that doing yourself in makes no sense, because things do get better, though it's harder for kids today because of the drugs. What I've learned from Christie and from being a father and from the whole maturation process is that you've got to forgive yourself at times and to grow from failure, instead of letting it destroy you. The thing is never to give up."[5]

Like Billy Joel, singer Tracy Chapman has taken the history of her life and her people and combined them with her talents. She started "strumming for dollars in Harvard Square" and has gone on to realize a dream that is more than most singers could hope for: the Grammy Award for Best New Artist in 1988!

Roddy McDowell began his acting career when he was only ten years old, but he found his true love while he was in his mid-teens. While acting has always been a part of his life, much of his great joy comes from being on the other side of the camera. As a young man, Roddy started taking candid pictures of his friends. His friends were "classic figures in Hollywood," names we would all know. Now in his sixties, Roddy McDowell's late entry into photography is a "source of anguish." He wishes he had started sooner. Roddy has published two books of his work, *Double Exposure* and *Double Exposure II*. He has taken his talent and turned it into a successful venture. He dreams that some day there will be a *Double Exposure III*.

What are your talents and abilities? Are they holding your dream? Perhaps they could be turned into a dream that blossoms into a full-time career like those of Billy Joel or Tracy Chapman. Maybe your dream will fill a sideline direction like that of Roddy McDowell. *Remember, the success of your dream isn't measured by dollars but rather by the quantity and quality of personal satisfaction it brings you.*

My son-in-law Chuck loves Jaguars, especially the classic early 1960 "E" types. His dream would be to own a Jaguar junkyard where he could play with his cars all day long. He is very mechanical and has the ability to fix almost anything that is broken. While owning a Jaguar junkyard is not something that is feasible at this point in his life, he has been able to turn his dream into a successful sideline. Every morning he scans several papers for Jaguars for sale. Each week he searches the *Auto Trader* for Jaguars, and once a month he gets a national publication that features classic cars. Just reading the ads is exciting to him. But reading those ads has paid off. Chuck has made several smart investments in both the cars themselves and in miscellaneous parts. People call him for advice on "E" types. He has won awards on his cars for his restoration work and in rallies with his local Jaguar club. Knowing he has toy cars in the garage lifts his spirits. And when he decided to go back to the University of San Diego and get his masters degree, he was able to sell one of his prized Jaguars and pay for his tuition.

Look to Fill Needs

In the midst of talks of a national recession, I tuned into a television show where a perky lady was telling how she had gone into business for herself. With her was an exuberant man who interjected that "when the economy is down, it is time for you to look around, find a need, and fill it." He asked how she had gone from being a corporate manager to her current business, and she explained that she found herself out of a job and asked herself what she had needed most when she was working. She realized she never had time to go shopping or do errands, so she decided she'd do that for busy people. She started her own business doing other people's marketing, walking their dog, taking their shirts to the laundry, or sitting and waiting for the television repairman to come to their house. Her hours are flexible and her profit is clear. She has always loved to shop, so now she has time to shop all day and earn a living while doing it.

Do your dreams sound outlandish? Are you afraid of what others will say, or that they will laugh? Perhaps your dream is something many of us have thought about and said, "I wish someone would come up with. . . ."

Do you ever wish you didn't have to deal with some of life's unpleasantries or that you could send a "stand-in double" to take your place? Well, that's just where Mr. Hideto Katamine aims to please. This eight-year-old company which grosses a hundred million yen a year (over seven hundred thousand dollars) will rent stand-in wedding guests from the best man to an eloquent father of the bride who will toast the young couple magnificently. Thinking of quitting your job? He has told off bosses for his clients, handed in resignations, and demanded final paychecks.

Mr. Katamine says his company is perfect for present-day Japan, who he says has become lazy and busy. He is even thinking of franchising his business, becoming a kind of "McDonald's of Sham" from Japan. I am sure there are those who heard Hideto's dream and said "Who would be crazy enough to do that?" or "Who would pay for this kind of service?" Obviously there are several takers in this arena who are willingly paying Mr. Katamine to "stand in" for them. Nothing seems to be too far out of the question for those people who have learned to *dare to dream*.

As a young man, Bobby Griffin recalls feeling like a failure, someone who would never amount to anything in life. After dropping out of school at the age of seventeen and being wounded while serving his country in Korea, Bobby Griffin at a discouraged twenty-one returned home with scars, bad memories, little education, and no marketable skills. Who would have thought he would *dare to dream* of being a millionaire?

In 1959, he and his wife Frieda won a trip to Sarasota, Florida. In the parking lot of a used-car dealership, Bobby received an inspiration for a business. As they were about to climb into the front seat of a car they liked but could ill-afford, the salesman said, "Stop! You have sand on your shoes." As they stood by humiliated, the man put down a piece of cardboard on the floor to protect the carpet. A dream was born! Bobby went home to design a disposable floor mat to prevent future customers from the same embarrassment. He thought of putting advertisements for banks about financing car loans in big print on the floormats.

After Bobby had many rejections, one banker told about Bobby's idea at an installment loan convention where other bankers could benefit from the advertising. It wasn't long until Bobby began receiving orders from all over the country for his disposable floor mats.

Bobby reflects that he encountered much ridicule and rejection early on, and because of this he travels five months out of the year speaking to others to encourage them in their dreams. Griffin advises, "If you feel you have a good idea, don't let anyone discourage you. Pursue it to the fullest."

What happened to Bobby Griffin? He had a dream, he believed in his product, he vowed to overcome his circumstances and background, and he pursued the dream with lots of hard work. Bobby says he likes to share his "dream" story so others can realize that they, too, can achieve their dreams, regardless of how much or how little education they have— if they have vision, determination, patience, common sense, and a burning desire to see that dream succeed.

From here on, each time you step on one of those floor mats, think of Bobby Griffin who took a moment of humiliation and provided a positive answer. He saw a need and he filled it. Look around and learn an important lesson from this: *We must not allow failures, or rejection, or personal handicaps, or even lack of education to keep us from daring to dream.*

When I give my *Silver Boxes* message, I quote Oliver Wendell Holmes, who said, "Many of us die with the music still in us." This statement makes many people think about where they're headed and what progress they're making.

Ralph Lagergren spent ten years trying to get his Bi-Rotor invention produced and marketed. This harvesting combine is engineered to reap grain with 70 percent fewer moving parts than existing combines and will enable farmers to harvest faster while losing less grain and yielding fewer damaged kernels than anything on the market. Ralph and his cousin Mark Underwood have been fluctuating between frustration and exhilaration for all these years and have finally received some money from the state of Kansas to help finance the lab tests. Ralph has quit his sales job to go into the promotion of his invention.

After listening to my *Silver Boxes* tape, he wrote me:

> The key statement that I took from your speech was, "Many of us die with the music still in us." Ms. Littauer, that helped me confirm that I'm pursuing the right avenue. I'm banging my cymbals, and playing every other instrument I can. The music is not going to die in me.
>
> My parents have always encouraged me to achieve and have been supportive even though I left a $50,000 job to pursue this project. They know I have to go after my goals. Their support has meant a great deal to me. I want to achieve this goal so they can see that their efforts paid off.

Carol-Marie has a successful business selling her own line of cosmetics and doing makeovers on her customers. She shows women how to project the image they need for their job and lifestyle. While working on women's faces, she came across some that were either temporarily or permanently disfigured. She saw a need to help these women so they could feel better about themselves, and she decided to get some special training to help her meet that need. After that she opened a Para-medical Camouflage Clinic in Apple Valley, California, one of a very few in the entire United States. Carol-Marie is not only filling a unique need, she is ministering personally to those who didn't even want to go out of the house. How rewarding it is to bring help and healing to those who had lost hope.

Having a dream for the future is much more than just a "pipe dream" or a "daydream." In order to make that dream come true and be successful, we must prepare wisely and work hard. It may mean doing a demographic study to see where the market is for our "business dream" and then uprooting the entire family.

Such was the case for Jesse Grover Bell.

Jesse was a young Kansas salesman who manufactured cosmetics in his basement. Jesse read in his newspaper that Cleveland, Ohio, was within five hundred miles of half of the population of the entire country. This piqued his curiosity and so he did further research, only to find that most of the top-selling salesmen were working in Cleveland. With this knowledge, Jesse set out to move his family of five to Cleveland that same year, 1927. Jesse knew that if his cosmetics company was to be successful, he must expose his product to a large general public. Cleveland would give them the exposure that was needed to realize his dream.

Most of us today have heard of Bonne Bell and its famous Ten-O-Six lotion, but in that day no one was producing a medicated skin wash.

Jesse was ahead of his time. He dared to step out to achieve his dream, and he had taken time by reading and researching to get prepared for the dream.

Up to this point, Jesse had been doing "direct sales," going door-to-door, but when Jesse's son Jess came into the business years later, he began to shift the emphasis from direct to indirect sales in drugstores. "Cosmetics for Young Women" was the targeted market. Jess began a plan to put the cosmetics into the hands of a much bigger market by offering consumers free samples of new Bonne Bell products. Jess was a pioneer of a "Teen Board" and "College Board" of sales staff, consisting of young women who went to the drugstores and did beauty makeovers. At this time, Bonne Bell also increased their advertising campaigns in teen magazines. By the mid-1950s with the booming teenage market, Bonne Bell was profiting as never before. The tradition of daring to dream had been passed from one generation, Jesse Grover Bell, to his son, Jess, in the next generation. They each identified their market trends and were ahead of their times.

In the 1960s Jess identified yet another trend—the emphasis on physical fitness. When many other cosmetic lines were hitting older, sedentary women, Jess pushed out in a completely different direction. He helped to sponsor the U. S. Ski Team. The country's growing interest in athletics was impetus for the company's next product, "Lip Smackers," a fruit-flavored lip balm for the active, healthy woman.

All was going very well, and yet it was in the 1970s that Jess almost lost everything that he and his father had worked so hard to achieve. He was taking too much time for the national obsession—athletics, his in the form of tennis—and he began drinking heavily. He almost lost his business and his wife. He needed to take time out to do some "repair" work in order to keep his dream intact. In 1972 he was able to quit drinking and start running. His life, his marriage, and his business were saved. Because of the repairs made to his personal life, Jess decided that his personal growth could be duplicated in corporate growth.

Bonne Bell gave cash incentives of fifty cents a mile to those who walked or ran during their lunch hours or before work. Anyone employed there who gave up smoking for six months received two hundred and fifty dollar bonus, and employees who lost weight in a six-month period were paid five dollars for every pound they lost. Anyone exercising during the lunch hour could wear their athletic clothes the rest of the day. And it's working! More than 60 percent of Bonne Bell employees take advantage of the fitness incentive program.

Bonne Bell believes in sharing their successful dream. J. G. Bell and his son Jess visualized success by daring to dream. They identified success by preparing to dream. They capitalized on success by repairing the dream. And they multiplied success by sharing the dream with the Bonne Bell family of employees. And the dream is wearing well!

Sometimes others tell us we dare not dream because "it's too risky, no one else has succeeded in this area before in quite this way."

Yet those who do succeed in daring to dream have ventured into areas where angels fear to tread. Such is the case for Australian-born Paul Hogan, star of the hit movie "Crocodile Dundee." A former painter who helped paint the Sydney Harbour Bridge, Paul Hogan had a dream to be on television. In less than a decade, he and his partner John Cornell changed the rules for independent television production. They perceived a need in the quality, variety, and creativity of Australian television. In order to fill the need, they dared to form their own production company, against the advice of veteran colleagues. "You are foolish to go it alone," they were told, but they proceeded anyway. Paul's partner negotiated deals with the channels and they wrote, performed, and produced within their own production company.

Paul Hogan suddenly found himself a national celebrity, star, and entertainer, with offers to do concerts, make club appearances, and do more commercials. It was then that he agreed to let his partner manage his career.

Because of Paul's sheer audacity to insist on owning everything he did on television, it allowed him to make the money that ordinarily would have gone to the network. What he and his partner did was truly pioneering and they dared to go against the norm. In light of Paul Hogan's history of success, the Australian government listened and gave their approval for a tourist campaign. Paul offered his services free of charge to help get the campaign off the ground in the hopes that the exposure would make up for his time and effort. The commercial went on American networks with outstanding results. In only five weeks, Australia went from being number forty-nine on the "most desired destination" list to number one. It was the most successful tourist commercial in America in ten years. It was also a boon for Australia's struggling commerce: The average tourist stays in Australia two weeks and leaves behind fifteen hundred dollars! The first week after the commercial aired, Australia's tourism took a giant leap forward.

Are there those who are throwing water on your dream with phrases like "it's never been done that way" and "it's too risky"? Don't let that dampen your dream. Reach for that star and dare to dream that dream!

I was personally so caught up in Hogan's smiling pitch that I believed him, and on my first trip to Australia I firmly expected to see

Paul Hogan at the airport to welcome me, to take me home, and to "throw another shrimp on the barbie."

When I first met Joel Schiavone, he was an awkward young man with a very noticeable stammer when he tried to speak. As friends of his wealthy parents, we could see how his handicap bothered them even though they never spoke of it. Joel went to Yale and then to Harvard Business School, but instead of doing something normal he started a chain of taverns called "Your Father's Moustache" where he played the banjo. He seemed to be transported to another world when he was on the stage with his banjo. After twelve years of this business, he had accumulated enough to buy the Connecticut Limousine Service, a pet store chain, and the New Haven Nighthawks, a local hockey team. He also bought the Bridgeport Cable Television for three hundred thousand dollars, and after building it up he sold it for fifty-eight million.

In 1979, he realized that the downtown of his home city of New Haven was rapidly deteriorating and he decided to fill a need. He took on a project a lesser person would not have touched, to revitalize a dying city. Besides putting in about twelve million dollars of his own, Joel Schiavone encouraged others to invest. Together they turned a vacant hotel into apartments, the abandoned Union League into an elegant office building, the decrepit Palace Theatre into a music hall, and the Schubert into a beautiful restoration of its former self.

"To re-create an effective downtown," he says, "you need people to work and live and play downtown. We don't do shopping centers. We do neighborhoods and try to create day life and night life."

The local newspaper called him "a private sector superman . . . a banjo banging entrepreneur who takes no pains to sugarcoat his opinions or soft pedal his intentions."

Joel Schiavone could have lived off his father's money or his "Father's Moustache," but he chose to fill a need to salvage and redecorate the center of a sick city.

Look to Areas of Leadership

Politics has lost much of its past glamour, but there are still possible dreams in the area of leadership. If we keep alert to what's going on in the world and have some leadership skills, we could have a new profession.

Who would have dreamed that the Eastern European communist bloc countries would be seeing their dream come true . . . the dream of a freer society, a relaxed government stance, and the burning of communist membership cards outside the Kremlin in Red Square? The walls that were built to keep freedom out have crumbled . . . the Berlin Wall is gone. Who would have dreamed a poet could become the president of Czechoslovakia? And yet who better than poet Vaclav Havel could inspire a country that had just about given up hope to dare to dream again.

God's Word says, "Without vision the people perish" (Proverbs 29:18), and little Czechoslovakia had all but perished when the embers of a dream began to ignite. Soon, little by little, the fire engulfed the dry wood in men's hearts until the raging inferno had spread and all were aflame with the cry of "freedom!" There was a revival in every sense of the word in that little country. After forty years of hearing lies about their "state of the country" in speeches by the previous regime with words like "we are so prosperous, so happy, we trust the government . . . ," the people were ready to hear the truth.

In Vaclav Havel's 1990 New Year's Day address to his country, he presented the reality. "Our country is not prospering. The great creative and spiritual potential of our nation is not being used to its fullest, our outdated economy is squandering energy, a country once proud of the standard of education ranks seventy-second in the world, we have (ecologically) the worst environment in all of Europe, but the worst thing is we are living in a decayed moral environment."

Vaclav Havel voiced thoughts long kept private when he said, "We have learned not to believe in anything, not to care about one another, and only to look after ourselves. Notions such as love, friendship, companionship, humility and forgiveness have lost their depth and dimension, and for many of us they represent merely some kind of psychological idiosyncrasy. . . ." The previous government had been arrogant and intolerant of free thought and creativity, and they used people as cogs in the big machine of communism. When people are used as cogs, one turning against the other, they eventually wear down from the constant grind—mentally, emotionally, physically, and spiritually.

Vaclav Havel also depicted them as a morally ill people because they had all allowed this to happen; they accepted the totalitarian system as inalterable, thereby keeping it going.

He presented the reality and the reason for it and challenged the people and himself to see their responsibility for it—they had been willing victims. It's a truth all of us need to understand: Until we truly see the error of our ways, we may not understand how we got there and how to prevent it from happening in the future. "We cannot lay all the blame on those who ruled before us, not only because this would not be true, but also because it could detract from the responsibility each of us now faces—the responsibility to act on our own initiative, freely, sensibly, and quickly. . . ."

Even Vaclav Havel found it difficult to fathom what had happened in his own country. "How," he asked, "had a people who no longer believed in anything suddenly managed to find the enormous strength in the space of a few weeks to shake off the totalitarian system in a decent and peaceful way?" He also asked, "Where had the younger generation who had grown up totalitarian found their source of aspirations for truth, freedom of thought, political imagination, civic courage, and insight? And how was it that the parents (also considered lost) joined in with them, and how was it possible all of them immediately grasped what had to be done?" A good set of questions! The obvious answer must be, "The dream for freedom and a better life never really died."

Havel challenged them with the memory of how many lives had been lost and sacrificed for the freedom they were now enjoying. He told them it was up to them to see this new-found hope of freedom came to fruition and their civic, national, and political self-confidence would come alive in a historically new way.

Vaclav Havel, a dreamer, a poet, a president, is a pioneer in the field of dreams for Czechoslovakia. What inspires *you* to dream great dreams? What aspirations do *you* have deep in your heart that are only embers now? Fan the flame . . . dream! Dreams can come true. Just ask Vaclav Havel.

> "Great visions often start
> with small dreams."

My first introduction to Brig Hart was when I was picked up at the airport by Billy, the limousine driver for the weekend seminar. As Billy and I became acquainted in the rides between the convention center and the hotel, I discovered he was more than just my driver for the weekend. He had been brought in especially for the occasion.

Billy was actually the personal valet and chauffeur for Brig Hart, the energetic and enthusiastic host of our weekend seminar. Brig was the center of attention and a bundle of energy. Everywhere he went, people seemed to follow him. He and his adorable wife Lita seemed to be born to a life of riches and excitement.

But Billy told me about a different Brig, long before he ever dared to dream.

Brig had once been in the Marines, but he found life at the beaches to be more his style. Billy and Brig spent their days surfing, and in his spare time Brig operated a floundering surf shop. Surfing and partying were his main interests, and Billy told me he doubted that Brig would ever amount to anything. To Billy, Brig was just another beach bum who rented a room from his mother.

Brig's surfing shop was failing miserably, and he knew he needed help. So when someone suggested he attend a meeting for local businessmen, he jumped at the chance. With his long blonde hair and deeply tanned skin, Brig looked out-of-place among the other businessmen there.

The speaker that night had driven seven hundred miles to share the plan of network marketing. Only a handful of people were in attendance, a couple of well-dressed businessmen and one long-haired beach bum. The speaker quickly discounted Brig as a network marketing potential, and focused his attention on the other men present.

It wasn't long until the smartly dressed businessmen concluded that the concept of network marketing wasn't for them and they left in the middle of the presentation. Only Brig remained in the audience. Disheartened, the speaker stopped and prepared to pack up his materials when Brig said, "Hey, man, I'm here. Go on with the program." Although he figured he was just wasting his time with this long-haired beach bum, the speaker continued his presentation. At the conclusion, Brig decided to join the business.

The minute Brig saw the possibility for his future, he began to prepare the dream. He attended a weekend event for the business, and while he was there two things happened that changed his life. He saw his dream actually being lived out by others. They became his friends and his mentors. He also saw another dimension to their lives, and he committed his life to the Lord. Following the guidance of these men, he began to mature both professionally and spiritually.

In just a matter of years, Brig has been transformed from an aimless surfer struggling to survive to the head of a large networking group. The room he rented from Billy's mother has been replaced with a ten-room waterfront home of his own, a motor coach, a boat, and lots of other toys. Brig dared to dream, and as a result, his whole life has changed. He no longer worries about how he can pay the rent. His main problem these days is finding a convention center large enough to hold everyone who wants to come hear him share his dream. Brig Hart has become the motivation to thousands of others, teaching them how they, too, can *dare to dream*.

On my first visit to New Zealand, I addressed a group in Auckland called "Women with a Difference." As I walked through the foyer in Clifford House I heard excited whispers, "The mayor is coming!" Since I wasn't the mayor, I knew these women were thrilled over the anticipated arrival of a local dignitary.

"Our mayor is a woman," the chairperson stated, "and I had to really pull strings to get her to show up. She's so busy, but she did agree to come and greet the business women of the city. I told her she'd like you, so be sure you're charming."

I hadn't planned to be disagreeable, but I thanked her for the warning.

"Her name is Dame Cath Tizard. That rhymes with lizard."

Instantly I pictured an elderly, plump dowager with white hair and a dour disposition, someone aloof and forbidding, perhaps a dignified version of Miss Marple out of an Agatha Christie novel. As this flash passed through my mind, I heard an excited, "Here she comes!" I turned expecting a chauffeur-driven limousine and instead saw a small car draw up to a no-parking zone. Out stepped a sharply dressed fiftyish matron in a black pantsuit with a bright red blazer. Dame Cath with her stylish salt and pepper hair strode into the foyer alone and glanced around with an air of confidence and a winning smile.

As the seminar began, Dame Cath was introduced. She gave a brief greeting from the city, and encouraged women to seek leadership positions. But instead of leaving after her greeting as she had planned, she sat down in the first row and listened intently as I explained the characteristics of personalities. She responded with laughter as she found herself a twin to me: outgoing, optimistic, fun-loving, talkative, dynamic, active, and controlling.

After the morning break, Dame Cath was back in her front-row seat and readily took notes as I gave the steps for constructing a speech. At lunch we had fun exchanging stories and finding out how much we had in common. Even though she had business awaiting her attention, she stayed until the end of the session and was even willing to give a summary of what she had learned. She used all the principles of speaking I had given, put them into practice, and gave her own personal application. I was impressed with her brilliance and her ability to summarize the whole day in a brief and motivating message. She touched us all emotionally as she concluded, "I came to scoff, and I stayed to worship."

As time went on, I learned more about Dame Cath. She was a girl from a working-class background who dared to dream. She went to college and married a man who ran for Parliament in 1957 and was there for the next thirty-three years. During the early years of her marriage, she returned to the university to prepare her dream. She managed to maintain a B average while raising four children and being active socially as a parliamentarian's wife. Her husband persuaded her to put her name forward for the Auckland City Council, and in 1971 she was elected to a seat. She had done her homework and she was ready. Because she faithfully did more than her duty demanded, she wore the dream well. Even though her husband later left her for a younger woman, Dame Cath continued on, repaired the dream, and in 1983 was chosen as the first female mayor of Auckland. The *New Zealand Herald* describes her personality, "Quick-witted, sharp-tongued, and disarmingly friendly, she's been called many things. But never dull. Never quiet."

When I met her in 1989, I was fascinated with her quick wit and engaging personality. Actually, I was a little envious of her position since I'd always wanted to be in politics. I hoped I would someday be appointed, because I didn't want to run for something and take the chance of losing. But Dame Cath was obviously a winner.

However, the public is often fickle, and when some unpopular situations arose in city government, Dame Cath was the easy one to blame. For years there had been talk of amalgamating the towns around Auckland into a new city, and under her leadership this feat was finally accomplished. But in the process, a collective debt of one hundred and fifty million dollars was announced, layoffs of public employees were necessary, and an 18.5 percent tax rate increase had to be imposed. Added to these problems was the completion of a new civic center at the cost of $128.5 million, more than double the estimated cost. Infighting over the contracting and a public report of the costly changes caused the people to rise up in criticism of the council. Unfortunately for Dame Cath, the buck was made to stop with her.

It is obvious that the critical attitude, negative attention, and her inability to fight back because of legal constraints were extremely draining on Dame Cath. Her powerful personality needed a sense of loyalty and appreciation for all the work she had done in seven years as mayor. But the loyalty which had been high in her good years quickly disappeared. Dame Cath said, "It has been distressing to become the personal target of disillusioned council employees and disenchanted rate payers. They've looked for a focus of their anger and their distress and whoever the mayor is, they're a target for that. I find it very sad when my relationships with the staff have always been very good to find spiteful little cartoons and poems and pamphlets going about which target me personally."[6]

In August of 1990 when the council workers went on strike, Dame Cath was called a few choice names and spat on by a protesting laborer who knew nothing of her working-class background and how simply she really lived.

On the confrontations Dame Cath commented, "He didn't know me and he knew nothing of my record in council. His assumption was that I was rich. . . . I know it's silly to get upset over one ignorant person, but it is distressing to find yourself the target when you're tired and personally stressed and these things get out of proportion."[7]

One journalist noted, "Dame Cath Tizard doesn't feel funny any more. She of the rapid-fire one-liners and damning put downs, has misplaced her sense of humor somewhere during the sheer, grinding exhaustion of recent months. She's changed incredibly."[8]

During the depths of these depressing times as Dame Cath was assessing the situation she received a call from Government House asking if she would accept appointment as governor general of New Zealand, a highly coveted position with perks including a pension for life. This post removed Dame Cath from the controversy of politics and placed her in a post of honor. She even flew to London to be personally confirmed by Queen Elizabeth II.

Dame Cath dared to dream once again. "At nearly sixty," *The New Zealand Herald* said, "she does not expect her new role to change her much. People who have been confronted by an angry Dame Cath in full flight, or a rather merry Dame Cath out to have a good time may quail at the prospect of her in such a dignified role."[9]

But Dame Cath responds, "Throughout all my time in public life I have realized you can play your role without losing your integrity or ceasing to be yourself. I will continue to be myself, although I might from time to time feel it necessary to bite my tongue."

We all want to be real, to stay true to our birth personality, yet we know that our real identity is not an excuse for poor behavior. Like Dame Cath, sometimes we may need to bite our tongue.

As word spread that Dame Cath had been appointed as governor general, the criticism vanished and Dame Cath was the center of attention at a celebrity roast given for her at the civic center, the very place whose construction costs had caused her so much grief.

Later, at an art gallery, Dame Cath made a grand entrance. A local columnist referred to her as "the very elegant, very gracious, very regal, happy and glorious Dame Catherine Tizard." And when asked when she would step down as mayor, she replied, "There's no rule that says you can't be governor general and mayor of Auckland at the same time, and if some of these pushy mayoral candidates keep pushing too hard, I may not step down at all!"

Dame Cath is back to normal!

When I was in New Zealand in October of 1990, Dame Cath, and I met for what turned out to be a three-hour breakfast at an Auckland hotel. We discussed politics and personalities and I asked her what had happened that ended her marriage. She told me a story that showed both her sense of humor and her maturity. During World War II, her husband Bob had been in the military and had met a Canadian woman named Beryl. They had talked of marriage, but distance kept them apart and instead Bob met and married Cath. Whenever they had disputes, Cath would retort, "Why didn't you marry Beryl?" It was as if Beryl were hiding in their bedroom closet waiting to step out at the first sign of a separation!

While Bob was in session for Parliament, Cath ran the household and raised the children, even though she knew their living in different cities allowed him to be discreetly unfaithful. He subsequently fell in love with a young woman and left Cath after thirty years of marriage for this tempting diversion. Amidst jokes about his mid-life crisis, Bob married his mistress and they had a baby boy. But this tempestuous relationship ended quickly in divorce and Cath quipped, "I told him he should have married Beryl!"

At a World War II reunion in Canada a few years ago, Bob once again met Beryl and he came back to New Zealand to announce to the family, "I'm going to marry Beryl." And he did. Dame Cath laughed as she told me about going to the wedding. "I even offered to perform the ceremony. If he had married Beryl in the first place, he would have saved us all a lot of trouble."

In discussing her trip to England to visit the queen, Cath explained that if a woman's husband is knighted she becomes a Lady, but if she is honored for her own achievements, she becomes a Dame. She also told me that she was to be given two more Dame designations while at the Court of St. James.

She concluded with her typical wit, "I've heard of people who were double-damned, but I will be triple-Damed."

When Dame Cath Tizard assumed her title as governor general, the first woman in New Zealand to hold this post, she became the personal representative of the Crown in New Zealand, took residence in palatial dwellings in Auckland and Wellington, and was given a staff of servants, including a lady-in-waiting. Not bad for a poor working-class girl!

Dame Cath, Governor General of New Zealand, dared to dream that she could rise above her humble beginnings. She prepared her dream at the university by being alert to life, by always speaking the truth in a clear way, and by using her personality strengths while working to overcome her weaknesses. Her life has not been easy, as governor general she will share that dream as she travels, speaks, and officiates, and as she adds a regal, if roguish, air to any reception as the representative of the queen.

Four days before his own death, Sir David Martin made final arrangements with the Sydney City Mission for the establishment of the Sir David Martin Foundation: Caring for Young Australians. Sir David was concerned for homeless, deprived, or addicted youth of his country and he felt the Sydney City Mission could be trusted to implement his ideas. According to foundation material, "Sir David had a vision for Australia's youth and charged the Mission with the responsibility of fulfilling his dream." Sir David dared to dream that even after his death his wishes would come true. "While it's still today," he once said, "let's help equip our young people for tomorrow."

There is such a need for people in all countries to use their leadership skills to help change the lives of others.

Don't Look to Luck

"Sweet dreams may millions find you,
sweet dreams, leave all your worries behind you,
and in your dreams, whatever they be,
dream a little dream of me. . . ."
—California Lotto theme song

Even the California Lottery has capitalized on the notion of making dreams come true by luring the population to "get rich quick" and to "grab for the brass ring," to look for the "pot of gold" by playing Lotto. Every single one of us, whether we have plunked down a dollar or not, has probably given at least a little thought to the question, "What if I won the lottery?"

When people were asked, "What could you do with twelve million dollars?" there were both practical answers and fairy-tale dreams. Some of the answers given were amusing: "Pay off our four maxed-out Mastercards, buy each of the four magazines that sent rejection slips back with my manuscript, buy a candy company and refuse to sell candy to anyone under 135 pounds!" Other dreams had to do with security: "Own our own home, not have to work for a living." Then there were dreams of multiplication: "If we could invest in a sure thing, we would make millions on our millions." Revenge dreams made the list also: "We would buy that computer store and fire all the credit personnel that turned us down for credit in 1985, we would buy 51 percent of the stock of the auto insurance company that wouldn't pay off on our claim."

It seems all of us have our own "pet dreams" about what we could do if we ever were *lucky* enough, but perhaps if we spent as much time *working* toward realistic goals, the dreams could and would become a reality! If only we would dare to dream a little dream! We might really leave our worries behind us.

> "This was my dream:
> What doth it bode,
> God knows."
> —William Shakespeare

PART TWO

Prepare
the
Dream

> "I will study and prepare myself
> and then someday my chance will come."
> —Abraham Lincoln

Ignore the Things That Don't Help

Have you ever looked at someone who made it to the top and wondered why? Have you ever said, "I'm smarter, better looking, with more education. How come he got ahead?" Those who appear to be overnight successes have usually worked for years, for little money, honing their skills, getting ready for that magic moment when it all comes together and appears to be a stroke of luck.

Ron Chapman (formerly Ralph) didn't become that overnight success by luck, but he did work diligently for thirty-five years in radio before receiving national acclaim. He was always able to see the humor in life, to quickly size up every situation, and to give his best even in events with little acclaim or promise.

When asked about his school days Ron says, "I always knew I wanted to be a disc jockey and I just ignored the things that I thought weren't going to help me." With his single-minded goal in life, Ron was able to sift out those things that wouldn't help and excel in those that would provide practice for the future.

The only way we could ever get Ron to do his homework was to allow him to read it aloud as a radio show. He'd go into the den, play a record, and then say to a mythical audience, "Today we will read another exciting chapter in *Ivanhoe*." He seldom finished even one chapter because he had to pause to play a platter and talk to the folks.

Ron felt reading was a waste of active time and he devised different ploys to get out of doing book reports. In his senior year of high school he dated Barbara, a serious student, who had just completed *Gone with the Wind*. Since Ron's teacher had assigned a certain number of pages to be read for book reports, Ron thought if he could only use *Gone with the Wind* he would cover his whole year's requirements in one fell swoop. This idea so excited him that he got Barbara to write up a lengthy book report and he got Mother to type it. Mother was willing to do anything to help Ron out, so she stayed up late into the night to prepare his report. He passed it in, got an A, and was through for the year.

That was until Mother went to P.T.A., where she was bemoaning how hard it was to get him to read. As she expressed these thoughts to his teacher, he replied, "That's odd you say that as he just read *Gone with the Wind*."

"*Gone with the Wind?*" Mother cried. "He never read *Gone with the Wind!*"

When she came home and asked Ron about *Gone with the Wind*, he couldn't believe her. "You're the one who typed it!"

"Well, I guess I didn't pay much attention to what I was typing," she said with a sigh.

The next day Ron's teacher rescinded the A and replaced it with a zero for the year's reports, bringing his average so low that he barely passed English.

For years after that, my mother would burst into tears at the mere mention of *Gone with the Wind*.

While my mother worried about how poorly he was doing in school, Ron was out with his tape recorder interviewing celebrities at Salisbury Beach. As a teenager with no credentials, he managed to get into the dressing rooms of the visiting stars and made friends with the Ames Brothers, Patti Paige, and dozens of others. He'd bring his interviews back to WHAV and they would put them on the air. No one on their staff was able to get to these people and so Ron added a touch of glamour to our Haverhill station. Once he graduated, WHAV had little choice but to put Ron on the air and give him his own show.

At eighteen he was where he wanted to be for life, but the government intervened and sent him to Korea as a private in the United States Army. Once the troopship got under way, an announcement came over the loudspeaker that tomorrow morning the jobs would be given out for the two weeks on board. Ron's mind went into high gear to figure out how he could avoid the menial tasks, those things that weren't going to help him, and spend his time on more fulfilling activities. The next morning he took a clipboard and stood next to the sergeant who was giving out the orders. As the sergeant assigned the first fifty to scrape paint, the next group to clean latrines, and on down the line, Ron stood nodding in approval taking notes. "Well done," he said in affirmation.

The sergeant hardly dared ask him, "What is it that *you'll* be doing here on the ship?"

Ron answered, "I'm in charge of the talent show," of which there was not one at the moment.

Not wishing to appear ignorant or out of touch, the sergeant replied, "Oh yes, the talent show." Throughout the two weeks, everyone assumed someone had assigned Ron to put on a talent show as he busied himself around the ship interviewing men to cull out their latent talents. While others scraped and scoured, he created a show in his mind, and the night before they docked he pulled off the highlight of the whole trip. With his warm sense of humor he was able to hold together a series of acts that no one would have ever dared to do on dry land.

After being in Korea a few weeks, he received a scroll from the United States government for having lifted the morale of the troops while onboard ship. He was the only one able to avoid the assigned work and the only one to receive a commendation for having done it.

Once settled in Korea, Ron became the Voice of the United Nations Command and was able, while the others were out at the front, to reside in the air-conditioned trailer with his radio equipment. He was an early Robin Williams and his "Good Morning, Korea" was a hit with the troops. He worked hard to eliminate his Boston accent, to improve his vocabulary, and to develop his own morning DJ personality. Ron was preparing his dream.

Some Korean businessmen who appreciated his clear articulation asked Ron to tutor them in conversational English. They recommended him to others, and soon he was teaching English at the University of Seoul. When he wrote me about that job I wanted to go back to Haverhill High School and tell his crusty old English teacher that Ron was now *teaching English in a university!*

At this point, Ron was doing his good morning show plus tutoring and teaching, and there were just not enough hours in the day to do it all. An idea came to him to tape a month's worth of generic shows and then he wouldn't have to do a live one ever again. No one seemed to notice that on the first of May they heard the same program they had listened to on April first and March first. This creative system allowed him to hear the alarm at 6:00 A.M., turn on the tape, and go back to sleep, saving his strength for more creative activities.

His reputation as an articulate speaker spread and he was asked to put together an instructional television program to teach Koreans how to pronounce English words. Surrounding him on the show were petite Korean beauties who smiled, bowed frequently, and handed him anything he needed.

This format of Ron with his scantily clad showgirls became so popular that his English program moved up to number one in the national ratings.

Many of the servicemen in Korea did their tour of duty and went home, but Ron worked every minute he could, learned all he was able, and prepared himself for what would become his life's profession. He had learned to sift out what wouldn't advance his aims and to dedicate his creative energies on what would work.

Another broadcaster says of Ron, "He is going to be remembered for years and years to come because he got himself into a position where he instinctively knew what to do. And that happens so rarely on radio." From childhood Ron was busy preparing his dream to become a radio personality.

What about you? Some of us are not sure that we have life under control or that our desires are within reach, so let's begin with the basics and go back to the starting gate.

Personality Introduction

After years of corporations concentrating on business seminars that show executives how to manage money and achieve success, some are developing a new soft heart and a spirit that cares for the private life of each individual. Many businesses are now aware that when an employee is unhappy at home, he or she is not functioning well at work.

As drug and alcohol problems have become too obvious to ignore, insurance companies have accepted rehabilitation as a health necessity and expensive programs have developed overnight. Costly clinics have copied Betty Ford and taking the cure has become not only socially acceptable, but even somewhat chic. Helpful as many of these programs are, they all take place *after* the damage has been done. It's like patching the tire every day instead of looking for the spike in the road.

Suddenly a new idea has come along: "Let's look at people's lives before they fall apart, let's show them how to get along with each other before it's too late." Perhaps if we teach them how to wear their dreams, we won't have to spend so much time and money repairing them. Perhaps Lee Iacocca said to himself, "If I can't hold a marriage together for at least a couple years, maybe I don't know as much about human relationships as I thought."

Perhaps Donald Trump, with his Taj Mahal toppling like the tower of Pisa and his marriage left in the dust, finally had a second thought about his priorities.

To examine our lives and know our strengths from our weaknesses, we need some kind of a tool so simple that we can grasp it quickly without having to go back to college. Is this a possibility?

Who Am I?

People are always interested in analyzing themselves. We all want to know, "Who am I?" This eternal question has been asked by the ancient philosophers, the Jewish patriarchs, and the Renaissance man. It is the major question college students discuss and ponder over, and is of such concern to adults today that I have spent twenty-two years of seminar teaching helping people to find answers.

Oswald Chambers says, "Personality is that peculiar, incalculable thing that is meant when we speak of ourselves as distinct from everyone else. Our personality is always too big for us to grasp. An island in the sea may be but the top of a great mountain. Personality is like an island, we know nothing about the great depths underneath, consequently we cannot estimate ourselves."[10]

Our personality is too big for us to grasp and it is difficult to estimate ourselves. If only we could find some simple tool, some measuring stick by which we could get a handle on our own natures.

In the human quest for answers to life, we have divided ourselves into all kinds of categories. We can check our body types: endomorph and ectomorph; we can analyze our brains: right and left; we can ponder over extrovert or introvert, aggressive or passive. One humorous article in *USA Today* even did a profile on the type of person who gives fruitcakes for Christmas presents: a man, fifty-five or older, who lives in the country. These exciting statistics came from a poll of over seven hundred adults' holiday behavior revealing the demographics of the fruitcake giver. Whether we wish to think about our bodies, our brains, or our propensity to give out fruitcakes, there is only one theory of personality evaluation that has been around for over two thousand years.

The four temperaments were first labeled by Hippocrates, a noted Greek philosopher and physician and author of the Hippocratic oath taken by the medical profession over the years. As he dealt with complex human problems, he felt it would help people to understand themselves if he could simplify their personality traits and label them. Using the fluids of the body as types he said the *sanguine* (blood) was the talker who wanted to have fun. The *choleric* (yellow bile) was the worker who wanted to be in control. The *melancholy* (black bile) was the thinker who wanted everything perfect. The *phlegmatic* (phlegm) was the balancer of life who wanted to keep peace and avoid conflict.

When Fred and I first came across this theory in 1968, it revolutionized our marriage. I had always thought he was the only person in the world who reasoned that if you could only make out a chart on any given problem, you could solve it rationally. He thought I was the only one who felt it was more important to enjoy myself than to get the details down perfectly. When I learned that he was melancholy and there were thousands like him, I backed up and looked at him in a new light. When he found out that I was sanguine and that having fun didn't mean I was without purpose, he relaxed his grip on my training program. For the first time in fifteen years of marriage, we began to accept each other as we were, not as we had always hoped the other would become.

As we studied further, we found we both had an ample amount of choleric and for all these years we had been trying to control and remake each other. Typical of my nature, the minute I learned these new truths I had to tell someone else. I invited in ten couples and played with the personalities as a parlor game. The experience was so revealing that suddenly clouds of confusion cleared up and people began to see each other in truth for the first time. They looked at the sanguine and said, "Now I see why you're so happy all the time and why you talk so much."

To the choleric, "Now I see why you're so bossy and why it aggravates me that you are always right."

To the melancholy, "Now I see why you say if it's worth doing, it's worth doing right." To the phlegmatic, "Now I see why you never get excited over anything and why you like to take it easy and avoid trouble."

In one evening with limited knowledge, I could see that the theory worked. People who thought there was no hope they could ever understand each other suddenly looked at each other with clear eyes.

From that time on, I became an avid student of personality theories. As I developed my own examples, groups began to ask me to come and share with them. From those early speaking engagements sprang up a career of answering the question, "Who am I?"

Physically, I am a human being who had all the genes within me at conception to predetermine my coloring, shape, intelligence, and personality.

Spiritually, the Bible says that God knew me when I was conceived in that secret place, before there was anything on my frame. God knit me together in my mother's womb. I am fearfully and wonderfully made (Psalm 139).

Now science agrees with Scripture. Adam Matheny of the Louisville Twin Study, the oldest of U.S. twin study groups, says, "The mechanism for change is laid down the moment a child is conceived" and that the genes program a "rough sketch of life."[11]

Emotionally, I react to life's situations based on my birth personality and the amount of childhood trauma and abuse put upon me. If I live a relatively normal life with a low degree of stress, my personality and responses will be consistent from the time I am a child until I die.

Author Melvin Konner writes:

> "Who am I?" is the most basic question we ask. Education and environment don't count, geneticists say. We are who we are when we are born and much more so. Words like personality are now being shaken by a biological revolution. Ancient and medieval ideas about our constitutional predisposition to certain character types (choleric, or quick to anger, for example, or phlegmatic and unemotional) are rising again, in altered form, with data to back them up.[12]

Personality is the outward display of our inner self. We are all born with a certain predisposition and set of responses. We are not little blank pages waiting for fate to write upon us. If I am born a sanguine, all my life I will be optimistic and bounce back quickly from negative experiences. If I am born a choleric, I will refuse to let bad times get me down and take immediate action after negative experiences. If I am born a melancholy, I will always have the tendency to think everything over carefully, tend to be pessimistic, and get depressed over negative experiences. If I am born a phlegmatic, I will stay balanced, seldom show my feelings, and look the other way in negative experiences. Because our personality is so closely tied to our responses, we get a clearer picture of ourselves from our reactions than from our cultivated behavior. Taking charm courses may improve our manners, but it doesn't alter our heredity.

Oswald Chambers says, "Personality merges and you only reach your real identity when you are merged with another person. . . . Love is the outpouring of one personality in fellowship with another personality."[13]

Where Did Personality Studies Come From?

When I first started speaking on the personalities, the idea seemed relatively unknown. I had read Tim Lahaye's *Spirit Controlled Temperament* and Hallesby's *Temperaments and the Christian Faith*, and from then on I developed my own examples. There had been large gaps from Hippocrates' writings to Carl Jung, who had the same message but with different labels. He used "vapors" to describe us combining warm and cold, dry and moist. In more recent years have come Myers-Briggs, breaking the four basic temperaments into sixteen possibilities, and the

Taylor-Johnson temperament test charting out our highs and lows. Performax has produced a wide range of personality evaluations, and Gary Smalley turns us into animals. Today there are endless ways to examine ourselves, but each system reaches back to Hippocrates for its roots no matter what it uses for labels.

Was I Born with My Personality?

Hippocrates' theories are based on our being created with a direction of personality, a set of responses to the circumstances of life. As I have worked with this system of analysis for twenty-two years, I have experientially validated this theory of birth personality thousands of times. However, in the last decade there has been an amazing surge of scientific interest and proof that we are born with a set of behavior patterns and responses. The researchers have discovered that our most genetic trait is leadership and our least is achievement. Still, what we do with our personality is strongly influenced by our environment.

How Can Anyone Prove We Are Born with a Personality Pattern?

The most well-publicized study was done by the University of Minnesota on twins who were reared apart. The research started in 1979, and the complete results were summarized in the *Journal of Personality and Social Psychology* in June of 1988. Throughout these years, the team headed by David Lykken administered personality questionnaires to 402 pairs of twins. Of these, forty-four pairs were identical (monozygotic) and were reared apart. The questions asked about feelings of well-being, confidence in self, attitude toward achievement, social intimacy, avoidance of danger, desire for pleasure, and many other temperament traits.

The experiment proved conclusively that we do inherit our basic personality and that environment plays upon what we have inherited. Many of the examples showed that twins who grew up in different parts of the world, some even speaking different languages, had identical personality patterns despite varied religious upbringings, economic backgrounds, or family size. The most popular example from the University of Minnesota study is the case history of Jim Lewis.

> Jim Lewis and Jim Springer were separated at birth and brought together at age forty. Both had taken law enforcement training. Both had blueprinting, drafting, and carpentry as hobbies. Lewis

had been married three times, Springer twice. Both first wives were named Linda; both second wives, Betty. Each named his first son James Allan. Each had a dog named Toy. Of their first meeting, Lewis said, "It was like looking in a mirror." The first twins studied at the University of Minnesota, they were found to have similar IQs, personality scores, electroencephalograms, electrocardiograms, fingerprints, and handwriting. As Springer put it, "All the tests we took looked like one person had taken them twice."[14]

Can you imagine the feeling of finding a duplicate of yourself? Forty-four sets of twins found similar experiences.

Are There Other Studies?

The research done at the University of Minnesota isn't the only study on genetic personality.

Starting in 1976, psychologists at the University of Texas studied 850 sets of twins and also concluded their personalities were genetically, not environmentally, based.

In 1981 Susan Farber, a clinical psychologist, wrote a book *Identical Twins Reared Apart* stating that "The similarities were so striking as to be unnerving."

Hans J. Eysenck from the Institute of Psychiatry at the University of London has done extensive work proving the validity of genetic personality traits, as have researchers in Australia, Sweden, and Finland.

When I was in New Zealand in October of 1990, there was extensive publicity on the "New Zealand Adult Twins and Multiple Births Convention," held at Victoria University in Wellington. Four hundred twins convened to hear Dr. David Hay speak on the results of his fourteen-year twin study at Latrobe University in Melbourne, Australia. He concluded, "It now looks as though genetic influences may be more important than the environmental ones."

The National Institute on Aging, according to the *New York Times*, has conducted "the largest and longest studies ever to analyze personality and reveals a core of traits that remain remarkably stable over the years: a person's anxiety level, friendliness and eagerness for novel experiences."

According to Paul T. Costa, Jr., one of the researchers, "What changes as you go through life are your roles and the issues that matter most to you. People may think their personality has changed as they age, but it is their habits that change, their vigor and health, their responsibilities and circumstances—not their basic personality."[15]

With the up-to-date research results giving overwhelming proof that we inherit our personality, we can accept that each one of us started out with personality potential.

Where Does Environment Fit In?

Does our upbringing have anything to do with our adult personality?

Statistics vary, but in general we function as adults with 60 percent of our behavior based on genetics and 40 percent influenced by our environment. If our parents accept us as we are born and don't try to change us to suit their ideas of "good children," we will stay closer to our birth personality. But if we have heavily controlling parents or if we are abused physically, emotionally, verbally, or sexually, our original child is changed and possibly obliterated.

We learn to function in a manner which minimizes the possibility of abuse, and our circumstances begin to control the development of our emotional maturity.

My adopted son came to me with a melancholy personality. I had nothing to do with his genetic pattern. He has always been serious, deep, analytical, and somewhat pessimistic in a family with high choleric traits of action, achievement, direction, and control. And although we haven't changed his personality itself, we have influenced his basic nature in the area of goal setting, business knowledge, moral standards, and social skills.

How Does This Knowledge Help Us As Parents?

We must realize that each child is born with a specific personality direction. Our job as parents is to find it so that we can help them identify their strengths and choose careers that will fit their skills versus our desires. We can show them early in life where their weaknesses tend to be and how to avoid the pitfalls of their personality. When we function with the awareness of their inborn traits, we can then nurture them in the right direction. In my book *Raising Christians, Not Just Children*, I take each personality of a parent and show how each one will relate to the different types of children. This study has helped many to take the mystery out of raising children and answered the question, "Why do I have this one peculiar child?"

If we can only realize that the peculiar child didn't set out to be different, he was born that way, we can accept him much more easily and learn to adjust to his nature.

Personality Profiles

There is hardly a business, organization, placement agency, college, or church that doesn't use some kind of personality analysis. However, many times the individual who is analyzed does not see or understand the results. There are also many of you reading who are in your own business or no business at all who have never had a chance to evaluate yourself or your family. Our simple *Personality Profile* that we have used over our many years of teaching has opened the eyes of tens of thousands of people who never knew "Who Am I?" It has also served as a catalyst for family conversation, a practice close to extinct in our busy lives. Often people write us to say "We stayed up until 2:00 in the morning talking back and forth about each other. We've never had so much fun," or "This was the first time we've been able to talk about our weaknesses without a fight."

Knowing the personalities can make such a positive change in a family. One seminar attendee later wrote and told me of her experience.

> Words cannot express the insight and turnaround in my husband, Walter, and me concerning the personalities. I sat in awe as you spoke about the different temperaments. Things clicked in my thick skull, and I could hardly wait to get home to share with Walter. Motor mouth Joan got going because of the excitement of learning. He just grinned as he patiently listened, but I could see a sparkle begin to return to his eyes. Thank you for expanding on the various temperaments for it was what the Lord used to turn this hurting couple back to where we should be. Walter says I've changed; I say he's changed. But I know we've both changed and the sparkle is back.

In this book we are using the study of the personalities to prepare us for our dream. How can we go out into the world and deal with difficult people when we don't know much about ourselves?

1.   Take the *Personality Profile*. Check off one trait that most nearly fits you on each line across. You will have twenty strengths and twenty weaknesses. There is no personality that is better than another. With each set of strengths there are accompanying weaknesses. Once you have checked your forty off then transfer the marks to the scoring sheet. On the profile the traits are jumbled, but on the scoring sheet you will see that your personality begins to take form.

Remember, we are not doing our profile to pin a label on ourselves or put ourselves in a box but to have a tool to use to examine ourselves without having to go to a psychiatrist.

Personality Profile

Name _____

Directions— In *each* of the following rows of *four words across*, place an X in front of the *one* word that most often applies to you. Continue through all forty lines. Be sure each number is marked. If you are not sure of which word "most applies," ask a spouse or a friend, and think of what your answer would have been *when you were a child*.

Strengths

1	Adventurous		Adaptable		Animated		Analytical
2	Persistent		Playful		Persuasive		Peaceful
3	Submissive		Self-sacrificing		Sociable		Strong-willed
4	Considerate		Controlled		Competitive		Convincing
5	Refreshing		Respectful		Reserved		Resourceful
6	Satisfied		Sensitive		Self-reliant		Spirited
7	Planner		Patient		Positive		Promoter
8	Sure		Spontaneous		Scheduled		Shy
9	Orderly		Obligingly		Outspoken		Optimistic
10	Friendly		Faithful		Funny		Forceful
11	Daring		Delightful		Diplomatic		Detailed
12	Cheerful		Considerate		Cultured		Confident
13	Idealistic		Independent		Inoffensive		Inspiring
14	Demonstrative		Decisive		Dry Humor		Deep
15	Mediator		Musical		Mover		Mixes easily
16	Thoughtful		Tenacious		Talker		Tolerant
17	Listener		Loyal		Leader		Lively
18	Contented		Chief		Chartmaker		Cute
19	Perfectionist		Pleasant		Productive		Popular
20	Bouncy		Bold		Behaved		Balanced

Weaknesses

21	Blank		Bashful		Brassy		Bossy
22	Undisciplined		Unsympathetic		Unenthusiatic		Unforgiving
23	Reticent		Resentful		Resistant		Repetitious
24	Fussy		Fearful		Forgetful		Frank
25	Impatient		Insecure		Indecisive		Interrupts
26	Unpopular		Uninvolved		Unpredictable		Unaffectionate
27	Headstrong		Haphazard		Hard to please		Hesitant
28	Plain		Pessimistic		Proud		Permissive
29	Angered easily		Aimless		Argumentative		Alienated
30	Naive		Negative attitude		Nervy		Nonchalant
31	Worrier		Withdrawn		Workaholic		Wants credit
32	Too sensitive		Tactless		Timid		Talkative
33	Doubtful		Disorganized		Domineering		Depressed
34	Inconsistent		Introvert		Intolerant		Indifferent
35	Messy		Moody		Mumbles		Manipulative
36	Slow		Stubborn		Show-off		Skeptical
37	Loner		Lord over		Lazy		Loud
38	Sluggish		Suspicious		Short-tempered		Scatterbrained
39	Revengeful		Restless		Reluctant		Rash
40	Compromising		Critical		Crafty		Changeable

Now transfer all of your "Xs" to the corresponding words on the personality scoring sheet and add up your totals.

Created by Fred Littauer

Personality Scoring Sheet

Name _____

Strengths

1 ___	Animated	___	Adventurous	___	Analytical	___	Adaptable
2 ___	Playful	___	Persuasive	___	Persistent	___	Peaceful
3 ___	Sociable	___	Strong-willed	___	Self-sacrificing	___	Submissive
4 ___	Convincing	___	Competitive	___	Considerate	___	Controlled
5 ___	Refreshing	___	Resourceful	___	Respectful	___	Reserved
6 ___	Spirited	___	Self-reliant	___	Sensitive	___	Satisfied
7 ___	Promoter	___	Positive	___	Planner	___	Patient
8 ___	Spontaneous	___	Sure	___	Scheduled	___	Shy
9 ___	Optimistic	___	Outspoken	___	Orderly	___	Obliging
10 ___	Funny	___	Forceful	___	Faithful	___	Friendly
11 ___	Delightful	___	Daring	___	Detailed	___	Diplomatic
12 ___	Cheerful	___	Confident	___	Cultured	___	Consistent
13 ___	Inspiring	___	Independent	___	Idealistic	___	Inoffensive
14 ___	Demonstrative	___	Decisive	___	Deep	___	Dry humor
15 ___	Mixes easily	___	Mover	___	Musical	___	Mediator
16 ___	Talker	___	Tenacious	___	Thoughtful	___	Tolerant
17 ___	Lively	___	Leader	___	Loyal	___	Listener
18 ___	Cute	___	Chief	___	Chartmaker	___	Contented
19 ___	Popular	___	Productive	___	Perfectionist	___	Pleasant
20 ___	Bouncy	___	Bold	___	Behaved	___	Balanced

Weaknesses

21 ___	Brassy	___	Bossy	___	Bashful	___	Blank
22 ___	Undisciplined	___	Unsympathetic	___	Unforgiving	___	Unenthusiastic
23 ___	Repetitious	___	Resistant	___	Resentful	___	Reticent
24 ___	Forgetful	___	Frank	___	Fussy	___	Fearful
25 ___	Interrupts	___	Impatient	___	Insecure	___	Indecisive
26 ___	Unpredictable	___	Unaffectionate	___	Unpopular	___	Uninvolved
27 ___	Haphazard	___	Headstrong	___	Hard-to-please	___	Hesitant
28 ___	Permissive	___	Proud	___	Pessimistic	___	Plain
29 ___	Angered Easily	___	Argumentative	___	Alienated	___	Aimless
30 ___	Naive	___	Nervy	___	Negative attitude	___	Nonchalant
31 ___	Wants credit	___	Workaholic	___	Withdrawn	___	Worrier
32 ___	Talkative	___	Tactless	___	Too sensitive	___	Timid
33 ___	Disorganized	___	Domineering	___	Depressed	___	Doubtful
34 ___	Inconsistent	___	Introlerant	___	Introvert	___	Indifferent
35 ___	Messy	___	Manipulative	___	Moody	___	Mumbles
36 ___	Show-off	___	Stubborn	___	Skeptical	___	Slow
37 ___	Loud	___	Lord -over-others	___	Loner	___	Lazy
38 ___	Scatterbrained	___	Short-tempered	___	Suspicious	___	Sluggish
39 ___	Restless	___	Rash	___	Revengeful	___	Reluctant
40 ___	Changeable	___	Crafty	___	Critical	___	Compromising

Totals

___   ___   ___   ___

Strengths

	Sanguine-Popular	Choleric-Powerful	Melancholy-Perfect	Phlegmatic-Peaceful
EMOTIONS	Appealing personality Talkative, storyteller Life of the party Good sense of humor Memory for color Physically holds on to listener Emotional and demonstrative Enthusiastic and expressive Cheerful and bubbling over Curious Good on stage Wide-eyed and innocent Lives in the present Changeable disposition Sincere at heart Always a child	Born leader Dynamic and active Compulsive need for change Must correct wrongs Strong-willed and decisive Unemotional Not easily discouraged Independent and self-sufficient Exudes confidence Can run anything	Deep and thoughtful Analytical Serious and purposeful Genius prone Talented and creative Artistic or musical Philosophical and poetic Appreciative of beauty Sensitive to others Self-sacrificing Conscientious Idealistic	Low-key personality Easygoing and relaxed Calm, cool and collected Patient, well balanced Consistent life Quiet, but witty Sympathetic and kind Keeps emotions hidden Happily reconciled to life All-purpose person
WORK	Volunteers for jobs Thinks up new activities Looks great on the surface Creative and colorful Has energy and enthusiasm Starts in a flashy way Inspires others to join Charms others to work	Goal oriented Sees the whole picture Organizes well Seeks practical solutions Moves quickly to action Delegates work Insists on production Makes the goal Stimulates activity Thrives on opposition	Schedule oriented Perfectionist, high standards Detail conscious Persistent and thorough Orderly and organized Neat and tidy Economical Sees the problems Finds creative solutions Needs to finish what he starts Likes charts, graphs, figures, lists	Competent and steady Peaceful and agreeable Has administrative ability Mediates problems Avoids conflicts Good under pressure Finds the easy way
FRIENDS	Makes friends easily Loves people Thrives on compliments Seems exciting Envied by others Doesn't hold grudges Apologizes quickly Prevents dull moments Likes spontaneous activities	Has little need for friends Will work for group activity Will lead and organize Is usually right Excels in emergencies	Makes friends cautiously Content to stay in background Avoids causing attention Faithful and devoted Will listen to complaints Can solve other's problems Deep concern for other people Moved to tears with compassion Seeks ideal mate	Easy to get along with Pleasant and enjoyable Inoffensive Good listener Dry sense of humor Enjoys watching people Has many friends Has compassion and concern

Weaknesses

Sanguine-Popular	Choleric-Powerful	Melancholy-Perfect	Phlegmatic-Peaceful
E M O T I O N S Compulsive talker / Exaggerates and elaborates / Dwells on trivia / Can't remember names / Scares others off / Too happy for some / Has restless energy / Egotistical / Blusters and complains / Naive, gets taken in / Has loud voice and laugh / Controlled by circumstances / Gets angry easily / Seems phony to some / Never grows up	Bossy / Impatient / Quick-tempered / Can't relax / Too impetuous / Enjoys controversy and arguments / Won't give up when losing / Comes on too strong / Inflexible / Is not complimentary / Dislikes tears and emotions / Is unsympathetic	Remembers the negatives / Moody and depressed / Enjoys being hurt / Has false humility / Off in another world / Low self-image / Has selective hearing / Self-centered / Too introspective / Guilt feelings / Persecution complex / Tends to hypochondria	Unenthusiastic / Fearful and worried / Indecisive / Avoids responsibility / Quiet will of iron / Selfish / Too shy and reticent / Too compromising / Self-righteous
W O R K Would rather talk / Forgets obligations / Doesn't follow through / Confidence fades fast / Undisciplined / Priorities out of order / Decides by feelings / Easily distracted / Wastes time talking	Little tolerance for mistakes / Doesn't analyze details / Bored by trivia / May make rash decisions / May be rude or tactless / Manipulates people / Demanding of others / End justifies the means / Work may become his god / Demands loyalty in the ranks	Not people oriented / Depressed over imperfections / Chooses difficult work / Hesitant to start projects / Spends too much time planning / Prefers analysis to work / Self-deprecating / Hard to please / Standards often too high / Deep need for approval	Not goal oriented / Lacks self-motivation / Hard to get moving / Resents being pushed / Lazy and careless / Discourages others / Would rather watch
F R I E N D S Hates to be alone / Needs to be center stage / Wants to be popular / Looks for credit / Dominates conversations / Interrupts and doesn't listen / Answers for others / Fickle and forgetful / Makes excuses / Repeats stories	Tends to use people / Dominates others / Decides for others / Knows everything / Can do everything better / Is too independent / Possessive of friends and mate / Can't say, "I'm sorry" / May be right, but unpopular	Lives through others / Insecure socially / Withdrawn and remote / Critical of others / Holds back affection / Dislikes those in opposition / Suspicious of people / Antagonistic and vengeful / Unforgiving / Full of contradictions / Skeptical of compliments	Dampens enthusiasm / Stays uninvolved / Is not exciting / Indifferent to plans / Judges others / Sarcastic and teasing / Resists change

2. Read over the strengths and weaknesses chart and check off what most applies to you. This is a second measure of your personality.

3. Discuss how you feel about yourself with your family and encourage them to take the profile as well. Ask your co-workers to share opinions on whether or not they agree with you on your own personal evaluation. They will love to tell you! Don't go to anyone and say, "You ought to take this test. It will straighten you out." Instead, discuss your own results first and arouse their curiosity.

4. Enjoy some of the following stories that will give you the flavor and the heart of the four personalities.

The Popular Personality—Fun, Fun, Fun!

The fastest way to recognize a *sanguine* is from his or her continuous and usually exciting conversation. A cartoon showed a couple sitting on a park bench. She is obviously sanguine and he is phlegmatic, relaxing with no apparent expression. She turns to him and says, "I'd let you talk more but you're not as interesting as me." This represents the thinking of most sanguines. One said to me, "If it hadn't been for me, it would have been a dull party." To those of you who aren't sanguine you might find that a conceited thing to say. But the sanguine isn't bragging—he is just sharing the truth as he knows it.

Velm Holtz said to me one day, "The trouble with people who talk all the time is sometimes they say things they haven't thought of yet." Humorist Saki notes, "A little inaccuracy sometimes saves tons of explanation."

Joan Collins of "Dynasty" fame is a combination of the Popular and Powerful personalities. "She rarely uses twenty words when the same thing can be said in 200; indeed she believes that length means strength." So says a reviewer in *Options* magazine about her sanguine side, and then adds for her tougher nature: "She is a tiny tornado. Her brief grip suggests a will of steel. All the world knows of temper tantrums at airports."[16]

Jesse Jackson is a visible male sanguine who is always running for something. He concluded that the best thing for a talker to do for a living is talk. So taking advantage of his sense of humor and his gift of gab, he started his own talk show aptly named "Jesse Jackson." He says this show will not be "just reflecting and recording and research. (He also has the gift of alliteration.) We intend to communicate—to make things happen."

Reviewers felt that the show would be a lot better if Jesse would talk less and let his guests talk more, but he feels that people tune in to hear *his* opinions, not the guests'. Critics see his show as a launching pad for political office. One asked him if his talk show was a key to the White House, and he gave a quick and witty retort, "I see this as a key to all houses. Everybody's house will see this."

One columnist said, "He lives to talk. He looks at a defenseless ear the way Refrigerator Perry eyes a roast chicken."

Time magazine summed Jesse up, "There's never been a conflict in Jackson's ability to talk, talk, talk while he runs, runs, runs."

Kathy's husband says the word "adventure" takes on a whole new meaning when she uses it. "Kathy," he told her, "adventure is just your romantic cover-up for trouble."

The sanguine evaluates everything according to whether it is or isn't fun. "This is *fun!*" "This is *no fun!*"

Little Benjamin, eight years old, had to do a report on the Pilgrims. He wrote, "They spent a long time on an old boat. This trip was no fun!"

Sanguine Nancy Kintner wrote me this story. "Today I went to vote in the same grade school I attended as a child. Outside a first-grade room, I read some papers on the topic, 'If I Were a Caterpillar.' I fell in love with Amanda sight unseen because she wrote, 'If I were a caterpillar, I would live in the woods. And I would have fun!!!!!!!' Yes, seven exclamation points! Certainly Amanda is one of us!"

I called my eight-year-old grandson Jonathan and asked him, "How are you today?" He's always in good humor, but he replied, "I'm just a little bit sick." I pampered him a while and then spoke to his twelve-year-old brother, melancholy Randy, and asked, "Is Jonathan really sick?"

Randy sighed and replied, "Frankly, I think it's all in his head. He has a new teacher who doesn't think he's funny."

Later, when I talked to Jonathan about his sickness, he sighed, "I guess that's just the state I was in at the time."

We learned that Jonathan uses ailments and pseudo-symptoms to get attention. His weekly report came home from school with a "happy face" drawn out for "academics." On behavior there was a "sad face" and the teacher wrote, "I hope you're feeling better this weekend; you sure had a lot of aches and pains this week!!"

Julia Child, six-feet-two-inches with a size twelve tennis shoe, could have let her looks keep her from daring to dream, but with her sanguine nature she turned her liabilities into *fun*. "I was always one size bigger than you could ever buy." She laughs. But "Why languish as a giantess when it's so much fun to be a myth?"

Her cooking classes that began on television in 1963 are known not for their perfection but for the *fun*. Once when she was flipping a potato pancake, it missed the skillet and fell to the floor. She picked it up, shook it off, and holding it in her hand said, "Remember, you are alone in the kitchen and no one can see you." Melancholies probably never tuned in again, but the sanguines loved it.

Julia, close to eighty, is still going strong. "Perfectionism," she says, "never quite works out." She laps the beaters from the whipped cream and smiles, "Isn't this fun?" She then adds a little sanguine homily, "I still insist that an unhappy stomach is going to curdle your nutrition." Julia is still busy creating happy stomachs in her sometimes slapstick way. An obviously melancholy reviewer for the *New York Times* concludes that Julia Child is "still imperturbable in her own imperfection."

Forget and Forgive

The Popular Personality is the one person that can't remember facts, figures, or what happened yesterday. In my book *Personality Plus* I told the story of losing my car in a seven-story parking garage, and I've been deluged with similar examples ever since. Melancholies wouldn't want anyone to know if they made mistakes, but sanguines will tell anything if it will get a laugh. One lady recently told me that she had parked at a large shopping center and gone in with her three children, five, six, and eight. When she came out, she had no idea where the car was. She dragged the children around looking until the eight year old remembered they had gone in through a different store. Back they went, through the mall and out the correct store. They still couldn't find the car, so she, in a burst of organizational skill, assigned each child one aisle to walk up. "We'll meet at the other end and see who found it," she explained, brightly making this problem situation into a game. Each one took off happily to play "find the car." She found it herself and was so thrilled that she got into the car and drove away. As she was turning out onto the main street, she checked her rearview mirror and saw her little children running toward her with their hands up in the air. She could hardly wait to tell me this adorable adventure of child abandonment and she asked, "Will you put it in a book?"

My friend Carolyn wrote me about her new pastor. The Search Committee had been all phlegmatics and melancholies and it had taken them almost two years to decide on an appropriate replacement for the last phlegmatic/melancholy minister. They chose a sanguine who amused them, and Carolyn, who understands the personalities, knew what they had on their hands.

Our new sanguine pastor is living up to his personality. It is quite amusing to watch. One Sunday, two minutes before service, he was frantically looking for someone to play the organ. The organist had told him a week before that she would be absent—he forgot. The next Sunday evening, he forgot to take the offering. Yesterday he forgot the closing hymn until the organist started playing it as he walked off the stage. All those things are quite amusing but last week, without asking the choir, he appointed a temporary director whom none of the choir respected as a director. He had heard that the person had directed the choir years ago and without asking anyone's opinion, asked him to fill in since our other director has left. This may be the time for me to take a sabbatical!

My two brothers and I are about one-half sanguine and we have always been more interested in talk and fun than in statistics and records. I was reminded of the loose way young Ron ran his paper route when I read a note in the *New Yorker* written by a boy that could well have been Ron.

To All My Customers

I am giving up my paper route so that I can play baseball.
Thank you all for being so nice. It was a lot of fun.
I am sorry if I messed up sometimes. If anyone is behind in paying, please try to catch up, by the above date. If you don't know how much you owe, just take a guess because I don't know either. I had sort of an honor system paper route.
Thanks again.
Peter[17]

The Popular Personality has an honor system for all of life's business because they don't keep records and they forget from one moment to the next. The amazing thing about the sanguine that baffles everyone else is that they make even their mistakes so funny that everyone is willing to forgive.

I saw a bumper sticker one day on what had to have been a sanguine's car, "I can't be overdrawn; I still have some checks."

The Perfect Personality—Think, Think, Think

Where the sanguine loves to talk without thinking, the *melancholy* loves to think without talking. This latter is obviously a better choice for those who are more interested in facts than in fun. The problem is that the talkers always seem to marry the thinkers and spend the rest of their lives trying to get their partner to either shut up or open up.

Tom Landry is a high-profile melancholy. As a friend who's an avid football fan said of Tom Landry, "Florence, did you ever watch Landry on the sidelines? He was always deep in thought, analyzing and recording by memory every play to be reviewed later. His steel gray eyes were focused either on the field or the scoreboard, his lips drawn tightly, his arms folded across his chest, with one hand attached to his chin. He was unflappable, circumspect, without any evidence of emotion as many of his colleagues exhibit it, and immaculately dressed with sport coat and tie and the ever-present hat. Tom was always the same and expected the same—perfection."

Charlie Brown is another famous melancholy. He has "always been a melancholy sort, the Hamlet of the comic page who dares to ponder life's inponderables."[18]

I recently met a man who was pondering things I'd never thought of. He wondered if there was a way to catch clouds and squeeze water out of them to irrigate the desert. Doesn't that sound like Charlie Brown? But this was not a cartoon. This man was serious. He had built a Cloud Catcher and had already tested it atop a mesa in Arizona. He started with a long piece of awning material. He tied enough helium-filled balloons to the top of the fabric to hold it up off the ground but not enough to cause it to float away. Realize the delicate balance here. He put a series of buckets under the cloth and sat down to wait for a cloud. Would you believe one appeared, hit against the cloth, and was so upset that it wept into the buckets.

Can you just picture it if this Cloud Catcher catches on? It could become the new fad for weekend sport. Every family in Arizona could head out with their own cloth, balloons, and buckets to find an overcast mesa. Children could have a new paternal boast, "My daddy caught more clouds than your daddy."

My melancholy son-in-law Chuck provides me with many melancholy examples. He is so neat and organized and he likes everything to be clean and orderly. One day he said, "I wish there were some other way to get the news. TV never has it on when you want it and the newspaper is so messy. You have to get up and wash your hands."

He told me he prefers baseball to football because it's so organized and neat. One man throws one ball to another fellow who tries to hit it. When he does hit he runs to first base and all the men run in the same orderly direction. The bases are all numbered and you go to them in logical progression. Halfway through the game, little men come out on the field with wide brooms and tidy the place up. With football, however, players run any old way and soon the field and both teams are muddy. There's no order, it's confusing, and the players keep running into each other.

Chuck says, "Football is for cholerics who like to beat each other up and vent their own anger on another team. Baseball is for melancholies. It's a gentleman's game and you can keep score in those neat little boxes."

Melancholies love neat little boxes and they believe that the answer to all life's problems can be found on a good chart. Fred made a check-off list of all my virtues before we got married and then the areas where I needed to improve. I was reminded of this when I read the cartoon Single Slices by Peter Kohlsaat. A melancholy man was approaching a co-worker in his office. "You scored very well, Sandra. You fulfill 48 out of 50 of my requirements. Why don't I get your phone number, and we'll get together and work on these last two requirements, and just maybe you'll end up being the girl for me."

A full-page cartoon in the New Yorker showed a serious-faced man in twelve different scenes. It was labeled "The Twelve Labors of Hercules of Elmhurst" by Ziegler and represents typical planning of a melancholy's day. Done in line drawings, it showed Hercules's schedule:

- Brush teeth
- Eat high-fiber cereal
- Return videos
- Buy lottery ticket
- Get gas
- Scan newspaper
- Attempt crossword
- Do lunch
- Take nap
- Call weather service
- Consult watch
- Plan evening activities

The melancholy's planning and record keeping is often a blessing to those of us who don't have those same skills. Our sanguine daughter Marita and our melancholy friend Marilyn Heavilin are co-chairmen of the Southern California Women's Retreat. Observers wonder how two such different personalities can function together, but it is their understanding of the personalities that makes it possible.

While Marita excels in planning the retreat, negotiating with the hotels, and creating the brochures, Marilyn handles the registration, answers telephone inquiries, and deposits all of the registration money. A few years ago, Marilyn received several calls from women stating that their checks had not been cashed and they were worried that the re-treat was already full and their registration had not been accepted. After checking her records, Marilyn began to suspect that one of the deposits had been lost by the bank. She quickly called Marita and asked if she would check her records to see if the deposit had been listed on her last bank statement. There was a long pause. "Records?" In her sanguine fashion, Marita had all of the statements stored in a drawer, but she was unable to locate a current statement.

A quick call to the bank confirmed Marilyn's fears. The deposit of over two hundred checks was lost. Because of Marilyn's meticulous record keeping, she not only had a list of whose checks were in that deposit, but she also had noted the check numbers, the names of all of the registrations each check covered, the amount of each check, and even a note if the check was written by someone other than the regis-trant—in three different places! She was able to write to each woman, ask that another check be written, and all of the money was recovered.

As a melancholy, Marilyn's first reaction to the situation was, "It must be my fault—I'm going to quit." Because Marita understands the temperaments, she quickly called Marilyn and said, "Marilyn, remember it's not your fault, and don't you dare quit!"

Little Calvin in the cartoon "Calvin and Hobbes" brought his father his Christmas letter to Santa. Calvin must be a melancholy. He asked, "Want to read my letter to Santa?"

"All that?!"

"I hope I didn't forget to ask for something I want."

"This is alphabetized."

"Yeah, and I cross-indexed the accessory items he'll need to get. I try to help him out."

"This says 'volume one.'"

"'Atom bomb' through 'grenade launcher.'"

"You're going to be one sad little kid on Christmas morning."

Sink, Sink, Sink

The major weakness of the melancholy is their focus on the nega-tives of the world and of themselves. Broom Hilda walks around the comic strip with a black cloud over her head. The Ziggy cartoon shows him constantly depressed, the fall guy of jokes, and the one who feels worthless and helpless in the path of cruel fate. A melancholy friend sent me a Ziggy card summing up the feelings of this personality. On the cover he looks relatively bright with a slight smile and he says "Hi there. . . . There's no special reason for this card." On the inside it continues ". . . I just sent it on the off chance that you've been wondering what ever happened to me."

Ann McDonald listened to me tell about my melancholy son Fred with his Perfect Personality. I had explained in my Silver Boxes message that young Fred had slept through much of our trip to Europe and had not wanted to see "one more cathedral." Ann came up to share that she had a son just like Fred. Her son was stationed in Germany in the service and she kept writing and telling him to do some sightseeing and not waste his time there. Ann is obviously the Powerful Personality, wanting to make sure everyone keeps moving and accomplishing great and mighty deeds. After two years of urging, Ann's son finally went to visit one cathedral and sent her this message on a postcard:

> Dear Mom,
> I'm in a tourist trap here in Germany. There's supposed to be some priests buried in the basement.
> Love, Steve

Melancholies don't get too excited over what they consider trivia and they don't want to waste words.

My son-in-law Chuck is the brilliant intellectual who loves to study and who is working on his masters degree in family counseling. He has built an invention that holds his book on a pole so that he doesn't have to keep his neck bent for all-day reading. When he comes back from classes each day, he immediately types all of his notes into the computer and organizes anything the teacher may have taught out of sequence. He got a new computer program that analyzes writing style and ability. After completing a thesis on "Intergenerational Incest," he ran his words through the computer and it printed out on the screen, "Your whole report is too negative. Could you say this in a more positive way?"

We chuckled that the machine, without even knowing Chuck, judged his melancholy words as a little on the gloomy side. "What do they want," he asked referring to the little men inside the computer, "cheerful statistics on incest?"

The Powerful Personality—Lead, Lead, Lead!

One of the quickest way to spot the Powerful Personality of a *choleric* is to catch them pointing to others and moving in close to add emphasis. We call our little grandson Bryan a two-fingered choleric because he points his two index fingers at the same time. No one had to place Bryan on a stool and say, "Listen here, we want you to be strong and bossy, take control of everything you can get your hands on, point at everyone to make them feel insecure, and get right up into a person's face if you need to exert more authority." No, we didn't have to teach this to Bryan—he came with the knowledge prepackaged in his head. One day he and my husband were playing a game and Bryan made a wrong move. Fred, being a melancholy couldn't allow even a three year old to make a mistake and he said, "Bryan dear, you are wrong." Instantly Bryan retorted, pointing with two fingers, "I am not wong, I am wight."

I found him eating a box of chocolates I thought were hidden away and I asked, "Why are you eating so many candies?" A quick answer came, "My stomach told my mind, 'I need chocolate.'"

When he was four and a half we were all out to a steakhouse for dinner. Bryan asked his phlegmatic father if he could take his left-over drink to the car. His father said, "No Bryan, it's too much trouble." When his father wasn't looking, he quietly asked the waitress for "one of those big white cups with the cover." She brought him one and poured his drink in it. When we got up to leave, he showed his cup to his father and said with confidence, "I took care of the matter myself."

When we observe our children, we can clearly see that they are born with a personality that will be part of them forever.

The choleric is the born leader and greatest achiever, yet as Oswald Chambers says, "Some of us leaders are irritating dictators instead of indwelling disciples." Biographies of outstanding Powerful Personalities can be found in every newspaper and magazine because they are the people who are doing something. The reviews of their lives may be positive or they may be extremely critical, according to which point of view the writer has or how the choleric is performing at the moment. Of all personalities, this is the one most apt to carry his strengths to extremes.

Understanding the personality of any individual gives clues to their future. If we know which type a person is we can then make a calculated judgment on where their failings may come so that we can be aware and alert. Former CIA director William Casey was an excellent example of how strengths carried to extremes become weaknesses.

If we had been watching Casey, we could have seen some of his problems as they were on the distant horizon. We need only know his childhood nickname was "Cyclone" to guess he was a Powerful Personality. Roger Morris wrote a fascinating article entitled "Casey's past told us the 'Fixer' would get us into a Fix."

Although Morris didn't write this insightful piece based on the different personalities, his descriptions of Casey show a Powerful Personality who from youth was "a shrewd, energetic kid figuring all the angles and clearly on the make."[19]

Since we inherit our personality, we can see that Casey was born to control and he instinctively knew it. He worked his way through Fordham and St. John's Law School during the Depression doing something fitted to his desire for control: He investigated welfare applicants. He succeeded at everything he touched, and by age forty he was a millionaire lawyer and investor. He didn't need to work, but since a choleric's self-worth is measured daily by his accomplishments, he was eager to move on up. Morris says of Casey's work in the office of Strategic Services during World War II, "He rose, as always, by hard work and a canny, practical intelligence."[20]

Later he wrote more than thirty books on how to make money. One representing his love for straddling the fine line of ethics was called *How Federal Tax Angles Multiply Real Estate Profits*. Hardly a catchy title, but one indicative of his circumspect nature. "The essence of his recommendation," wrote *Business Week* editor Stephen Wildstrom, "was to do the minimum necessary to comply with the law. He was extraordinarily good at giving such advice and grew rich doing it. Later, his willingness to push the law to its limits would keep him on the edge of legal trouble throughout his public career. Casey was ever the fixer, preferably a secret fixer, quietly behind the scenes where things could be done without noisome regulations or publicity."[21] Casey was a perfect companion for Richard Nixon. Tricky Dick and Fixer Bill were made for each other as their minds were speeding down the same track. They both firmly believed the Powerful Doctrine: "The end justifies the means."

Unfortunately, when Powerful Personalities are in complete control, they don't mind bending a few rules here and there if it will bring the desired results. Author Joseph Persico says that William Casey was brilliant and loyal but, according to a friend, "never saw an ethical dimension to business. Is it illegal? If not, then you can do it."[22] The knowledge of this possibility can give us clues to future behavior. In these two cases, each man went on to deceptive activities which caused Nixon's downfall and which have led to a somewhat unflattering obituary for Casey.

Roger Morris says that Casey's practices were "on the murky margin of moral and legal standards," he "stirred controversy," was a "formidable and successful" CIA chief, had an "imperious manner" and was sometimes "nagging and nasty."[23]

All these traits fit the choleric's powerful personality, but Casey had that added need to do what he did covertly. He loved playing detective, and was a natural to be the person in the CIA responsible for restoring the power and glory to this somewhat tarnished institution.

Should it be a surprise to any of us that in the Iran-Contra hearings each path seemed to lead to the dead director? Wasn't the whole proceeding like a maze? Befuddled senators and lawyers weaving their way through blind alleys, faintly hearing the chuckle from the grave.

The Iran-Contra affair represented "the unmistakable resumé of a man whose wanton ignorance of the world, whose penchant for the quick fix and the back-room deal were exceeded only by his contempt for the inconveniences of democracy."

Casey's record was consistent, an example of a Powerful Personality whose strengths, when carried to extremes, became his weaknesses.

Persico tells that President Reagan, a Popular Personality, never did quite understand gruff and mumbling Casey. "I didn't understand him at meetings . . . I'd just nod my head, but I didn't know what he was actually saying." What a combination, a sanguine president with a choleric controller.

"Columnists walk a tightrope," says William A. Henry III in *Time* magazine. "To be either too bland or too savage usually erodes their following and, ultimately, their livelihood."[24] One of the columnists Henry wrote about has never liked the middle-of-the-road position and he could certainly never be thought of as bland. As many other Powerful Personalities, Patrick Buchanan goes as far as he can to be challenging, some say attacking, without taking that fatal step. On "Crossfire," "The McLaughlin Group," and "Capital Gang" he is admired for frank and pugnacious comments that ensure there will never be a dull moment. "Blending unyielding right-wing views with incendiary rhetoric, he stirs deep passions. Last week Buchanan was teetering on the tight rope," Henry says.[25] Last week was September of 1990 when Buchanan carried his strengths to the extreme by making a typical crack "which wrapped a core of fact in a coating of hyperbole"—his touch of sanguine.

For his job he has to be controversial and his personality fits his outspoken position, but when he implied that the Israeli Defense Ministry was encouraging a Mid-East war, the whole Jewish world rose up against him. He had fallen off the tightrope. A. M. Rosenthal of the *New York Times* called the statements "blood libel" and concluded "Buchanan can dish it out; let him take it a little." The attacks from even some of his friends would have caused a sanguine to say, "Nobody loves me," a melancholy to go into a depression, and a phlegmatic to leave town, but Buchanan enjoyed the fray and replied, "I don't retract a single word."

Ferdinand Marcos had a "fighting spirit that enabled him to survive years of scorn and degradation," according to writer Bob Sector. He called Marcos crafty, controversial, ruthless, defiant, brilliant, vain, and outrageously extravagant. By convincing his Filippino people that he was impervious to gun fire and impressing them with his exploits in the war, he became a national hero who was worshiped by the poor. Typical of the choleric personality, he wasn't content with having a lot; he wanted it all. He took a country that was considered the richest nation in Southeast Asia and in twenty years of personal greed and corruption, turned it into one of the poorest with horrendous debt problems. By the time he died in exile, his extravagances had so overshadowed his powerful positives that he is remembered for his excesses and not his achievements. Here was a Powerful Personality that pushed his strengths to such an extreme that they became weaknesses.

Sandy Sigoloff has created a position that fits the best of the choleric strengths. He takes over companies on the verge of bankruptcy, chops down dead wood, reduces the payroll, sells off bad properties, and either miraculously revives them or shuts them down. He loves crisis management and he gets five hundred dollars an hour for chopping up a company. Now in his early sixties, Sigoloff still looks like a young man and thrives on controversy and being called "Mr. Chapter 11." In 1980 he tried running a normal company with a healthy balance sheet, but he got bored by the lack of crisis. "I'm the kind of guy," Sigoloff says, "who goes on vacation and will look at that beach and the shells and by the third day I've counted and organized them all."

From reading about William Casey, Patrick Buchanan, Ferdinand Marcos, and Sandy Sigoloff, we can see degrees of the choleric leadership, characteristics in men as diverse as a cabinet member, columnist, dictator, and business expert. They all have had, in their day, the ability to rise to the top, but some have carried their strengths to extremes until they turned into weaknesses.

In an article about domineering, controlling business executives, anger was said to be one of their worst problems. "Most angry responses are due to unrealistic expectations about the way others should behave. Also, some people believe there are benefits in giving anger free rein— they think they can intimidate people into better performance or to doing things they don't want to do. But they confuse coming on strong with leadership qualities, mistakenly seeing their aggression as rein-forcing their perception of themselves as tough and decisive."[26]

By studying the traits of the different personalities, the Powerful Personality can begin to see himself more objectively and to under-stand why three-fourths of the people he deals with don't see things from his perspective. Cholerics are the most difficult to reach because whether men or women, they have endless energy and tremendous power, and they know in their hearts they will win. If they step on a few toes along the way, it's all in a day's work. Their mascot car should be the Ford Fairlane: "For those who are driven to win!"

The Peaceful Personality—Balance, Balance, Balance!

The one word that represents the behavior pattern of the phlegmatic's Peaceful Personality is "balance." Don't go too far to the left or the right. Don't be too loud or too soft.

"This is the way I feel, but on the other hand. . . ." I received a phlegmatic birthday card one year. On the front was a cartoon person with big eyes and a little smile. He said, "This is not a birthday card! How-ever, I do want to wish you a happy birthday. But I don't want to make you mad by reminding you that you're a *year older*! And on the other hand, I don't want to make you mad by forgetting your *birthday*, either."

When I opened to the inside it continued, "Nevertheless, I do want you to have a happy birthday, but if there's going to be trouble, I don't want to get involved. . . ."

The creator of the card may not have known much about the per-sonalities, but the phrases are perfectly phlegmatic.

When it was time to replace choleric Ed Koch as mayor of New York, the people chose a phlegmatic. They had lived with a Powerful Personality long enough, one whose "penchant for insensitive remarks heightened racial ten-sions."[27] *Newsweek* called Koch "the consummate, big-mouthed New Yorker who governed the city with a flamboyance bordering on the obnoxious."[28]

Strong words about a strong personality! After the period of Power, the New Yorkers opted for what they hope will be a period of Peace!

The *Newsweek* article went on to say, "David Dinkins has built his career on conciliation and consensus . . . he has always worked within the system . . . he has a gift for consensus."[29]

When Dinkins won the Democratic nomination for mayor, he responded with a truly phlegmatic promise, "Today, the healing has begun."

When people do not understand the basic personalities, they tend to expect all things out of all people and then give up when they don't measure up. The same senators who chose George J. Mitchell, a former federal judge, as Senate majority leader because of his phlegmatic, cool-under-pressure, non-partisan nature are now complaining that he is not also a choleric aggressive and partisan.

The *New York Times* says of Mitchell, "His logic is crisp, unassailable, his manner far removed from the thrust and parry of contemporary politics. He is the soul of judiciousness, highminded in his concern for governance. But some in his party would like for a bit more of the street fighter."[30]

Mitchell is a typical example of the American dream, a man whose father was a janitor and whose mother worked nights in a textile mill in Maine. He dared to dream that he could do better than his parents, and he quietly and methodically worked his way up the political ladder. Representative of the phlegmatic, Mitchell says he never claimed to be a fighter, that he has won by conciliation and consensus. He keeps the interests of the nation ahead of his party's desires, a rare trait for a politician. Mitchell is probably the most balanced and patient person the Senate could have chosen to preside over their prima donna per-sonalities. Ever cautious and humble, Mitchell says, "We have 100 equal senators. I am constantly reminded of the limitations on my authority on a daily basis."[31]

Mitchell, who claims he has a strong "patience muscle," has the right personality to keep peace while pleading with his colleagues to stop talking and get on with the work at hand. Typical of the phlegmatic, Mitchell is not showy, dramatic, or impressed with his own voice; he is more interested in doing the right thing quietly than fighting loudly for what benefits "the party." Seldom do we see a man in politics who can rise above the partisan fray and keep what he calls his "inner com-pass" in balance. What a shame that so many of his own party want to change the conciliator into a challenger.

Over the years, the choosing of a Supreme Court Justice has been based more on emotional issues than the individual's abilities. Intelli-gent, articulate, experienced men have been defeated or not even nominated because they had heartfelt opinions that they dared to mention. The only hope for Senate approval was to find a man who had no opinions and who had never done anything wrong that could possibly be traced down by a team of bloodhounds and Inspector Clouseau. The candidate couldn't be a sanguine—they all have talked too much, made too many foolish mistakes, and think serious things are funny. He couldn't be a choleric—they'd already tried that and found cholerics were too outspoken and didn't care a whit about conciliation or the other side of any issue. It couldn't be a melancholy because depth and brilliance scare the Senate: "Who knows what he's really thinking in there?" As Shakespeare wrote in *Julius Caesar*, "Yond' Cassius has a lean and hungry look; He thinks too much; such men are dangerous."

That narrowed the choice down to a phlegmatic, preferably one who had never left home, had no gossiping alcoholic wife, and certainly no rebellious children who would write books condemning his secret life. Can you believe it? They found such a man, a bachelor—who according to *Newsweek* "has left so few footprints" and has "committed no political blunders" that no one can find anything to complain about. And they tried. For the entire summer of 1990, FBI agents were swarming through the New Hampshire capital at Concord trying to find people who had opinions about David Souter, people that might have had romantic attachments or those who could even remember they went to school with him. After culling through the records in the local libraries and interviewing anyone with a memory, they could find no clue to the philosophy of the nominee. Some said he was "a decent if drab ascetic" who seems detached from reality.

Insight magazine said, "He's coming off a state court experience with next to no federal background, and he suddenly has to bring himself up to speed on this."[32]

The American Bar Association stated, "Souter's integrity, character, and general reputation appear to be of the highest order and without blemish."[33]

The *New York Times* said, "He has not been a combatant in anyone's ideological war."[34] To make sure that the nominee could complete a sentence without making any waves or stating an obvious opinion, they questioned him and were thrilled with his ambiguous conclusions. When asked, "Should the courts jump in to solve social problems when legislators fail to act?" Judge David Souter said wisely, "Courts do not self-define their jurisdictions and they do not have the authority to define them simply when they perceive what they think is a vacuum in the political process which leaves a problem unsolved."[35]

He was confirmed 97 to 0. He's just what the country ordered!

As I viewed the final segment of Jane Pauley's long reign as Queen of "Today," I found myself in tears as if I were losing a close personal friend. Review shots showed Jane atop the Great Wall of China, posed in profile before the Eiffel Tower, and standing regally on the steps of St. Paul's Cathedral reporting on the wedding of Princess Di. As I watched Jane's many years in retrospect, I realized that while we'd never met, Jane and I were friends. I'd flown to China with her, I'd felt her excitement in Paris, and I'd thrilled as she'd partied in Buckingham

Palace. Feeling a lump of nostalgia and sadness in my throat, I wondered why I felt a personal tug toward Jane.

Would I have cared if choleric Bryant had left, Bryant who knows it all and tends to look down on any hopeless human who wilts under his curt questioning? Could Gene be replaced without remorse? Gene with the fuzzy hair like a giant-sized Brillo pad and the moustache that droops to his chest? I guess I would miss super-sanguine Willard with his removable toupee—hair today, gone tomorrow. Willard who opens his mouth before his mind is in gear, who says of every woman over a hundred, "Isn't she the loveliest lady you've ever seen?" and of every city, "This is my favorite spot in the whole world!"

Each one of the "Today" cast is a different personality, each plays a specific role—but why is Jane special? As I watched that farewell segment ending thirteen years of Jane's reign, I asked myself, "Why do you care? What's different about Jane?" They must have known I'd ask, for each one in turn answered me. Willard, surrounded by a group of fans in Florida, led them all in shouting, "We love you, Jane." With tears in his big eyes he added, "You are a class act." Yes, Jane's been lovable and classy without being puffed up about herself.

Gene said he'd miss her smile, but then felt led to add he'd been around longer than she had. Deborah, whose addition to the show had been the catalyst for Jane's departure, said she hoped they'd still be friends. Bryant, not given to sentimental statements, squeezed Jane's hand and stated, "Consistency, that's what you've got, consistency." Realizing that wasn't a glowing conclusion, he added with a rare touch of embarrassment, "You know how I feel about you." The choleric always has difficulty stating anything that might be considered sentimental.

Jane has intelligence with no touch of arrogance; she gives consistency without boredom. Jane could be regal and yet keep the common touch. Jane could be stylish without hairspray, crisp without seeming starched, genuine without guile in a business where everyone's an act. Jane is real in an unreal world.

Jane is a highly motivated phlegmatic. *Life* magazine, in an article entitled "Our Loss, Her Dream," said of Jane, "Viewers perceive her as warm, natural, sensitive, intelligent, and charmingly feminine, a gentle madonna in the dream machine . . . the apotheosis of the acceptable, a role model of moderation who holds a pleasing mirror up to Middle America."[36] Her co-workers call her "the healthiest woman in broadcasting."

Her husband, "Doonesbury" cartoonist Garry Trudeau, says that Jane tries to be all things to all people. "What keeps her in balance is a sense of humor and a core of self-esteem based on a loving upbringing."[37]

Jane is real and emotionally healthy because she's never had to build walls of protection and defense. She was "loved unconditionally" by her parents, she has stated consistently over the years, and that has made the difference. With a solid foundation, Jane has built a successful career and not walls of partition.

Why did Jane leave her morning chair without criticism, "harmless and blameless, without rebuke?" Because she's a genuine person and we are attracted to people who are real. Even though we don't understand why, we are drawn to someone who has a quiet self-confidence and is not constantly groping through life trying to find themselves. In a world full of actors and pretenders, we like that person who has never put on a mask.

As I talked one day with a struggling pastor's wife about becoming real, she replied, "But what if I became myself and they didn't like me?"

"Do they like you now?" I asked.

"Well, no."

"Then wouldn't it be better for them to not like you for being real than to not like you for being a phony?" No one likes a phony. We all see through plastic personalities. We respect the real thing.

As I watched Jane's farewell and listened as tributes were given to her genuine heart for her people, I wondered what would be said about me as I might take my final bow. Would people say I was real, that I practiced what I preached, that I wasn't trying to be something I wasn't?

I think most of us want to be the real thing, not an imitation. And yet so many of us have built up great, impenetrable walls around ourselves, hiding who we think we are. Some have said to me, "I never let anyone get to know me. If you knew what I was really like you wouldn't respect me. I try to keep people at arm's length. I've played so many games I have no idea who I really am."

Wouldn't we all like to feel good about ourselves? Wouldn't we like to be stamped "genuine?" How can we throw off the masks of a lifetime? How can we experience personal peace? God's Word gives us a promise. "For He is our peace who has broken down that wall of partition between us" (Ephesians 2:14).

Jane moved on to host a show that fit her genuine nature, "Real Life with Jane Pauley." She dreamed that it would get a permanent slot and that she would be able to balance her family and her career. "I'm afraid I have to walk a careful line—lest I spoil the magic," she said.

My phlegmatic mother constantly admonished us to not get excited or "all gee-hawed up." She kept the balance among a family of sanguine-cholerics and tried to rein in our enthusiasm.

This balancing and calming influence is a strength of the phlegmatic, but carried to extremes it keeps them from making decisions or getting excited over anything. Some phlegmatics are just a step above furniture. One couple I counseled had an odd problem. She had slapped him across the face. When I asked why, she replied, "I just wanted to see if he was still alive!"

We have a phlegmatic in our office who is so pleasant and agreeable that all our clients love him. Jeff will go along with anything anyone wants. "You'd like Florence to speak naked at the Rotary Club? No problem. She'd love to." One day we sanguines were talking about having fun and Jeff replied, "I like to have fun as long as it's not too much work."

Early one morning, Barry was in his office next to Jeff's when he smelled something burning. He looked around the front office and then went into Jeff. "Is there anything burning in here?" Jeff pointed out that he had turned on the tall cylindrical space heater a while before and "it often smells funny at first." Barry left, but the smell got stronger and he asked Jeff again. "No, there's nothing burning in here." On the third venture into Jeff's office, Barry walked over behind Jeff's desk, looked down and saw Jeff's pants on fire! When he screamed "Jeff, your pants are on fire!" Jeff looked down and said calmly, "I hadn't noticed."

I walked in at that point and saw Barry laughing as Jeff looked in quiet amazement at the leg of his polyester pants that was a smoldering mass of black sludge. I suggested he cut the legs off and make Bermuda shorts for the summer.

It's a strength that the phlegmatic's Peaceful Personality is not easily excitable, but it approaches the extreme when you can sit at your desk with your pants on fire and not know it!

I once received an adorable phlegmatic card. On the front was a Peaceful mother in a lounge chair watching television—the great phlegmatic stress reliever. Around her on the floor were unopened newspapers, old magazines, letters under the slot in the front door, and trash from the overflowing wastebasket. The dog was scratching to get out, the fish were dead in the bowl, and even the cactus had fainted from lack of water. Dishes were piled high in the sink, cobwebs were in the corners, and books were holding up the broken leg on the coffee table. The message was, "There's a lot to be said for procrastination," and then inside, "but I'll tell you about it some other time."

> "May your heart always be young.
> May your dreams live forever."

When I arrived in Auckland, New Zealnand, to teach a seminar on leadershhip to business women, the chairman informed me that "Lady Muldoon" would be attending and presenting the opening welcome.

The chairman had thoughtfully taken two books on the Muldoons out of the library and I read them over to familiarize myself with this political family. The Right Honorable Sir Robert Muldoon, GCMG, CH, MP, was the Prime Minister of New Zealand from 1975-1984, and everything I read about him pointed to a Powerful Personality. As I asked people about him in casual conversation, I received affirming comments: "He's in control of everything he touches. His presence fills a room. He takes charge even if you didn't ask him to." All the statements included words that had to do with control and power, and without meeting him I could conclude that he was the typical Powerful politician.

When I asked about his wife, Thea Muldoon, I got phlegmatic answers: "She's quiet. She doesn't offer opinions. She stands behind him and smiles. She is calm and peaceful." As usual, Lady Muldoon was the opposite of her husband, although she was very active and had transformed Vogel House, the Prime Minister's residence, into a place of international standing. She and her husband became experts on the propagation of lilies, and she used her horticultural interest as a member of the management committee of the Kauri Point Centennial Park.

Armed with this background information plus the fact that Lady Muldoon attended yoga classes and was in excellent physical condition, I felt ready to meet her. As the word spread that Lady Muldoon was attending, excitement built. One woman said to me in disgust, "Why didn't they tell us she was coming? I would have brought more friends if I'd known there'd be someone here who was really important!"

Feeling suddenly unimportant, I stood strangely silent as she chugged off to repeat her opinion to others. Suddenly all conversation stopped and I saw in the doorway a diminutive lady, a real *lady*, in a dark conservative dress. She stood erect and quietly confident of her bearing. As we were introduced, she smiled and apologized that she'd have to leave at lunch time because "Bob" was returning from a trip and would expect her there to greet him.

The chairman introduced Lady Muldoon, who gave a brief and carefully prepared message of greeting. She then sat in the front row to listen attentively to my teaching on the personalities. To illustrate the differences of the Powerful Personality and the Peaceful Personality I used an example of a choleric pastor who had built a church from a few hundred to seven thousand because of his drive and determination. I told how he worked constantly and how his single-minded focus kept him from having time for family or friends. I shared how he had brought me in to analyze the personalities of his staff, but how he himself didn't have time to come to the staff meeting where I asked each member to explain his job description. When I got to the phlegmatic assistant pastor, I asked him what he did there, and he replied, "I follow the pastor through life and pick up the pieces."

On that line Lady Muldoon threw her hands up in the air and called out for all to hear, "That's me! That's me. That's what I've been doing—following him through life picking up the pieces." The audience laughed with her in sympathy and understanding, and from then on the group paid personal attention to the practical application of the personalities.

Lady Muldoon had given a clear example of the phlegmatic sense of humor about her quiet background position of picking up the pieces behind the Powerful prime minister.

Afterward, comments were made about how genuine Lady Muldoon was and how she put us all at ease—a trait so becoming in the Peaceful Personality.

Sanguine
- Greatest strength is the ability to talk anywhere at any time, with or without information.
- Carried to extremes they are compulsive talkers with little relationship to the truth.

Choleric
- Greatest strength is the ability to take control of any project, make quick decisions, and move into action.
- Carried to extremes they appear to be bossy, arrogant, overwhelming, jumping impulsively into things they don't understand, and telling everyone where to go.
- It is easy to see that when the choleric crosses the line into the extremes, everybody knows it.

Melancholy
- Greatest strength is the ability to delve deeply into life, see things philosophically, and quickly observe what might go wrong in any situation.
- Carried to extremes they are thinking so deeply they are over people's heads, they are out of touch with reality, and they are frequently depressed.

Phlegmatic
- Greatest strength is their ability to stay calm in tense situations, stay out of trouble, and relax those around them.
- Carried to extremes they react to nothing, make no decisions, and don't want to get out of the chair.

Can We Know Our Children's Personalities?

The Sanguine Child

If we have a Popular, sanguine child we must realize he is inherently light-hearted, humorous, and energetic, with little ability to organize or remember instructions. The sanguine's love of telling stories and wanting instant response often leads them into exaggerating the truth. They will get excited over every new project that comes along, but have little follow-through and will abandon one pursuit if a new one seems more fun.

When Marilyn Heavilin's granddaughter Kate was two and a half, melancholy Marilyn was explaining to Kate, "Grammie is going away for three whole weeks." While Marilyn was expecting a response such as, "Oh, Grammie, I'll miss you," sanguine Kate, who wants to see the bright side of everything, responded, "That's okay Grammie. You'll come back!"

The Choleric Child

If we have a Powerful choleric child, we already know it because he has tried to take control of us and all his siblings. The choleric is a born leader, strong in every way, and usually right. These children are out to win and they will stop at nothing to achieve their end. Just because we are bigger doesn't intimidate them. One lady told me she was trying to discipline her choleric three and a half year old. She told him to come downstairs and he stood at the top and said *no*. She repeated her command three times with the same response. Finally he put his pudgy little fists on his hips and replied, "Read my lips, *NO!*"

The Melancholy Child

If we have a Perfect, melancholy child, we will be constantly wondering why he is never happy. He's not unhappy; he just has a different level of pleasure. He doesn't like noise and confusion and prefers to be by himself much of the time. If he has a sanguine mother, he soon becomes exhausted trying to keep up with her whirlwind of people-related activities. This child is the best student and should be offered opportunities to pursue art, music, and drama, as melancholies usually have talent beyond the norm.

The Phlegmatic Child

If we have a Peaceful, phlegmatic child, we have the easiest one to raise because he will desire to please and want to stay out of trouble. This child has a dry sense of humor and is easily content. By the time he is a teenager and we see that he has no goals or burning desire to achieve, we begin to worry. Where have we gone wrong? In my experience, I have learned that phlegmatics are single-interest children, and our job is to locate that one interest and help them develop it. My phlegmatic son-in-law Randy has always loved stamps and coins. He started collecting as a boy, read books on what kings minted what coins, and started working in a coin store when he was in his early teens. Today he is president of that company, the Stamp and Coin Galleries of San Bernardino, California.

Does Our Genetic Pattern Influence Other Aspects of Our Life?

One of the amazing results in these recent studies tells that our personality type can show the kind of physical ailments we may develop in the future. Beginning in the sixties, a Yugoslav psychologist measured the personality characteristics of thousands of people, predicted the illnesses they would get, and then followed them for ten years to see what happened. From this study and others he is still doing in Heidelberg, he has concluded that personality attributes do lead to disease. He has witnessed in his case histories that hostility and anger, aggression and need to control, cynicism about life and other people's ability to do anything right, and excessive drive and need to achieve—all choleric weaknesses—lead to heart problems. He has also learned that repressed emotions, feelings of hopelessness, consistent passivity, an over-degree of patience, a doormat attitude, and a need to avoid conflict at all costs— all phlegmatic weaknesses—contribute to cancer.[38]

Johns Hopkins School of Medicine has come up with similar results labeling these two persons Type A: choleric, aggressive, and Type B: phlegmatic, passive.

Realizing these personality influences on our health should encourage us to work prayerfully and humanly to overcome our weaknesses and compulsions.

After a mastectomy and bone cancer, Marie Mosback, a Connecticut teacher, said, "I feel the cancer is related to the repression of my feelings and to chronic stress. Staying in a situation where there is chronic stress like my unhappy marriage is very weakening to the immune system."[39]

Massachusetts college professor Ray Berte, who has battled throat cancer and other types for years, wrote in *Psychology Today*, "I used to be too passive, too much a responder to life. I also buried a lot of anger and depression. I cut my feelings off at the throat. Now I'm accepting responsibility for what is happening to my body. That puts me at cause rather than effect."[40]

Other areas influenced by our natural personality have been reported in recent years. A Canadian study published in the *New England Journal of Medicine* confirmed that a tendency toward obesity is inherited. They say that environmental factors do have an influence, but genes are the principal determining element. Alcoholism studies have also shown a strong tie with heredity, and addictive personalities seem to follow family patterns.

Penn State psychologist Robert Plomiu has even connected heredity with watching television. "Some children are much more at risk than others to be really captured by TV. They find it harder not to watch and are more susceptible to its influence. Personality attitudes and interests, which we know all have a strong genetic base, account for the differences."[41]

This research ties in with the phlegmatic personality which I have personally observed over the years to be the one most drawn to television. Watching other people helps the phlegmatic to turn from dealing with his own problems, to blot out the world around him, and to deal with stress in a passive manner.

The article concludes, "Findings are consistent with mounting evidence from both twins and adoptive studies that genetics and non-shared environment account for the lion's share of personality differences; the role of family environment is minor."[42]

Speak the Same Language

One morning Marita placed an impressive breakfast before Chuck. Being sanguine, she wanted instant praise for her good works, but Chuck said nothing. Being melancholy, he saw nothing to talk about. "How do you like your breakfast?" she asked, forcing him to sing her praises.

"It's fine," he replied.

"Only fine?"

"That's what I said, It's fine."

When Marita shares this repartee in our seminars she asks the sanguines in the audience, "On a scale of one to ten, where is fine?" They scream out, "One," and they all groan. Instantly they relate to Marita fishing for compliments and getting only a "fine" in return. She then asks the melancholies where they place fine and they answer in a low-key manner "A ten."

Marita then tells of the day she called Chuck while we were on the road. "How's your day been?" She turns to the audience, "And what did he say?" The all call out, "Fine." By now they are all laughing because they've been there. She says, "I replied, 'What was wrong?'"

"I said it was fine."

"But that means you had a bad day."

"Listen, Marita, you have to learn that with me, 'fine' is about as good as it's ever going to get." At this point the sanguines yell out in pain and the melancholies nod in affirmation.

"What we've learned," Marita explains "is that when Chuck talks to me, 'fine' is not an acceptable word, but when he tells me his day was 'fine,' I tell him that's great. Now when I place a breakfast before him, he looks at it, forces a smile, and says, 'This is the greatest breakfast I've ever seen in my entire life!'"

If you and your family are trying to communicate on different levels and getting nowhere, sit down one night and ask them to give you their favorite words and what they really mean. As long as you're doing it in fun and not as a seminar, the whole family should enjoy it, and you might even begin to speak the same language for the first time in your life.

Not only are there differences in vocabulary but also in the concept of time and numbers. Melancholies are born with digital clocks in their brains, which can be a great asset to all who live with them if this knowledge is looked on as a positive. Often, however, those closest to the Perfect Personality become highly annoyed at the constant reference to minutes and dates, and this organized person, who feels socially insecure underneath, uses his computerized mind to intimidate others in a subtle way.

Picture this: a sanguine wife and her melancholy husband go to the store. As they drive up, he asks, "How long will you be in there?" This is a foolish question and forces the sanguine to create an answer that may or may not be anywhere near to the truth, "About five minutes" is a convenient response. Sanguines always precede numbers with "about" so that they can't be held accountable when the estimate is wrong; however, the melancholy takes all numbers literally and expects accuracy. The sanguine goes bouncing into the store happy to get free of the Great Computer.

Once in the store, the first problem is that the sanguine can't remember what she came for and this slows down her progress. "What am I doing here?" In contrast, when the melancholy goes in for five minutes, he knows exactly what he's after and can get in and out well within the allotted time. My melancholy husband has a set of thirty-six 3x5 cards in his shirt pocket at all times. One card is his "Buy List." He has it pre-divided into different stores he frequents, and when a need strikes him, he jots it down under the proper store. By this intricate system he can walk into K-Mart, go directly to stationery, pick up a dozen manila file folders, and be out the door in three and a half minutes. He looks neither right nor left, meets no one, and buys nothing extra. When I enter K-Mart, it becomes a social event. I find new friends and we discuss the merits of Windex over the cheaper K-Mart brand of glass cleaner. I wander around wide-eyed, finding all sorts of wonderful bargains I didn't need and listening to the Blue Light Special. The checkout line is an obvious place to converse with other bored people and establish new relationships, and I somehow have a knack for choosing a line where the lady in front of me has an item with no price on it causing a paging of the store manager who has just stepped into the men's room.

By the time I get out loaded with bargains but having forgotten what I went after, an hour has elapsed and Fred is sitting silently in the driver's seat. "Do you have any idea how long you were in there?" he questions routinely. Do I have any idea? This is hardly a fair question to ask me since historically I never have had an accurate answer.

Get Ready

As we prepare to dream, we need to do all we can to get ourselves ready to wear that dream. If there are classes we can take to educate ourselves, then we should enroll and study. We must also anticipate the opportunities that might come our way.

At a recent CLASS seminar, one of my staff, Pam Stephens, was talking with another staff member, Marilyn Heavilin. Marilyn was discussing the possibilities of including workshops for the following day and mentioned some topics that would be available. Pam volunteered to lead a separate workshop on "How to Prepare a Bible Study Lesson."

As Pam shared this story with me, she told me that many months before she had prepared a worksheet on the subject and carried it with her just in case she was ever given the opportunity to lead a workshop.

Another staff member spoke to Pam and voiced a desire to have been given the opportunity to do a workshop.

Pam asked her if she had something already prepared? "Not exactly," was the answer. So Pam gave her some suggestions on what to do for next time: Go home and prepare several different lessons on her varied areas of interest and expertise, make handouts for each one, and be prepared to volunteer her services when the time becomes available.

What was the difference in these two staff members? Each one was quite capable of leading a workshop, but only one was prepared when the time came.

When Marilyn Heavilin's husband Glen became newly employed in a computer company, he was more than qualified for the position he accepted. Further advancement did not seem probable for many years since the current employees would be in line for advancement first, but Glen had opted to take the position anyway because it would give him more time with his children, who were approaching their teenage years. Although promotion was not likely and further education did not seem necessary, Glen decided to pursue his master's degree in business so that he would be prepared for advancement if the opportunity ever came.

Within a short time after he received his degree, his boss contracted cancer and died unexpectedly. Glen and another employee who had much more seniority were both considered for the position of department director. When all their qualifications were weighed, Glen was given the position. His master's degree had given him the edge he needed.

Are you getting ready to see your dream fulfilled, or are you waiting until the dream is in sight before you start to get ready? When the opportunity comes, and it usually comes unexpectedly, the ones who are prepared will be chosen.

"Be ready for the sudden surprise visits of God. A ready person never needs to get ready. Think of the time we waste trying to get ready when God has called!"[43]

Learn to Listen

"It is the disease of not listening, the malady of not marking, that I am troubled withal."
—William Shakespeare

So many of us success-oriented people spend much of our human relationship time trying to impress some wide-eyed observer with our past academic achievements or some memorable moment of our summer vacation.

We don't feel we're bragging, but rather helping some poor unfortunate broaden his limited mind set. In my early years of marriage, I felt that God personally anointed me with a gift for filling in gaps in potentially boring conversations. My children noticed my talent as they were growing up and created their own biblical paraphrase, "Where two or three are gathered together, Mother will give a seminar." One day I heard Lauren explain to a friend after I had entertained them with a dramatic delivery of a familiar family fable, "That is the fifth time I've heard that story and each time it has a different ending."

Some fainthearted mothers might have taken this as an insult, but I chose to consider it as a testimony to my creativity. Didn't Lauren's friends agree that I was the most fun mother on Beechwood Drive? Wasn't I the only mother who had memorized the entire Dr. Seuss book, *Green Eggs and Ham* and was willing to recite it at the drop of a *Cat in the Hat*?

> Do you like green eggs and ham?
> Do you like them Sam-I-Am?
> Do you like them in a box?
> Do you like them with a fox?
> Do you like them on a train?
> Do you like them in the rain?[44]

At the conclusion of my recitation where Sam-I-Am has tasted green eggs and ham, and likes them, I would review the moral of the story that we should all try at least a little bit of each item offered. Then I would send the children home to eat their dinners with a new sense of surprise and anticipation.

At parties I would hardly make my grand entrance before gathering a little flock of ardent listeners to hear one of my latest exciting episodes based loosely on actual facts. Marita has said, "Mother's stories are all rooted in truth." But I never felt the truth should stand in the way of a good story. My perfectionistic husband would later correct my creative statistics and I would respond, "But they loved me, didn't they?" This light-hearted answer would put him into a depression not improved by my pointing out that while his conversation was certainly accurate, it could be considered dull.

One day Fred came up with a statement worthy of Socrates and those other sages: "Do you realize that when you are talking, you're not learning anything because what you're saying you already know?" I had to admit I'd never thought of that heavy homily before. He went on to point out that he felt I had come to a place in life where I should pay attention to what other people were saying, inferior and uninspiring though their thoughts might be. "You might even learn something," he concluded. I agreed to take up his challenge and I soon had an opportunity.

As I stood chatting with a dignified lady at a wedding reception, Fred joined us and said, "Tell me, Florence, what is your new friend's name and where does she live?" I had no idea. I hadn't asked. She graciously provided the information to help me out and I learned a humbling lesson. Now when I see Fred approaching at a social affair, I quickly ask, "And what's your name, honey, and where do you live?" When he then asks, I smile broadly and recite a few pertinent facts. At first it was a game, but as I saw how people responded to these simple questions and how they thanked me for caring, I noticed how empty was the adulation of an audience compared to the opening of another person's covered heart.

Fred's lesson fifteen years ago was a turning point. I began to develop questions to ask on a deeper level than "what's your name?" and "where do you live?" As I began to write books, I found that every person I met had a story inside waiting for someone to set it free. In fact, I've been able to continue writing each year because I've learned to listen.

Listen to People

Grocer Stew Leonard believes in letting his employees in on wearing the dream. In fact, on his store's wall it says, "Rule #1: *The customer is always right. Rule #2: If the customer is wrong, see Rule #1.*" Stew even took this a step further in 1985 by securing a three-ton piece of granite and having the two rules chiseled into the rock and set in concrete outside his store so that customers could see it as they came in. Stew says, "When I see a frown on a customer's face, I see fifty thousand dollars' about to walk out the door." His good customers buy about one hundred dollars worth of groceries a week. Calculated over a ten-year time frame, that adds up to fifty thousand big ones. Maintaining Stew Leonard's dream, his grocery business, means sharing the dream's goals and plans with employees so he doesn't have to take valuable time and money to repair the dream later. "Every time our customers walk by the chiseled granite, they are reminded that's how they should judge us. We'd better live up to it. There's no place to hide."[45]

Many have dared to dream and even prepared for the dream, but there are also, unfortunately, many who have gotten tired or lazy in the wearing of the dream, and before long they must be repairing the dream.

In order to wear the dream well, it does take maintenance, and not just of ourselves but of those who are sharing the dream with us, the employees or staff. Have you looked in the mirror lately at your dream? How does it look? How are you doing? Do any alterations, adjustments, or repairs need to be made? Make them now before the repairs are too costly and you lose your dream.

If you have ever been to Richmond, Virginia, you have probably seen the Ukrop's supermarkets. They are the ultimate in grocery stores.

I personally had the opportunity and privilege to be invited to the home of Joe and Jacquelin Ukrop for the family Sunday dinner when I was in Virginia speaking. The family Sunday dinner is a tradition in the Ukrop home. All of them, children and grandchildren, have their traditional seat at the table. I was particularly impressed at their singleness of purpose not only in their business but in their personal lives, as well. I also found that traditions are very high priority for the Ukrop's supermarkets.

Joe and Jacquelin Ukrop began to dare to dream back in 1942 as they were raising a family and building a business. One very large tradition was and still is the Golden Rule: they did unto others as they would have others do unto them. Each Wednesday after closing their own store, they and five employees went to help the families of farmers in the area who were away at war. They helped bring in crops that would have spoiled before getting to market. A tradition of caring resulted as five-year-old son Jim watched his parents helping and caring for others. Joe and Jacquelin prepared their son Jim to continue the dream as he learned his parents' traditions and they became his own. The store and son Jim, now president of Ukrop's, are fifty years old and the tradition continues. "The company has become an institution in Richmond because of its friendliness, cleanliness, and value . . . the Golden Rule applies equally to customers, associates and suppliers. The results are good things to eat, service with a smile, and an atmosphere in which the customer truly comes first."[46] And because of their personal touch it is a pleasure to shop there. Jim and Bob Ukrop have traditionally sought after suggestions for their supermarket and really want to hear from their customers. And what's more, they *listen*, which is a necessary trait for all successful people—they truly listen.

I saw that firsthand when Bob Ukrop, vice president of Ukrop's, invited me to tour the store while I was in Richmond. In the bakery, they offered me a sample of the rolls from lidded bins holding various versions of wonderful creations. The one I chose had a slight onion flavor and I exclaimed, "This is an onion roll," thinking he would be pleased at my connoiseur taste in breads. Instead, he walked right over to the bakery manager and had them remove all the rolls because some had picked up the onion flavor of other rolls through the plastic bins. This willingness to make immediate, necessary change is proof that Ukrop's really means what they say—they do want to be the best they can be and they aren't afraid to listen! And *that* is a great tradition.

> "Don't let anybody steal your dream."
> —Dexter Yager

Is your dream built on principles, upon traditions that have lasting values? Will those around you learn from you the value of right traditions and principles? Or will your dream die when you are no longer around? Are you listening to suggestions from those around you or simply mouthing the words in platitudes and excuses? Dreams are not maintenance-free. They do require upkeep and you must do your homework to keep yours up and flying! The Ukrops have certainly done that, and I am confident that tradition will be passed on long after they have passed on!

Just as Ukrop's has succeeded because they choose to listen and change what needs to be changed, there are thousands of other businesses that are failing or running in place because they choose to not listen to "bad news."

Fortune magazine evaluated K-Mart's Joseph Antonini, the chain's CEO, and came up with some "bad news." Although he has hired known names to pitch his advertising (golfer Fuzzy Zoeller, caterer Martha Stewart, actress Jaclyn Smith) and slashed prices on eight thousand items, he has stalled and is standing still profit and growthwise. *Fortune* also cites a bad distribution system for merchandise and trying to incorporate other operations that don't fit into the core of his business— such as ownership of the Waldenbooks chain—as reasons for this "stall." But the one that stands out to me for the major reason K-Mart isn't going to grow and succeed is this: "Antonini hates bad news. There is no one to tell him things are going wrong. The culture here is to tell the chairman what he wants to hear."[47]

Are you one who hates to hear "bad news"? Do those around you hide or suppress bad news because they know you will not want to hear it? If so, your dream may be on hold. It may be stalled because you refuse to listen and take action. Your dream may be limited because you really don't want to grow if it means changing anything. Self-deception only fools you, and sooner or later reality must seep in to evaporate the dream. Are you *listening*?

Ask Questions

At a recent dinner party I was sitting next to an adorable sanguine lady who had entertained the whole table and probably those nearby with her animated stories. When she paused for a breath, I asked a quiet phlegmatic man across the table what he did for a living. I have learned that the Peaceful Personalities all have at least one area where they have some expertise but their nature prevents them from bringing it up unless questioned. This man had sat with no change of expression throughout the monologue, but when I turned attention to him, he brightened up and told how he had ranches all over Texas, New Mexico, Colorado, and Australia. With only a little prompting from my questions, he shared how he held together a large family business that owned real-estate in downtown Midland, Texas, and a Bed and Breakfast in New Mexico for trout fishermen.

I listened fascinated at his humble stories of how his family had acquired their property and wealth. As I was focused on him, I could tell the talkative lady was having a whispering conversation with her husband. After dinner she reported to me that her husband had said to her, "See how Florence listens? She's the same personality as you so it's not natural for her to listen, but she's doing it. You, too, can learn to listen."

She made a pledge that night that she would curtail her conversation, ask questions of quiet people, and learn to listen.

Don't Know It All

So many of us think that people will only like us if they are impressed with our position or credentials, and yet the opposite is true. We really dislike people who appear to know it all and who don't ask for opinions but for agreements. They make us feel insecure and insignificant.

They never say, "I don't know," and they never ask questions, they just give answers. For example, they might say in a board meeting, "We all know what the obvious next step must be—close down the entire plant in Arizona." In effect, the board meeting is over at that moment— the know-it-all had already made the decision; there was no debate. He invited them to agree, but not to discuss.

The know-it-all, usually a Powerful Personality, is a dangerous person. He intimidates subordinates, irritates colleagues, and exasperates customers and clients. He speaks well of himself and moves with confidence, but his attitude rarely speaks well for his company. Knowing it all in business or in social relationships is remarkably self-defeating and counterproductive.

Once I was asked to approach a very successful pastor of a large church about his "bull-in-a-china-shop" approach to leadership. His board labeled his style this way because he plowed ahead with what he wanted to do without listening to others' opinions. Although he knew it all, he had made some major financial mistakes and the board could see it coming again. Since he, a Powerful Personality, had all Peacefuls on his board to assure a lack of dissension, they were too afraid to approach him with bad news. "He'll chew us up and spit us out," one said.

I had little enthusiasm for a confrontation, either, but since they had brought me in to solve their personality problems, I had no choice.

The pastor sensed I was not the "good news bear" and he was ready. He did the classic "how-to-win" approach, which may win points but loses in relationships.

He started with a compliment. That part is always positive. Then he shifted to something I had said in my message the day before that he didn't think was effective for the average person. He had, of course, understood it well, but "you have to think of the simple people."

By this approach he had cleverly taken the control of the conversation away from me and he was putting me down in a most cordial manner. He then cheerfully enumerated the positive side of the points I had ready to bring up. "The board is a wonderful group of men who all agree with what we are doing here. I wouldn't take a step without their approval. I listen to each one. It's never too late to learn." He went on with further proof of the harmony within the group and then stood up, dismissed me, and rushed out to another meeting.

He did a masterful job of snatching the control and refusing to listen. He already knew it all, but he didn't have a clue! For there were scattered bodies of bleeding people all over his church who had tried to voice an opinion. Because there was no hope of meaningful communication, a brilliant man was later dismissed from his position where he could have continued the church growth he had started—if he'd only been willing to listen.

Say "I Don't Know"

There is nothing wrong or weak in saying, "I don't know." It is an effective way to get rather than give information. Its meaning is clear, and no one can misunderstand the answer. In order to learn from others, we must listen and sometimes say, "I don't know."

Mark H. McCormack, author of *What They Don't Teach You at Harvard Business School* and chairman and CEO of International Sports Management Group, says, "Today, when I presumably know more than I did twenty-five years ago, I find myself using the phrase more than ever. I even say 'I don't know' when I do know—to find out how much the other person really knows. This willingness to appear ignorant is considerably more effective than pretending to be a know-it-all."[48]

As one executive said, "Making a sale is a two-step process:

> Step one: Ask very specific questions.
> Step two: Wait for the answer.

The person with the "know-it-all syndrome" forgets step two. No one has the answers to everything. In fact, it may mean you have stopped learning and growing if you aren't *asking* questions, and then *listening* for the reply. Don't be fooled by that one who wears the "know-it-all" mask—often it is just a "know-nothing" disguise!

Turn the Question Around

Often the best answer to a question is another question. I frequently have people ask me controversial questions. I've learned that they don't want *my* answer, they just want to give me *theirs*. "Do you think Saddam Hussein is the anti-Christ?"

How would I know? I just ask, "What do you think?"

"Well, I have done a lot of study on prophecy and I know. . . ."

I have saved potentially explosive situations by turning the question around to "What do *you* think?"

They always have an opinion.

To be a good listener, we must focus on the person who's talking and look alert. There is nothing more insulting to the one trying to communicate than a person who is looking around the room trying to find someone more amusing. Nod, be affirming, add a story that amplifies their point—and they will consider you a brilliant conversationalist.

Overcome Your Conversational Weaknesses

Because we are all different, generic advice on conversing will not apply to everyone. So let me break down my ideas into personality groups.

The Popular Personality: Those of you sanguines who love to talk and easily become the center of attention and the life of the party need to learn to listen. Stop at the end of an adventurous story and look around you. What can you remember about anyone there? Who has talked besides you? Are people still hanging on to your every word? If any of these answers are fuzzy, perhaps you need to give your vocal chords a rest. Don't say, "But then there'll be silence." Mrs. J. Borden Harriman wrote a maxim just for sanguines. "Next to entertaining or impressive talk, a thoroughgoing silence manages to intrigue most people."

You can always ask someone *else* a question. They just might surprise you by having something to say.

The Powerful Personality: You tend to be the choleric know-it-all whose every statement sounds like a mandate from God Himself. Realize that you can convince without being in control and yet not appear wishy-washy as you might fear. Ask others' opinions, don't interrupt when you don't agree, and don't start arguments. The Powerful Personality loves to drop seeds of dissension in a low-key group and watch them spring up and attack. This is not only rude, but it may even cause your mate to want to divorce you if you try it one more time. People need your wealth of information, but keep it pleasant.

The Perfect Personality: Realize, my dear melancholy, that there is no perfect gathering of imperfect people and that waiting to say something until you get a group worthy of your words will keep you silent forever. Be willing to listen to inconsequential people who have only trivial pursuits. Call it "recess" for your mind. Let it rest and dabble around in the murky waters of other people's confused thoughts. You might even find it fun. When you do converse, try not to sound like an encyclopedia. We don't need to hear how many miles you get to the gallon or the wind-chill factor in North Dakota in order to enjoy the adventure of your last trip. And don't feel you have to correct the statistics of each person who speaks. No one else took note of them, and even if they did they wouldn't remember them. Having been the butt of Fred's corrections, I got him to agree to let me talk freely unless I said something so far off that it might cause international conflagration.

The Peaceful Personality: You phlegmatics are never rude, argumentative, compulsive, or corrective. You are the most pleasant and easy-going of all personality types and you will never be offensive. However, you may be considered dull because you refuse to respond to other people or even nod and smile. My phlegmatic mother prided herself on the fact that no one ever knew what she was thinking. That was true, but take it from me—the rest of us would *like* to know what you're thinking. Inject a thought now and then. You have a wonderful dry sense of humor. Let us hear from you. In social situations try to keep standing. It will help you stay awake. If you don't wish to talk, force yourself to be alert and act enthusiastic occasionally.

Dr. Mark Leary, an expert on what is considered boring, says that "all shy people are concerned with how they are coming across. That is a central component of shyness." He feels that people who show little emotion or who don't respond to others are considered boring. "They are boring because they show that the person is not involved in the interaction. A monotonous voice, no facial expression, little eye contact—they imply disengagement."[49]

> If you talk too much, cut it down.
> If you talk too strong, tone it down.
> If you talk too serious, lighten up.
> If you talk too little, brighten up.
> Let's not ever be boring again.

Read Good Books

For years, Charlie "Tremendous" Jones, a big teddy bear of a man, has been challenging audiences all over the world with a now familiar statement, "What you will be five years from now will be influenced by the people you meet and the books that you read." Charlie motivates his listeners to become interested in the lives of those around them and to read "good books." He and I agree that if you don't continue to feed your mind with informative material, it will die for lack of nourishment. Yet in this age of television and videos, it takes a dedicated person who really wants to succeed to turn off the knob and read. Without setting an example for our children, we can't expect that they will settle in and read. It's so much easier to lie down and watch what others are doing. We can't sit glued to the television and think our children will want to do differently.

One of the things I admire most about the training received in the Yager branch of Amway distribution is their emphasis on reading motivational books. They agree with Tremendous Jones that you won't be any better in five years if you don't read. They choose a book of the month and make it available to all their "downlines."

One man spoke to me at a convention where I had been speaking and said, "Before I became a distributor I never read a thing, but then I was ashamed when the other men talked about what books they'd just finished. So in self-defense I started to read. I can't believe how much time I was wasting before because now I read at least a book a week."

Bob and Nona Mayers of Enfield, Connecticut, told me a similar story. Once they decided to change their lifestyle and dare to dream, one of their first steps of discipline was to get the family to read. They have seven children and they knew they could not implement changes unless the whole family knew they meant business. You can't "sort of" change. You need to *really* change. So they had a family meeting and made a two-year commitment.

1. No soccer
2. No moustache for Bob
3. No TV

Nona said although there was initial resistance, the whole tone of the family has changed. Instead of lying around and watching television, the children are reading worthwhile books, studying more, and arguing less. They can't believe the difference that a disciplined life can bring.

As she was going through the manuscript for this book, my editor related to me a story from her own experiences growing up. When Sheri was a little girl, her parents were missionaries, so she spent her first school years in Colombia.

"I always loved to read," Sheri says. "My older sister taught me how before I even started kindergarten, and with our only other entertainment choices being Spanish soap operas and game shows on the little black-and-white set, we chose books and read constantly. But when we moved back to the States, one of the family's first purchases was a color television. It intrigued me for about two hours (this was 1970 and I had never seen a color set before), then I settled back into my six-books-at-a-time routine. Our younger brother and sister, however, were toddlers at the time and grew up in front of the set with 'Sesame Street' and 'The Brady Bunch.' Consequently, they associate reading with boring school textbooks and mandatory assignments, and even today as adults they both hate to read. Television remains their entertainment choice.

"Reading will always be one of my great passions," she continues, "and I fully intend to instill that passion in my own kids. Lucky for me, my husband is a bookworm, too. Our favorite evenings are spent cuddling with a good book, sharing 'listen to this!' excerpts with each other, and learning incredible things in the process. Reading is a fundamental part of our lives."

A Gallup poll shows that the average sixteen to twenty-four year old listens to twenty-four hours of music a week, spends seventeen hours with friends, fourteen hours watching television or video tapes, and twelve hours studying. There is not even a mention of reading for personal growth. What a shame!

What Do I Read?

In spite of television, videos, and CDs, there are more books being purchased today than ever before. There's hardly a subject we could think of that doesn't have at least a tome or two telling us how to do it and how to review it. When I was a child, with no television to keep me entertained, my buddies and I all went through the Bobbsey Twins series, then Nancy Drew and the Hardy Boys. We talked about them as friends and tried to figure out who had the secret key to the brass-bound trunk before Nancy figured it out. All these literary heroines lived in large houses, had loving families, and had days filled with high adventure. Going to Paris with Cornelia and Emily in *Our Hearts Were Young and Gay* allowed us all to dare to dream of a journey we had little hope of ever taking. Books provided us with friends, travel, mystery, and romance—and they can do the same today.

Every city center or shopping mall has a bookstore, and many even have lounges where you can sit in a coffee-shop atmosphere and sip as you peruse a potential purchase. Every town of any size has a library, and there are book clubs that will promptly send you a book-of-the-month.

Browsing through stores that sell used books is a fascinating hobby, and when I have a spare hour, I love to look around. I've found Bibles in little-known translations, old novels that I read as a child, and collections of poetry that I taught my pupils back in Haverhill High School. These volumes are always a bargain and I love the thrill of discovery.

Don't let the ease of television eat up your time. Make the commitment to start reading good books.

"So what should I read?" I can hear you asking.

1. *Select a subject.* What are you interested in? Is there something related to your work or home life that you wish you knew more about? For the last two years I have been reading books on dreams in preparation for the writing of this book. I've read *Living Your Dreams* by David Seamands, *Free to Dream* by Neva Coyle, and *Don't Let Anybody Steal Your Dream* by Dexter Yager. I've not been specifically influenced by them, but they have provided my background, my reservoir of information. Once we decide on a subject, we begin to see books, articles, cassettes, and videos that will inspire and instruct us.

2. *Get acquainted with a person.* We could read a biography a week and never run out of possibilities. I love to read about real people and see how they overcame the adversities of life. I get excited when I realize how many great people have lived whom I have never read about or understood. During World War II, my father had me listen to Winston Churchill on the radio. We heard firsthand as he encouraged the British people in their dark before the dawn and told them to never, never, never give up. Later, when his series on the war and his *History of the English Speaking People* came out as bookclub bonuses, I bought them and actually read them. I was doubly blessed when an old college acquaintance, William Manchester, started a series of books on Churchill entitled *The Last Lion.* The first two volumes of over nine hundred pages each have become my favorite books, and even though I have no spare time, I managed somehow to complete them. When I went to England, I searched out the bunker under the streets of London from which Churchill ran the war. I had Fred take my picture next to Churchill's statue and we toured Blenheim Castle where he was born. I got a treasured little book of his *Wit and Wisdom,* which I have read several times. Who would not be moved by the following paragraph from Churchill's biography of "Marlborough: His Life and Times"?

It was only in love or on the battlefield that he (Marlborough) took all risks. In these supreme exaltations he was swept from his system and rule of living, and blazed resplendent with the heroic virtues. In his marriage and in his victories the worldly prudence, the calculation, the reinsurance, which regulated his ordinary life and sustained his strategy, fell from him like a too heavily embroidered cloak, and the genius within sprang forth in sure and triumphant command.[50]

When in Australia, I received a huge volume *Churchill's Wars* from a business client who knew my interest in this English hero.

If you choose a person to read about, this pursuit can take a lifetime, provide your friends with gift selections, and expand your knowledge. I was thrilled when my daughter found a cassette tape of selections of Churchill's most notable excerpts from his war-time messages. Often when I face a day of writing, I listen to Winston's Powerful Personality and get motivated to creative action.

Understanding the personalities will add a new dimension to your reading. When I pick up a book, I keep a highlighter pen in my hand and accent all descriptive words that refer to the character's personality. When I first started reading about Churchill, I assumed he had some melancholy in him because I remembered his depressions during the time before World War II. He would say, "My black dog is on me again." As I studied further, I found that his depression was not that of a melancholy who wanted life to be perfect, but rather that of a choleric's Powerful Personality when out of power. No one was listening to him and they ridiculed his statements that Hitler was not a nice man who deserved a piece of Poland. In *The Last Lion*, I pulled out words that represented Churchill's choleric nature: uncompromising, determined, dictatorial, hissing wrath, bellowing and raging, fiercely defensive. There were also descriptions of him that showed he had a sanguine touch when he pulled back from the fray: flamboyant, swashbuckler, dramatic, intuitive visionary, entertaining, and exhilarating. Seeing Churchill's personality gave me a new understanding of him and his need for Power and Popularity. Between 1932 and 1940 he had good reason to be depressed. He was out of power and extremely unpopular.

3. *Pick a period of history.* Can you see the endless possibilities of reading fiction and non-fiction of a chosen point of time? When I was teaching English I loved Dickens' *A Tale of Two Cities* about London and Paris during the French Revolution. This fascination led me to other histories of that era, and I have a burning desire to know more. General Dwight Eisenhower studied the Civil War, replotted the army strategies, became

an expert on that period, and ended up living in Gettysburg at the battlefield site.

When I began the preparation for my book *Personalities in Power*, I started buying new and used books on the presidents from Franklin Roosevelt through George Bush. As I did their personality profiles, I learned how each one was a man for his season and for his period of history. I became so fascinated with each man, each wife, and each set of circumstances, that I've continued adding to my collection of political biography even though I've completed the book.

4. Become an armchair traveler. We can't all go around the world, but we can read about different countries, their geography, and their people. The travel section in bookstores is filled with fascinating volumes of places I never knew anything about. As a child in Haverhill, I was far-sighted to dream of going to Boston, but as my horizons broadened, I dared to read and dream about faraway places with strange sounding names. Now that I am on the road to somewhere twenty-five out of thirty days, I buy a book of each country and read about it while I'm there. I have a travel shelf in my office, and my grandchildren know that when they study a country in school that Grammie probably has a book on it. I bring back hotel brochures and any items of local color to add to my collection. Before my first trip to Australia, I read *The Thornbirds* and *The Fatal Shore* to give me background, understanding, and feeling for the people. My future desire is to read more about Florence, Italy, because of my name and to visit it again with more knowledge of the art, sculpture, and government than I had before.

One book I thoroughly enjoyed was *Romantic European Hideaways* which consists of colorful descriptions of all kinds of hotels, inns, and castles. A girlfriend and I took this book with us when we went to Europe, and we stayed only in places that sounded like fun to us. Although we weren't looking for romance, we found each hideaway to be exactly as the description had said without any journalistic expansion.

Whether or not you can fly off to Portugal, the reading of travel books will broaden your horizons and the subscription to a magazine like the Condé Nast *Traveler* will bring adventure right into your living room.

5. Get motivated. Never was there a time when more books on success were available. You can examine your erroneous zones while planting seeds of greatness and avoiding the sharks as you climb to the top in pursuit of excellence, before opening your colorful parachute as you bail out to be a co-dependent no more and free your mind from memories that bind. By browsing through the sections on psychology and business, you can find specific instructions on how to sell insurance, start a business in your home, dry apricots in your own backyard, or get along with difficult people. You can improve your knowledge of the stock market so you can buy and sell for profit, or you can develop a plan to double your personal income by wise investments. You can learn how to dress for success, choose a wardrobe that will accent your personal color palette, and entertain with style and flair while operating on a shoestring. There are endless subjects to be digested, and publishers are always looking for a new twist to an old topic.

In this age of how-to books, there is no excuse for any of us to say, "I'd be a success if only I knew how."

6. *Enjoy romance and mystery.* Some of us spend so much time learning how to do things correctly and for profit that we have no light touch to our lives. We become so single-minded that we can't do anything for the sheer pleasure of it. In the last twenty years of my life, I have read widely but always in the areas of my speaking and writing at the time. I couldn't afford to be frivolous, and reading for fun was a thing of the past.

While in England, however, I saw a display of a newly packaged series of Agatha Christie mystery novels. I quickly thought, "You're on vacation. It would be all right for you to relax and enjoy a romp on the Orient Express." It seemed right to read an English novel while in England, and I loved trying to outguess Miss Marple as she gathered clues to the murder at Paddington Station. My mind became momentarily mindless to the things around me and the work awaiting my return. I just had fun.

Sometimes we need that. The bulk of my reading will still be related to my speaking and writing topics. I will be forever learning, processing, creating—but from here on, I'm going to add a dessert now and then to my diet.

The December 1990 issue of *Working Woman* (a magazine designed for choleric females) had an article entitled, "What Execs Read for Fun (Not Profit)." It told that in the eighties we were all too busy to read, but that now even top executives are realizing how important it is to read for pleasure rather than just for profit. Designer Carolyne Roehm loves Agatha Christie mysteries and eighteenth-century historical novels. Cathleen Black, publisher of *USA Today*, varies her reading according to her moods but is "dying to read Scott Turow's *The Burden of Proof*." I liked Lloyd Bentsen better than I had when he ran for vice-president when I found he had just finished reading *Churchill Alone*.

Linda Allard, director of design for Ellen Tracey, does practical reading. "Lately I've spent all my free reading time on architecture books because I'm building a house."

The mood of the nineties is no longer business as usual but a new searching for culture and intellectual pleasure.

7. *Reread the classics.* Many of us, when we were taking high school English literature classes, looked upon the classics we were forced to read as unintelligible and definitely inapplicable to our times. We didn't care if the albatross ever left the Ancient Mariner's shoulder or if Silas Marner ever donated money to charity. Some of us may have thought that Kipling's "Mandalay" was a Marriott Hotel, that Tennyson's "Crossing the Bar" was ordering a drink at *Cheers*, and that *Ivanhoe* was an ancient gardening tool.

Now that we're grown up and still don't know some of these answers, wouldn't it be fun to go back and read the poems and novels that left us cold in the past? Libraries and bookstores have whole sections on the classics. You might enjoy reading some of the love poems out loud to your mate or take turns reading Dickens' *Great Expectations* to each other in place of "Roseanne" and "The Simpsons."

You might even be able to interest your children in *Treasure Island* and *Moby Dick* if you read it to them. It's hard to inspire our children to lofty learning if we're not setting a classic example.

After I saw the movie "Dead Poets Society," I was led to look up a copy of "O Captain, My Captain" by Walt Whitman. I found it in an old high school book of American Poetry I had taught almost forty years ago. I had not remembered from the movie that the poem was a tribute to Abraham Lincoln and was written after his assassination. Knowing that adds meaning to the poem and helps us realize who the fallen captain was and what heartache the people felt at his death. Here is that poem.

O Captain, My Captain!
On the Death of Lincoln

Walt Whitman

O Captain, my Captain! our fearful trip is done;
The ship has weathered every rack, the prize we sought is won;
The port is near, the bells I hear, the people all exulting,
While follow eyes the steady keel, the vessel grim and daring;
But, O heart, heart, heart! O the bleeding drops of red,

Where on the deck my Captain lies, fallen cold and dead.
O Captain, my Captain! rise up and hear the bells;
Rise up—for you the flag is flung—for you the bugle trills,
For you bouquets and ribboned wreaths—for you the shores a-
    crowding,
For you they call, the swaying mass, their eager faces turning;
Here, Captain, dear father! this arm beneath your head!
It is some dream that on the deck, you've fallen cold and dead.

My Captain does not answer, his lips are pale and still;
My Captain does not feel my arm, he has no pulse nor will;
The ship is anchored safe and sound, its voyage is closed and
    done;
From fearful trip the victor ship comes in with object won;
Exult, O shores, and ring, O bells! but I with mournful tread
Walk the deck where my Captain lies, fallen cold and dead.

I feel sorry for those who don't take the time to read or for those who only read books that increase their business productivity but don't expand their minds, their creativity, or their wide-eyed awe of life.

I agree with Alexandra Long, author of *The Year of Christiana Cleaves*:

> You see them everywhere; houses without books. Their blood-
> less residents argue without values, travel without knowledge of
> other places and go for months without encountering a point of view
> different from their own. Occasionally they attend dinner parties
> in other bookless houses and nervously discuss their own choices
> and those of others. But these discussions are like walking through
> quicksand, because the speakers have no solid foundation of eth-
> ics, no points of reference from other times and world views. It is
> useless to tell them that beauty and charm are ultimately irrel-
> evant, that unrequited desire is cured by the passage of time, and
> that wealth and status do not bring happiness.
>
> You might think that I became a writer because I like books,
> words and spelling, but it's not true. I write because I like life. And
> one of the things that taught me to like life was books. Now I see
> patterns and resolutions where once I saw confusion and despair.[51]

If you see before you confusion and despair, start reading. Learn to love life!

It was Thoreau who said, "How many a man has dated a new era in his life from the reading of a book."

Improve Your Vocabulary

From the time I was a child, my father put an emphasis on vast vocabulary and he made learning words a fun experience. He taught Ron and Jim and me that we needed to know words not to impress people, but to be accurate. An extensive vocabulary is not so people will be amazed at what huge words we use, but so we can communicate clearly and people will understand what we are saying. Our father didn't tell us to study words; he did it with us.

In high school I loved vocabulary and especially enjoyed our text *Word Wealth*. It not only gave us challenging words, but most important to me was the section on prefixes, roots, and suffixes. Once I knew that every time I saw "port" in a word it had to do with carry, "fact" meant to make, and "voc" referred to a call, I was able to figure out words I'd never known before. I've included here a sampling of these keys to word wealth.

Study Guide—Prefixes

Uni- .... Mono- .... one
Unity (*oneness*) prevailed.
We studied *uni*cellular (*one*-celled) animals.
He raised his *mon*ocle (*single* eye-glass).
The *mono*logue (*one* person talking) continued.
Cf. *unite*, *unify*, (to make as *one*), *monopoly* (only *one* selling), *mono-plane* (*one*-winged plane).

Du(o)- .... Bi- .... two
They sang a *duet* (music for *two*).
*Du*plicate (*two*fold) prizes were given.
*Bi*monthly (every-*two*-months) payments are expected.
Man is a *biped* (*two*-footed creature).
Note: *di*- means *two* in words like *dicotyledon*, a plant having two seed leaves. Do not confuse with *dia*- (through, between, or across) in words like *dialect*, *diameter*, *diaper*, *diapason*, *diocese*, *dielectric*.

Tri- .... Tri- .... three
*Tri*plets were born.
Type it in *tri*plicate (*three*fold).
It is a *tri*ennial (every-*three*-years) event.
Cf. *Trinity* (*three* parts of the Godhead), *tri*sect (cut in *three* parts).

Quad(ri)- ....Tetra- ....four
Quadruplets (*four* babies at one birth) are rare.
A *quad*rant is *one fourth* of a circle.
A *quad*rangle is a *four*-cornered court or lawn surrounded by build-
   ings, usually in a college.
A *tetr*arch (Tee-trark) ruled *one fourth* of a province.
Lead *tetr*aethyl (*four* ethyls) is used in gasoline.
Cf. *quadruplex, quadruplicate.*

Quin(Que)- ....Penta- ....five
The Dionnes are called *Quín*-tu-plets. (Note accent on first syllable.)
Our basketball *quin*tet played well.
A *penta*style is a building with *five* columns in front.
*Pente*cost comes the *fiftieth* day after the second day of the Passover.

Sex- ....Hex- ....six
A *sex*tet is a group of *six* (singers, usually).
A *sex*agenarian is a person in his *sixties.*
A *hex*agon is a *six*-sided figure.

Sept- ....Hept- ....seven
*Sept*ember was really the *seventh* month until the beginning of the
   year was changed from March to January.
A *sept*agenarian is a person in his *seventies.*
A *hept*agon has *seven* sides. It is a *hept*angular because it has *seven*
   angles.

Octo- ....Octa- ....eight
An *oct*et sang.
An *oct*agon is a figure having *eight* sides.
An *oct*ave is the *eight* tones of a musical scale.
*Oct*ober was once the *eighth* month.

Nona- ....Nov- ....nine*
A *nona*gon is a *nine*-sided figure.
A *nona*genarian is in his *nineties.*
*Nov*ember was the *ninth* month in early Roman days.
A *nov*ena is an act of worship (Catholic) through *nine* successive days.
Note: *Nov*(a)- and *novo*- mean *new*, as in *novelty.*

Dec(a)- ....Deci(m)-..ten
A *deca*de is a *ten*-year period.
The Ten Commandments are known as the *Deca*log or *Deca*logue.
To *deci*mate an army is to destroy every *tenth* man or a considerable part of.
Cf. *decimal, decasyllable.*

Cent(i)- .... Hecto- .... one hundred
A *centipede* has *one hundred* legs.
A *century* is *one hundred* years.
A *hectograph* makes *one hundred* copies.
A *hectometer* is *one hundred* meters.

Mill(e)- .... Milli- .... Kilo- .... one thousand
A *milliard* is a *thousand* millions.
A *million* is a *thousand* thousand.
A *milligram* is *one thousandth* of a gram.
A *kilogram* is a *thousand* grams.

Note: These *thousand* prefixes occur chiefly in units of the metric system. In this system, *milli-* means *one thousandth* and *cent-* *one hundredth*.

Study Guide—Roots

1. -Ceive- .... -Cept- .... to take or seize
He managed to inter*cept* (*take* or *seize* between sender and receiver)
   the message.
Are you an ex*cept*ion (one *taken* out from)?
Here are the other words so common that the root has lost much of
   its original meaning:

receive—reception	inception
deceive—deception	precept
conceive—conception	susceptible
perceive—perception	accept

2. -Dic- .... -Dict(a)-to say (often in sense
                                                                of command)
A *dictator* arose.
He issued an e*dict* (*command*).
A *dictatorial* manner is one like that of a dictator.
A dictaphone is a mechanical ear that records *dict*ation.
Cf. *indicate, addict, dictate.*

3. -Fact- .... -Fect- .... -Fict- .... to make or do
A *factory* is a place to *make* something.
To manu*facture* is literally to make by hand (*manu-*).
Fiction is *make*-believe.
Cf. *confection, affect(ion), effect.*

4. -Fid(e)- .... faith, trust
fidelity—faithfulness
in*fidel*—one having no *trust* (in God)

per*fidy*—breach of *faith*, disloyalty
con*fidence*—*faith* in something

5. -Fract- .... to break
A *fractured* (broken) leg resulted.
In*fraction* (breaking) of the rules will be punished.
Cf. *fraction, refract, diffract.*

6. -Meter- .... a measure or measurer
The gas *meter* leaks.
The speed*ometer* (speed *measurer*) is broken.

7. -Mit(t)- .... -Miss- .... to send, sent
e*mit*—*send* forth .... e*miss*ion
dis*miss*—*send* away .... dis*miss*al
trans*mit*—*send* across .... trans*miss*ion
*miss*ion—a *sending* .... com*miss*ion
*miss*ionary—one *sent* .... com*mitt*ee

Note: Some of these show how the meaning is affected by prefixes
     which you have not studied yet.

8. -Mov- .... -Mot- .... to move
motive—idea which *moves* one (to act)
pro*mote*—*move* forward
e*motion*—*moving* forth of feelings
Cf. *move, motion, motor, promotion, motivation.*

9. -Ped- .... -Pod- .... foot
pedestrian—one who journeys on *foot*
Cf. *equestrian*—one who journeys on a *horse.*
pedicure—care of the *feet*
The burden im*pedes* (puts *foot* against or hinders) his progress.
Cf. *pedal, pedestal, impediment, chiropodist.*

10. -Pos- .... -Pon- .... to place
To com*pose* is to *place* together.
A com*position* is a *placing* together of words, paints, or musical notes
(For those wishing to improve their vocabulary, *Word Wealth* can
     usually be found in college bookstores.)

Isn't it amazing how clichés have become such a daily part of our
vocabularies? One of the silliest examples I've seen on how we let col-
loquialisms creep into our language is this spoof using animal clichés:

     Leapin' lizards, we can scarcely get through a day without
     meeting crestfallen, pussyfooting chickens who stick their heads

in the sand; henpecked underdogs who get goose pimples and butterflies and turn tail; scared rabbits who play possum and cry crocodile tears before they go belly up; spineless jellyfish who clam up with a frog in the throat whenever the cat gets their tongue; mousy worms who quail and founder and then, quiet as mice, slink off and then return to the fold with their tails between their legs; and shrimpy pipsqueaks who fawn like toadies until you want to croak. Let's face it. It's a dog-eat-dog world we live in. But doggone it, without beating a dead horse, I do not wish to duck or leapfrog over this subject. It's time to fish or cut bait, to take the bull by the horns, kill two birds with one stone, and before everything goes to the dogs and we've got a tiger by the tail, to give you a bird's-eye view of the animals hiding in our language![52]

If we don't have a good command of words, we tend to speak in clichés and we might sound like this section from Crazy English.

Check Your Handicaps

In our preparation for our dreams, we need to evaluate any handicaps we have and decide to pursue goals where our particular problem doesn't matter or plan a program to overcome them.

I can remember when I was on the staff of the Long Wharf Theatre in New Haven, Connecticut. Because of its proximity to New York, New Haven was a city where would-be actors came to be discovered. The old Shubert Theatre was a testing ground for pre-Broadway productions, and the Yale School of Drama was turning out a new crop of actors and actresses each year. The Long Wharf was established in a cinderblock cold-storage warehouse. Arvin Brown, who is now a New York director-producer, was the director of the children's theatre and he trained Gary Burghoff as the lead in the Saturday afternoon shows for the little ones. Gary went on to become Charlie Brown on Broadway and later to play the unforgettable role of Radar on "M.A.S.H." At the time we had no idea that Arvin would win awards on Broadway or that little Gary would make it big on television.

Perhaps the least likely to be a winner was a young man named Stacy Keach. He had an obvious harelip and I personally wondered how he dared to dream of becoming an actor. What I didn't understand at the time was that Stacy had determined to overcome a handicap that could have slowed others down. He had worked on his body so that his physique was impressive on the stage and he also had trained his voice so well that when he opened his mouth we all forgot his harelip. Years later when I saw him in Los Angeles performing Hamlet at the Mark Taper Forum, I was overwhelmed with his magnetic presence on the stage and his magnificent control of his voice as he made Shakespeare's poetry come alive. When he became Mike Hammer on television, he grew a moustache to cover the harelip and no one could ever tell. I'm sure there were people along the line who discouraged him, but he prepared for his dream and he made it. Unfortunately, his success led him into drugs, and he had to serve a sentence in England. I hope he'll be able to repair the dream with the same determination he had in the beginning and be willing to share his courage with others.

Another actor who overcame amazing odds is Lou Ferrigno, the "Incredible Hulk." As a child he had an ear infection that took away seventy percent of his hearing, leaving him with a speech impediment. In spite of his handicap, he dreamed of being a movie star and he prepared as if it were possible. He concentrated on body-building and won the Mr. Universe title. Because of this honor, he was cast as the Hulk in a non-speaking role. Seeing a chance to continue on television, he immersed himself in speech training and studied acting. Ferrigno, who wears two hearing aids, stated in an *America West* magazine interview, "I've wanted to be an actor since I was twelve. I never told anybody because they would laugh. But I've always taken the negatives and somehow turned them into positives. And I never feel sorry for myself."

The article also added that "it took years of effort, but Lou Ferrigno made that dream come true. Such confidence comes from strong preparation."[53]

The Hulk, six-feet-five-inches tall and weighing two hundred and fifty pounds, has gone on to other roles in "Wolf" and "Cage," parts that he could only dare to dream about a few years ago. Lou Ferrigno wants his life to count as an inspiration to others who may feel they don't have a chance. He wants to share his dream. "People can see the obstacles I've overcome," he says, "and I hope they decide they can emulate me in their own way."

Find a Mentor

Have you ever wondered why some people seem to instinctively know where their career should go next, or who to talk to about it to get advice? They seem to have those on "their team" pulling for them and introducing them to the right people. Perhaps they have what is called a "mentor." A mentor is someone who comes alongside another person, usually of lesser rank, and teaches, guides, advises, and directs them business-wise. Very often the mentor sees the "student" in a role that will eventually step into the mentor's job.

John Hermann, President of Total Employee Relations Services in Irvine, California, says he owes a debt of gratitude to San Francisco Labor attorney Fred Long. "He gave me my start and he did it by constantly getting me involved in situations that were way over my head."[54] It was Fred Long who offered to help John go out on his own and helped him finance a competing business. Now twelve years later, there's still a mutual respect and loyalty. You might call Long the "dream mentor."

However, mentoring is taking a different form than it used to because many fields are so specialized and the length of time in one office is not as long. People are much more transient.

Firms such as Security Pacific Bank and Rockwell Corporation have assigned mentors to provide one-on-one career counseling for certain employees. Marilynne Miles Grey, a partner at the Mentoring Institute in Vancouver, British Columbia, says they've seen a lot more companies setting up mentoring programs. They have developed formal programs for more than sixty U.S. firms.

Would you like to have someone become your "mentor"? Would you like to benefit from someone far more experienced in your field? Do you learn better and understand faster with someone you can ask questions and the proverbial "why"? Then this is something you may want to look into. Mentors are usually people who aren't afraid of sharing information and encourage others to stretch, challenge, and surge ahead in their fields.

Below are some tips in locating a mentor figure:

1) Look within your company first, but consider going outside your immediate department.

2) Don't be afraid to approach someone higher in your organization if you think he or she can help you. Most people are flattered to be viewed as experts.

3) If you can't find someone within your company that you admire or feel you can learn from, look outside.

4) Don't rule out peers. Just because people are at or even below your level doesn't mean you can't learn from them.

5) Don't stop at one. Most successful people have more than one mentor.[55]

Once you have found a mentor, don't be afraid to be a mentor to someone else. Share your dream with them. In the National Speakers Association, we have a mentor program where those of us with years of experience make ourselves available to encourage new members. There is nothing more fulfilling than seeing someone you've helped succeed. Sharing isn't losing; it's multiplying success! •

PART THREE

Wear the Dream

Wear the Dream

He's not just surviving; he's thriving.

"The fact that we're doing basically the same thing we started twenty years ago—and succeeding at it is pretty remarkable."[56] So says Ron Chapman about his twenty years on KVIL Dallas-Fort Worth as morning drive-time DJ. Is the same thing boring? Is it time for a change? Not when what you're doing works. Not when stations around the country try desperately to imitate your style. Not when the DJ's you've trained have left to teach seminars on the secrets of your success.

How does he do it? The *Dallas Times Herald* notes that in a city hungry for success stories, Ron Chapman is number one. "Curiosity about the secret of Chapman's success is hardly idle. Radio stations in other cities have sent spies to town to tape 'Ron Chapman and the Morning Group,' hoping to decipher the formula for obtaining such enormous audience loyalty. Yet Chapman's success remains uniquely his. Imitators have come and gone. Chapmanesque formulas have been tried and failed. And Chapman remains king of the morning rush hour."[57]

How has he remained king? How has the "towering genius" become the "First Citizen" of Dallas? Through the years I have learned some rules that can help all of us find that potential lurking deep inside.

1. Understand your personality and work with it, not against it. So many people I meet daily are dissatisfied with what they are doing. Often they are in a career that doesn't fit their personality because a parent pushed them into it, a guidance counselor wished he were in it, or it seemed like the safe and secure road to success.

Ron has known from the time he was a child, long before I began a study of the personalities, that his future was in his different personality strengths—the *sanguine* ones: talkative, outgoing, optimistic, creative, fast-paced, and hilarious—and the *choleric* ones: strong-willed, determined, single-minded, goal-oriented, and persevering. As he dared to dream that he might become a radio personality, he prepared the dream using every ounce of talent he possessed. He was not dissuaded by a mother who sighed over his unwillingness to settle down and be normal, by teachers who couldn't get him to be serious about ancient history or accounting, or by a traditional world that said no one can make a real living on the radio. He knew what he was good at, and he refused to be talked into a regular job that could have kept him struggling in his weaknesses.

Every day Ron does what he was meant to do. He doesn't get sidetracked on draining details, he just keeps stretching his strengths. As Ron has learned with me about the personalities, he can see that he is a Popular and Powerful person. He was born to have fun and be in control, and he knows that life is a lot more fun when he's in charge. He uses his sanguine strengths to have fun on the air, and he becomes choleric the minute he steps out of the sound booth and takes control of his staff and all the creative decisions.

From the time he was a child, Ron has been in control of the family fun and in charge of his own life. Even though his teachers had little hope for him, he had the Powerful Personality that determined he would become a success, with or without education. Ron says, "The guiding light in my life, my operational phrase, was 'I'll show 'em.' It wasn't angry. It was just ambition. Everyone I know went to college. And I was going to run faster, work harder, get street-smarter. Whatever it took!"

Ron did whatever it took, and by using his choleric confidence and sanguine charm he could get what he wanted and enter in where angels feared to tread. I remember when he, my phlegmatic mother, and I went to New York to see "The Music Man." Ron had his little tape recorder and after the show he went backstage to see if he could find Robert Preston. My mother was petrified for fear we'd all be arrested, but Ron announced to the guard, "I'm here for my interview with Mr. Preston."

"Right this way," the guard said with a smile. Ron walked briskly behind him while Mother held back saying, "What will they ever do to us when they find out he doesn't have an interview?"

"Let's find out," I replied as I pulled Mother by the arm.

We went down a dark back alley into a parking lot and up two steps into a trailer. The guard announced, "Mr. Chapman is here for your interview."

Mother gasped, "This is it. It's all over now." But much to her surprise, Robert Preston motioned us all into the trailer and welcomed us warmly. He had on a burgundy brocade dressing gown with black satin lapels and looked exactly like what I pictured off-duty movie stars to be. He asked no questions to validate our authenticity, he answered all Ron's questions graciously, and he even offered us all a chocolate from a crystal bowl. As we thanked him for his hospitality and left the trailer, Mother sighed, "That took ten years off my life," but I was proud of Ron's daring confidence and his ability to entertain anywhere at any time.

2. *Determine to succeed.* While other DJ's hope they can make it or wonder if it's possible, Ron is determining daily to stay on top. One of Ron's formidable rivals says, "He's one of the greatest of all time. He's a fierce competitor. He doesn't give up."[58] Another veteran radio personality states that Dallas-Fort Worth "is probably the most competitive radio market in the nation. So that makes Ron's success and longevity even that much more astounding. But the main thing is simply the fact that he is a great talent and hard worker. I don't think there's any question that KVIL's success is due to Ron Chapman."[59]

As opposing stations have brought in "twenty years' worth of six-month wonders," Ron has remained King of the Road. It all sounds so easy in retrospect, but when Ron left his successful television show "Sump'n Else" to take on the biggest challenge of his career trying to revive a station so low that it wasn't even on the ratings charts, people thought the move was a big mistake.

"KVIL was awful in those days. It was a loud rock 'n roll station that called itself 'your power pal.' Of course, the power they were referring to was only one thousand watts AM. All of the disc jockeys were named David. The whole point was that little David was going to take on big Goliath, which in those days was KLIF.

"I looked on it as a challenge, though. After I left Channel 8 in early '68. I had other offers. I could have gone back to KLIF. I had an offer from Channel 11 to do TV. I also had a very lucrative offer in Pittsburgh for more money than I ever thought I could make. But they were just jobs. KVIL seemed to be something you really could do something with.

"But what really motivated me was a couple of conversations I had with people in the industry who told me, 'Ron, we love you, but there's no way that this KVIL thing is ever going to get off the ground.'

"And it was that kind of comment that gave me just that much more energy and that much more determination to say, 'Just stand back and watch us smoke.'"[60]

It took a while for the smoke to rise as no one seemed to know there was a KVIL. Ron was pouring his heart out through an empty mike and he says it was over a month before he knew anyone was listening. Everywhere he went he'd mention his show, and one night at a party he met a woman who said, "You know, I'm there with you every morning." The next day he started by saying good morning to this lady. Others began to call in so their names would be broadcast, and ultimately Ron had too many names to mention.

Ron's "overnight success" took twenty years of hard work and dedication. One of his competitors says of Ron, "He is a promoter beyond anything I've ever seen in any market. He has worked so hard to be uniquely Dallas-Fort Worth. No one has shown the patience to establish a program and compete with him. For years others have tried to get Chapman. You can't because he has the years on you. I truly believe he is untouchable."[61]

At a time when radio was narrowing its focus to reach certain markets, Ron presented a well-rounded selection of music and created what is now known as adult contemporary music. As with all forerunners, Ron had to listen to those who said, "You can't do that. You can't try to please everybody. You've got to select your audience and go for it." But Ron was determined to win, and he has made enough people happy to stay on top for over twenty years. "This is not a case of twenty years and here I am in the twilight. It's twenty years and we're still winning," Ron says happily. "That is really a kick. In fact, we're winning better than we ever have before." Ron Chapman is still spinning and winning.

3. *Keep working and have a passion for your product.* I know of no truly successful people whose aim was to retire as soon as possible. Some of them do achieve their goals and retire early, but they didn't get to that point by aiming to relax. Instead, their success was due to their being willing to work.

Ron Chapman has been willing to pay the price to reach the top. "My dad is married to that station," says his daughter Melanie, an SMU graduate and promotion director for a Denver station. "He is a workaholic. He works twenty-four hours a day. He is always thinking of ideas. When I was young, I really didn't know him because he was working thirteen-hour days. He always brought work home with him. Not files, but ideas dancing in his head."[62]

Ron's racing mind is always at work and everything he sees becomes a potential bit for the audience. Before he goes on the air in the morning, he has already whipped through several newspapers to pick up the hot topics of the day. He knows what Carson, Letterman, and Arsenio Hall talked about the night before and by the time he steps into his studio and croons the first good morning to his faithful flock he is already flying high.

Other star DJ's love to have producers who will take care of all the mechanics of spinning the records, but not Ron. He does it all himself. To watch him flip the switches as he moves to the music is almost like viewing a ballet from the first row. Ron never sits down for his four hours on the air. He is on his toes one minute and rocking on his heels the next. During the music he tapes every call that comes in from his listeners who phone in opinions on the topic of the day or feed him appropriately humorous material. I've watched in awe as he weaves together the lines from several callers, makes a series of laughs, one topping the other, and plays the edited tape back to the expectant audience. No one depending on an engineer to push the buttons could create on-the-spot original humor five days a week. Ron calls his upbeat patter "verbal handholding." He lets his people know that the day is safe; they can get up and go out into the hard cruel world with a smile on their faces.

"I couldn't get up each day without your brother's encouragement," a lady told me.

"He's my best friend," said another who had never met him.

Ron's ability to work twelve hours a day and make it all sound like fun shows the combination of his personality strengths and his willingness to devote his time and energies to the cities of Dallas and Fort Worth.

Ron's single-minded purpose to keep KVIL on top causes him to keep tuned into it himself twenty-four hours a day. If a DJ has thirty seconds of dead air in the middle of the night it will wake him up. He'll make a note of it and when the DJ comes in for his shift the next night, there will be a warning message with the exact minute of the mistake. No one makes many of those mistakes twice.

Anyone who wishes to get an education in how to be successful in radio could do no better than to work under Ron Chapman. Although Ron is not the melancholy type of perfectionist, he has the choleric determination to see that things get done his way *now*. His way has worked. He has high standards for himself which he lives up to, and he expects those working for him to do the same. If you do, you learn; if you don't, you leave.

When asked if he hated Ron as a competitor, one morning DJ replied, "Hate him? No. My only regret is that I never worked for the guy. There's so much to learn from him."[63]

"KVIL and Ron are a benchmark to which many radio stations aspire," says a broadcasting consultant. "Nobody works harder than Ron Chapman."[64]

4. Sense the needs of your people and meet them. In the midst of his extremely hectic days, Ron still finds time to be a mentor and bring the new kid on the block along. His producer comments on Ron's high standards for himself and others: "He will not settle for less than the very best. It's like playing for Vince Lombardi." And the station manager says, "He is absolutely without question the driving force of KVIL."[65]

Ron is willing to train others and he holds nothing back. He listened to one of his DJs and noticed many pauses in his patter. It seemed as if he had to think the sentence out before he gave it. Since Ron's mind and mouth are at high speed twenty-four hours a day and he even creates commercials in his sleep, he couldn't tolerate this halting performance. He taped a half hour of this young man's show, edited out every gap, and produced a tighter replica of the original. He brought the man in for a review of his progress and asked him to sit down so they both could listen to a tape together. Naturally the man was shaking in his cowboy boots, but as the tape went on and he was so much better than he'd thought, he began to relax. By the end, he was smiling and quite proud of himself. "Would you feel content if you could sound like that everyday?" Ron asked.

"Yes, sir, I would."

"Well, you could, but you don't yet." Ron then switched on the original tape with the gaps and played it as the young man sank in his chair. Ron gave him both tapes and sent him on his way. The point had been made.

Ron was listening one afternoon to his drive-time DJ who was fresh out of radio school and working hard to sound deep and philosophical. His tone was lofty and did not have the warm touch that KVIL is noted for. *D* magazine says that what Ron and his group are communicating is, "Yes, my dear, the world is still a warm and safe and funny place to be, and you are on top of it with us, you know everything we do, which is a lot, and life keeps getting better."[66]

Because this young man was busy waxing eloquent and missing the mark, Ron took him out on the road in his car one afternoon. While a substitute was doing his show, this young man was stalled in traffic on Central Expressway. "Look around at the people," Ron said, "See that woman in the next car? Her window's open so we know she has no air-conditioning. She looks exhausted after a hard day in the steno pool and she's on her way to pick up the children at the baby sitter's so she can get them fed before going out to work as a cocktail waitress for the night. Do you think she cares anything about your college degrees and your platitudes on life?"

The next day this DJ had a new compassion in his voice. He had seen his audience face to face and Ron's time with him made a difference in his life and in his focus.

Whether you are running a household full of children, selling used cars, or talking on the radio each day, you won't be successful unless you know what the people want.

"I swear I can tell you how this market feels on any given subject by nine o'clock any morning," Ron says. Knowing that a large portion of his success is his intimate understanding of his people, he stays in close touch.

When Ron first started at KVIL he made a conscious choice to meet the needs of his people. The only problem was he didn't have any people. He looked around and saw two key steps to bringing in an audience: treat women and Fort Worth with respect.

The seventies was a time when macho men were focusing their humor around sexist jokes that demeaned women. Much of radio humor was at the expense of women, and Ron set out to bring about a positive change in that area. Because of his innate respect for women and the desire to right a wrong, Ron put forth some new directives: no dirty jokes, nothing derogatory about women. He got a picture of a woman who looked like what he anticipated his audience could be and he showed it to all new staff.

"Looking at her picture," he told them, "teaches us what not to do. Locker room jock talk is not going to play with that woman. Nor is sexist humor. Dolly Parton jokes, dumb receptionist stories are out. She's a no-nonsense, hard-working professional, and we treat her with respect."

Not only does Ron treat the women well, but so do his other DJ's— or they hear about it. Because of this conscious effort to please the ladies, KVIL has developed a fiercely loyal following in the eighteen-to-forty-nine-year-old female bracket.

The *Dallas Times Herald* says, "Long before today's sophisticated demographics, Chapman instinctively knew this was his audience and played to it."[67]

Ron's second change was to revise Dallas thinking about Fort Worth, the step-sister, the poor relation, the cowtown. No more aspersions on Fort

Worth. From here on we treat her with respect. By treating Fort Worth as a lady, as an equal, Ron was able to double his listeners. He takes new staff to the top of the oil derrick at Six Flags Over Texas, an amusement park located between the two cities. Ron tells them, "Here's the concept. The Right Hand of God is Dallas. The Left Hand of God is Fort Worth." He claims that once a person has seen the two towns from that high perspective, they don't do one-city things. They look at the area as a whole. "That's the main thing I teach people when they come to work at KVIL. We project in their mind that they are not in a studio on Central Expressway."[68]

That dedication to serving his constituents reaches the heart of the people. They think of him not in a studio on Central Expressway, but in their homes and their cars as part of the family.

5. *Build trust and be reliable.* To have people respond in blind faith to a DJ's request for money doesn't happen overnight. How do you build trust in a business noted for hype? How do you get people to believe in you more than they do their own family members? You always give them what you promised. You don't cut corners or change your plans mid-stream. Over the years Ron Chapman has built absolute trust in his listeners. When he says he'll give out a new car a year for life, all taxes paid, he does it. He doesn't surprise the winner with conditional clauses. If he says he'll prove that two prize-winning couples are racing across the Sahara Desert on camels, he'll beam it into a Dallas television station by satellite. If he says he'll be on the cruise to the Bahamas in person, he won't send a substitute at the last minute. Ron Chapman has built a trust in people who have never met him that surpasses that of many married couples. He delivers the prize when and where he said he would. They can count on him.

"Chapman isn't just a DJ to his devoted fans," a journalist explained, "he's like a longtime neighbor, a friend they trust. Not only do they pay homage to him whenever they see him in public, they also have been known to staunchly defend the man when someone has spoken unkind words about him or his show. Whenever KVIL issues a new bumper sticker, they eagerly slap it on their cars; some vehicles have four different designs glued to the fender. One year, Chapman asked listeners to pull the old stickers off and mail them back to the station. He received 100,000."[69]

It is this devotion to Ron Chapman as a trustworthy man that made his renowned request for money possible. A commentator for another local station said KVIL listeners responded in the manner they did because Chapman "epitomizes everything that is good" about broadcasting.

"What Ron Chapman has proved is his listeners are responsive, they listen to what he says, they pay attention to what he says and they do what he says, which puts a lot of responsibility on him.

"You know that he's going to do something responsible with the money. People are going to say, 'Wow, that's what I'd do with the dough.'

"No one is going to be mean enough to say give me back my twenty bucks. These people want to be excited by what happens. They can boast about it. Everybody who sent that money can say, 'I was part of that.'"[70]

Everyone did want to be part of whatever Ron was about to do. They didn't respond with $243,000 on a whim, but because he had built trust and they knew he'd be responsible.

Forbes magazine featured an article entitled, "Are You a Born Sucker?" They told multiple stories about Wall Street predators bilking the public and in the middle of the article they put Ron's story, the only positive in a sea of sham. They told of his simple request for twenty dollars. "No reason was given, no contest was named, no fund-raising program identified. He simply directed listeners to their checkbooks." They went on to conclude, "Chapman, who concedes that if he were not an honest man he could have a tremendous future in the investment fraud business, allowed his listeners to reclaim their money, and donated the rest to local charities."[71]

How do you become a role model? How do you get people to believe in you? Be honest, always stay true to your word, and fulfill every promise you make.

6. *Stay out of trouble.* So often when we achieve a comfortable level in life, we compromise and take chances that we would not have done in earlier times; however, Ron has kept his life clean and even when reporters have searched for trouble they have found no skeletons in his closet. During the publicity about the twenty dollars, the New Orleans *Baptist Message* wrote an article saying that no one would send in money for no reason unless they trusted the person involved. They concluded that he must be more than an overnight success even though they had never heard of him and that the people of Dallas must believe in him.

The article was sent to me by a friend who recognized my brother's name. In appreciation for the positive article, I wrote a letter to the editor which they quoted. In part it said:

> I was delighted to read your kind words about my brother, Ron Chapman, the Dallas disc jockey who asked people to send twenty dollars for no specific reason.
>
> You were correct in stating that people believed in him, but he was no overnight success. He has spent thirty years giving good clean fun to the listeners of Dallas and has been consistently the number one DJ in the area. "Billboard" recently chose him as tops nationally in his field.

Because he has proven honest and honorable over the years, the people of Dallas knew that he would do something right with the requested money, and they wanted to be part of whatever it was.

It is possible to make it to the top without resorting to swearing, vulgarities, cheap tricks, or loose living. My brother is more than another DJ—he is a positive role model for aspiring radio personalities. Thank you for your tribute to his reputation.[72]

7. *Keep a sense of humor.* Be happy. When I ask people I meet in Dallas what they like best about Ron Chapman, they all say, "He makes us laugh and he keeps us happy." Day after day, Ron keeps people happy. One morning as I was stuck in traffic on Central Expressway, I was listening to Ron and he was especially humorous. At one point, I laughed out loud and noticed the people in adjoining cars were doing the same thing. I rolled down my window and called to the man next to me, "That's my brother!"

"I don't know if he's your brother or not, but he sure is funny."

Soon other windows came down and we listened in unity, a vast audience of new friends, laughing together, making the best of a bad situation.

Ron has always been able to make fun of life in such a way that he lightens the load of his listeners and wipes out their worries.

"The fact that we can make you feel good about yourself," Ron says, "and make you laugh when you don't want to, is an enormous service."[73]

Right from the beginning of his tenure at KVIL, Ron insisted that all of the staff send out positive messages. According to the *Dallas Times Herald*, "The marching orders for his crusade include an edict not to confront listeners with too many negatives. People just getting up in the morning do not want to hear about murders, plagues, and disasters."[74]

Ron adds, "We are here to look out the drapes before you and make sure it's okay for you to go to work again. We give the listeners something to cling to."

Isn't that what everyone needs at the start of each day—good news instead of bad, positive versus negative, something to cling to?

"What they are clinging to is Chapman's fervent belief that most of life's woes can be eased with good humor, positive thinking, and hard work—the classic recipe for the American Dream."[75]

Perhaps you could wear your dream longer and better if you started each day giving good news to those around you. Perhaps your family would look forward to getting up each morning if you could give them something to cling to.

Follow Ron's example as he keeps the pulse on his people and senses his listeners' dreams. "We know we're part of something special here, and we want to keep it alive—to keep Camelot open awhile longer," he says.

- Ron Chapman understands his personality and has fine-tuned his strengths to keep him number one.
- He was determined from an early age to succeed in spite of discouraging words.
- He keeps working as hard at the top as he did on the way up.
- He is willing to spend time with his staff and not keep his secrets of success to himself.
- He senses the needs of his audience and gives them what they want.
- He has built a trust over the years so that his people believe in him.
- He refrains from negatives, criticism, vulgar language, and bad news in favor of positive, up-beat, fast-paced humor.

"As he prepares to send his message radiating into those hundreds of thousands of receptive minds," a Dallas magazine said, "he is more aware of them than perhaps anyone has ever been in the history of this city."[76]

Ron knows his listeners and he has a passion for his people.

Practice the Personalities

Few of us have the public profile that Ron Chapman has, but we are all faced with the dailiness of life. We have to hang in there and it's not always easy. Some achieve a certain social and career level, but then they relax to the point that they lose their position or become workaholics— to the detriment of their health and family life. Some I've talked with have said it was easier to dare to dream and prepare the dream than it was to wear the dream. For others the cloak seems too heavy and just keeps slipping off their shoulders.

One of the first steps in keeping our life together is to practice the personalities so that they become a useful tool in understanding ourselves and getting along with others.

If we want to be good at anything in life we have to work on it. Few blessings drop out of the heavens with no reason. If we want to play the piano well, we must practice our scales. If we want to win the marathon, we should run each day. If we want to understand the personalities and make their function an automatic part of our lives, we need to practice with every person we meet and then test out our first impressions as we observe other people's behavior.

Remember that our use of the personalities is not to pin labels on other people or to say, "Aha, now I see why you talk so much." We benefit from this knowledge when it becomes a subconscious part of our nature and we can know quickly how to converse with each person and be able to pre-judge their probable reactions for our benefit.

There are two ways to practice your personality skills. One is to observe people from a new perspective in single or group encounters. The second way is to underline personality traits in any biographical material you read about anyone, as I did with Winston Churchill.

1. *Observe people's personalities in real-life situations.* At two o'clock in the morning a fire alarm awakened Fred and me in our hotel and an announcement came blaring through the halls. "The hotel is on fire. Do not panic, do not use the elevators. Walk calmly down the inside stairs." We jumped up quickly and reached for our robes. As Fred organized our journey by gathering up some small valuables and thinking out what we couldn't afford to burn up, I went to the bathroom to see how I looked. How do you look at two in the morning? The view was depressing so I began to fluff up my hair and put mascara on so my eyes looked somewhat open. Just as I reached for the tube of lipstick, Fred appeared in the door and stated, "You can burn to death just as well without lipstick."

I had no intention of burning to death. I just wanted to be presentable in case I met anyone I knew.

As we left the room I looked longingly at the clothes I was leaving behind and began to estimate how much I had invested in those outfits that were soon to be reduced to ashes.

The walk down the stairs was a slow and plodding one from the fourteenth floor. People had their heads down in hopes no one would recognize them in their disheveled state. A sanguine bubbled, "I've never been in a hotel fire before." A choleric grumbled, "These things aren't usually fires at all and it makes me mad that they make us get up before they have checked it out."

A melancholy said, "I hate to get my sleep interrupted because when I don't get enough rest I'm miserable all day." A phlegmatic moaned, "I wish they'd let us use the elevators. It would sure be a lot easier."

Once we all hit the lobby, there were firemen dragging hoses through the crowd of people toward the kitchen where the fire had begun. There seemed to be no immediate danger, so we all settled in to await further directions.

If there ever was a place to analyze personalities, it was here. When standing in a lobby in your pajamas, you can hardly put on airs or pretend to be anything you aren't. We were looking at each other stripped down to reality. Fred and I leaned against a high marble planter full of phony philadendron and perused the people.

A melancholy lady was trying to get over to the elevator to go back for her jewelry. She was crying and pleading for permission from a three-hundred-pound phlegmatic guard who was not about to give in. He was dressed in a uniform and broad-brimmed hat that made him look like the Canadian Mounted Police without a horse. He was immovable and when she asked why she couldn't go up when the fire was in the kitchen he replied, "I don't ask why, I just do what they tell me."

Pushing through the crowd was a choleric woman with her ailing father in a wheelchair. The poor man had tubes in him and a bottle gurgling over his head, and he looked like a link between senility and death. She was angry that she had to bring him out in the middle of the night and she plunked him up against a wall facing an *exit* sign. As she banged him around to get him settled, she turned to me as if I were the chairman of the complaint department.

"Do you know there is not one person on this hotel staff that knows how to do CPR?"

I tried to remember what CPR was, but she went on without a comment from me. Pointing her finger in my face, she said, "My father could die right here before our very eyes and there wouldn't be a soul to save him!"

I mumbled about that being too bad and she continued, "The town I come from has only seven thousand people and we all know CPR. We had a course and everybody came. We all can help each other, but not here. You could gasp your last breath here and the hotel wouldn't care."

By this time she was right up close in my face and I found myself sincerely apologizing for the wanton disregard the hotel had for dying people.

At this point an announcement came over the speakers letting us know the fire was over and we could go back to bed. There's nothing more dangerous than an angry choleric wielding a wheelchair. People sensed this and parted the Red Sea for this woman and her father who seemed to still be breathing without CPR. As I finally got near the elevators, an adorable sanguine lady came bouncing along. She had her make-up on and she had even taken the time to glue on her false eyelashes. She smiled at me and said, "I love your robe."

"I like yours, too," I replied.

My attention encouraged her and she went on. "I got a new robe for Christmas. It's white with little blue flowers all over it. It has ruffles with blue edges all the way down the front and right at the waist there's this precious bunch of forget-me-nots." She took a deep breath and concluded, "If I had only known I was going to be in a fire, I would have brought my new robe."

Knowing the personalities adds a touch of humor to any situation. You'll never be bored again, whether you're biding time in a doctor's office, in a hotel fire, or the old ladies' home.

Dorothy wrote to tell me she was teaching my Personality Plus at the Royal Retirement Residence. The only way she could get her mother in was to volunteer to amuse the patients. "The sanguines have blue hair and purple lipstick and have bells on their wheelchairs. The cholerics keep using their canes to wake up the dozers. The melancholies make sure all the wheelchairs are in an even row and facing the right direction, and the phlegmatics are glued to the TV with a few of them close to comatose." She then encouraged me by saying, "Your Personality Plus has now entered the senior circuit. I'm preparing the way for you so when you need to check in, know that I, like John the Baptist, will let them know you're coming."

2. *Observe people's personalities in print.* The second way to practice the personalities is to keep a pen in hand each time you read the paper or a magazine and highlight every descriptive word about anyone. These words will instantly form a personality pattern.

Even the vocabularies of the personalities are different. The sanguine uses the word "fun" frequently. In an interview reported in *USA Today*, television star James Garner said that getting beaten up every week for six years as private-eye Jim Rockford "was no fun." Of his "Nichols" role, he said "It was very funny." In "Grand Prix," he liked his part "just for the fun of driving on the best circuits in the world."[77]

Garner reveals his secondary personality as phlegmatic when he uses trigger statements like, "I'd like to be retired and rest." When he can, he plays golf and watches sports on television. He also says he doesn't enjoy producing. "It takes up too much time, it's too hard to do." And acting in another series would be out of the question, "It would put me in the grave."[78]

From just these few sentences we can see that James Garner is a mixture of a sanguine who likes fun and a phlegmatic who finds that some of life is just too much like work.

To help you practice, I've pulled out some key words or quotes from news magazines about a few well-known people that you may have never analyzed before. Some are all one type of personality and one is a combination of two. See if you can sense the personality and then guess who this might be. Jot down your opinion and then turn to page 154 for the answers.

1. "I haven't ever felt that I was out of control." "I don't have time to think about my problems." "Nobody pushes me around. Do you understand?" "They dislike me out of jealousy." "I love to have enemies. I like beating my enemies to the ground." "No one has done more for this city than me!"[79]

2. "She's extremely sensitive not only to people but to art." "She has managed to preserve her dignity through crises." "She is a legend, a myth, an ethereal being." "She is secure in social situations." "She is elegant, charming, classy, a princess." "She loves literature, classical music, and poetry." "She's not ostentatious and is quite simple underneath."[80]

3. "He's a comic genius, eager to please, craving applause." "Every interview is an original performance." "He'll help you forget your troubles and be glad you're alive." "Uncanny ability to shift in and out of different characters." "He'll have you clutching at your sides in laughter." "I had to perform to get the adulation."[81]

4. "Could argue either side of an issue." "Brilliant, domineering, a heroic genius." "Rules his home as an absolute monarch." "He does not know how to give in." "He has a disdain for other's opinions." "He was a bundle of bad temper." "He could be mischievous, twinkling and adorable." "He was flambouyant, dramatic, a swashbuckler." "He found war romantic and exciting."[82]

5. "Inspiration is not his talent." "He's a sweetheart of a human being." "He's the ultimate team player." "There's not a bitter bone in his body." "He passes the peace pipe and heals wounds." "He has verbal dyslexia." "He's like a chameleon and takes his color from the environment." "He's not interested in getting even."[83]

6. "He's a world-class stickler for details." "He cares about the exact shade of marble and the wattage of the lighting." "He creates ingenious geometric schemes." "What he designs is refined, expensive, tasteful, but never flashy."[84]

7."He is spontaneous, genial, and where women are concerned, flirtatious." "He has an all-gums smile, an exuberant and affable manner." "He seems like an overgrown kid surveying a candy store." "His manic energy sends the signal that anything can happen." "He often appears disconnected."[85]

8. "He moved up in a cautious steady progression." "He has a gift for conciliation and repairs rifts." "He's pragmatic, willing to give and take." "Keeps his political opinions to himself." "He's not opposed to making significant compromises." "He leans back casually in his chair." "He's relaxed."[86]

9. "If you don't do what I say, it's over." "She's a cross between a tycoon and a tigress." "She reduced him to a spineless wimp." "She interrupted me and screamed at him." "She's an imperious queen standing guard." "Chintzy with the help, lavish with herself." "She's an elegantly coutured ruler." "She's Cinderella turned Medusa."[87]

10."Master of the media and magnetic story teller." "He has that essential magic spell." "He's always looking for the rainbow." "He looks through the lens of best intentions." "He drifts into oft-repeated anecdotes." "He's sometimes disengaged." "He has an erratic and selective memory."[88]

Answers to Personality Quiz

1. Donald Trump: (choleric) Each statement quoted here was uttered by "the Donald" himself and shows his Powerful Personality. Trump is a living example of the choleric strengths carried to extremes and then becoming weaknesses. He is also a warning to all cholerics not to make work your god and not to be so sure of yourself that you turn off those around you. It's good to love our work, but not to the exclusion of life itself. Trump's book *Trump: The Art of the Deal* became a best-seller and gave him about $1.5 million in royalties, but by the time his next book came out, his fortunes had turned and his cocky advice had a hollow ring. Will Donald Trump learn from his mistakes? It's unlikely, for the Powerful Personalities can't bear to see their weaknesses and can always rationalize that their failures were someone else's fault.

"The Donald" says: "When you start studying yourself too deeply, you start seeing things that you don't want to see."

But isn't it time to start looking?

2. *Jacqueline Kennedy Onassis:* (melancholy) Although Jackie has passed her sixtieth birthday, she still has the aura of a young princess, the heroine of Camelot. Her dignity and her ability to keep her composure during times of tragedy have caused the world to respect her. Her melancholy love of art and her tasteful redecoration of the White House gave us all a view of her depth and talent and made a decade of young women want to be like her. Jackie never made social errors, she never said the wrong thing, she brought out the desire for wealth and class in all of us. Jackie is the Perfect Personality.

3. *Robin Williams:* (sanguine) As a typical Popular Personality, Robin has craved applause and attention from the time he was a child. And with his comic genius, he has been able to command it. With a sanguine sense of humor and timing, he has gone from flunking out of college to a nomination for an Oscar for his hilarious performance in "Good Morning Vietnam." He dared to dream that his talent and hard work could get him to the top. He says, "My father gave me the belief that if you find something you love, something that gives you that sense of bliss, then you should go for it."[89]

Quite a contrast from the father in "Dead Poets Society" who refused to let his son try his talent on the stage but insisted he settle down and become a doctor. Williams admits that his success and the adulation of the crowds went to his head and he got involved in drugs along with his close friend John Belushi. Robin Williams didn't wear his dream well, but the death of Belushi brought him to a point where he saw the need to repair his dream before losing it completely. He has emerged from what he called his "early mid-life crisis." He also spent time in self-examination. "Therapy made me examine everything," Williams says, "my life, how I related to people, how far I could push the *please like me* desire before there was nothing left of me to like."[90]

Williams has learned to pull in from his extremes and use his Popular Personality to its fullest potential.

4. *Winston Churchill:* (choleric/sanguine) Here is a man that could be considered a 200 percent person. He appeared to be 100 percent the Powerful Personality who challenged his embattled nation to never, never, never give up, and yet there was that Popular Personality that could bring irrepressable laughter out of his worst enemies. As a student he was more interested in fun than in homework, and he refused to be disciplined. He found that the only way his sanguine nature got attention from his social-minded parents was to misbehave. When the headmaster got exasperated with young Winston's pranks, he would send for his parents who were then forced to come to see him. He had the

Popular's need for attention and he didn't care how he got it. Teachers saw little hope for mischievous Winston, but he knew better. He dared to dream that he could be a soldier, a hero, and a politician and the Powerful part of his personality said of his detractors, "I'll show them."

Winston used his strengths to carry him to the top, and he was usually able to hold his weaknesses under enough control that they didn't cripple his dream.

As a daring war correspondent he was renowned for his courage, crossing three hundred miles of enemy territory in order to escape a Boer prison camp. As a cabinet minister, his sanguine ability to communicate championed the development of the military tank.

As a historian, he disciplined himself to write fifty-six books and he won the first Nobel prize for Literature ever awarded for the quality of the *spoken* word as well as the written word.

As a Popular politician, he became the embodiment of the will of his country, leading them to their finest hour. His Powerful Personality took control of World War II, and he is credited with winning the battle of Britain.

As an artist, his paintings surprised the critics and won him a place of honor for his landscapes in the prestigious Royal Academy of Arts.

He dared to experiment in different arenas that interested him and found that he was more than competent in many. It has been said that the ability to do more than one thing well is the difference between competence and excellence. In the case of Winston Churchill, it was the difference between excellence and brilliance. Here was a Powerful and Popular Personality who dared to dream, prepared for his dream, and was able to wear the mantle of greatness, the cloak of a hero!

5. *George Bush*: (phlegmatic) George is the Peaceful Personality who wants to have a kinder and a gentler nation and who has reached out the hand of peace to hostile nations. From the time George was a boy, he was the one in the family to stay calm in time of turmoil, to give half of everything he had to others, and to mediate any family conflicts. Throughout his political career he's been sent in to calm down problem situations, to keep peace in China, to restore faith in the CIA, and to back up Popular President Reagan without drawing any attention to himself. A friend of mine who lived next door to him in the seventies told me he never said an unkind word, he was openly friendly, and he never tried to impress anyone with who he was.

For our peace-loving president to have chosen to go to war is against his personality, but his political upbringing in a home with a father who was a senator has inbred in him a sense of justice. Don't let the bullies take advantage of the little people. One trait of the phlegmatics is that once they take an action, they will persevere to a successful end. May his Peaceful Personality ultimately bring peace to a troubled world.

6. *I. M. Pei:* (melancholy) An impeccable architect, I. M. Pei is the perfect example of the Perfect Personality.

Now in his seventies, he is a creative genius, a master of his art, a designer beyond compare. His buildings have elegance, refined details, and obvious class. He is a master of geometry. When Hollywood agent Michael Ovitz wanted to build a headquarters for Creative Artists Agency, he hired Pei. "I wanted something very classic. His philosophy and taste were everything that I could hope for."

As an architect of such different buildings as the Morton H. Meyerson Symphony Center in Dallas, the Louvre pyramid in Paris, and a science building for Choate Rosemary Hall School in Wallingford, Connecticut, Pei is most excited about the stunning seventy-story skyscraper in Hong Kong for the Bank of America. Pei's father founded the Hong Kong branch in 1919, and at that time no one could have imagined that one day his son would design this highlight of the city skyline. When I was staying in Hong Kong, the view out my window included what *Newsweek* described as a "spectacular tower of triangular shapes that seems to twist as it soars up 1,100 feet—the world's tallest building outside the United States."[91] I. M. Pei is a classic perfectionist of enduring quality.

7. *Arsenio Hall:* (sanguine) As an overgrown kid surveying a candy store Arsenio is a visible example of the Popular Personality. He wants to have fun, receive applause, and keep everybody happy. He represents the sanguine who never grows up, like Peter Pan. He has the bright-eyed look of the sanguine wonderment of life and he is constantly in motion. I have a friend who's on his staff and she says Arsenio is the same in real life as he is on television. He is outgoing, optimistic, and friendly. He greets everyone personally each day and lifts up the spirits of the workers. One of his staff had formerly worked for Johnny Carson, where no one was allowed to even say hello to the star. When this man came on with Arsenio, he was stunned at his natural warmth and his constant personal encouragement.

Arsenio, who grew up in a Cleveland ghetto, didn't do well in school. As a typical sanguine, his mind was always on something else and his teachers wrote on his report card, "Arsenio needs attention. Is there anything you can do about it?"

Arsenio, like my brother Ron, pretended to be a show biz personality as a child. He set up chairs in his basement and played the part of Johnny Carson. He says, "Johnny is the architect of all my dreams."[92]

Arsenio Hall dared to dream he could get out of the ghetto and become the Johnny for a whole new generation. He prepared for his dream, and now he's wearing it.

"I take the view that the public has elected me as a new late-night talk-show host," he says enthusiastically.

"I've worked all my life preparing for it, putting together a platform—my kind of guests, my kind of music, what I think is funny. I've been warming up in the eighties, but I'm really for the nineties."[93]

8. *General Colin L. Powell:* (phlegmatic) What better personality could there have been in charge of a war than a man with a Peaceful Personality? Chairman of the Joint Chiefs of Staff, General Powell is a balanced pragmatist who has worked his way up through the military structure without causing any trouble or ruffling any ranking feathers. Born to Jamaican parents in Harlem, Powell had to really dare to dream. Like Arsenio Hall, Powell didn't have the background for success, but he had a quiet determination to get ahead. While attending City College of New York, he joined the ROTC with the hopes of becoming an officer. He received the Purple Heart and Bronze Star in Vietnam and has now become the first black, in addition to being the youngest man, to hold the nation's top military post. As a typical phlegmatic, General Powell has a gift of conciliation and is a master of compromise. We can be sure that whatever happens, Powell will not be impulsive or irrational. He will aim to establish peace.

9. *Leona Helmsley:* (choleric) "Only the little people pay taxes," stated Leona as she stood guard at one of her hotels in New York. The imperious queen, a Powerful Personality, dared to dream that she could marry the boss, but to do it she had to ruin his marriage of thirty-three years and take control of his life. Phlegmatic Harry fell for her tricks and she got him to leave his wife and marry her. The former cigarette girl, daughter of a Brooklyn milliner, became a billionaire overnight. She not only owned the Empire State Building but an $11 million mansion with a $1 million swimming pool, a $130,000 sound system modeled after one at Disney World, and a $13,000 barbecue pit. That plus a chain of hotels should have kept anyone happy, but Leona had an insatiable greed and a need to totally control Harry, reducing this helpless man to a "spineless wimp." Her unauthorized biography by Ransdell Pierson is appropriately titled *The Queen of Mean* and gives graphic accounts of her insults to the little people. Her ego has kept her picture on full-page ads boasting "the only palace in the world where the queen stands guard." She has her picture in every hotel room and sells decks of cards where she is

the Queen of Spades. Does it seem that Leona has carried her ability to control to an extreme?

10. *Ronald Reagan*: (sanguine) After four years of melancholy Jimmy Carter depressing us with the news we were in a national malaise, we Americans wanted a cheerful change. Popular President Reagan promised us Happy Days and Good Morning, America. He could turn every cloud into a silver lining and his sense of humor kept us smiling. His sanguine love of excitement provided us with Constitution parties, Fourth of July parties, and Tall Ship parties. From his childhood in the Depression, with an alcoholic father and religious mother, "Dutch" Reagan had to really dare to dream that he'd become anything. He started by announcing baseball games, and in his biography he writes:

"Before going to Hollywood, I spent four years at station WHO in Des Moines, and they were among the most pleasant of my life. At 22, I'd achieved my dream: I was a sports announcer. If I had stopped there, I believe I would have been happy the rest of my life.

"I 'covered' hundreds of baseball games played by the Chicago Cubs and the Chicago White Sox via remote control. Wherever they were playing, a telegrapher tapped out a report in Morse code after each pitch and each play. In Des Moines another telegraph operator decoded a burst of dots and dashes from the stadium, typed a few words on a slip of paper and handed it to me. I then described the play as if I'd been in the press box."[94]

Only a sanguine would dare to cover a game he wasn't even at!

When he got to Hollywod his personality and good looks made him the hero of B movies. Becoming the spokesman for General Electric gave him credibility in the business world, and when he ran for governor, we Californians decided that a charming actor was just what our state needed to play our ceremonial roles. With television becoming a major part in national elections, Reagan's engaging smile and sense of humor magnetized the American public and brought him to the presidency. He cast his magic spell and helped us see the rainbow. His persuasion also brought about unprecedented peace in many parts of the world, and his sanguine personality gave us all a few laughs when we needed it most. *Time* reviewed Reagan's book *An American Life* and called him "The Dreamer" and said "Reagan was and remains a stubborn dreamer."[95]

Ronald Reagan dared to dream that he could be president. He prepared for his dream, and he lived it with style and class. Even after a would-be assassin's bullet found its mark, Ronald Regan repaired his dream and now he's retired and willing to share his dream with others. "If I can be president, you can, too."

Know Your Strengths and Weaknesses

One of Ronald Reagan's favorite international personalities is Margaret Thatcher, and she is also one of mine. Let's practice the personalities by looking at her and her successor and thinking about our own strengths and weaknesses.

I've always had an admiration and emotional attachment to Margaret Thatcher, the "Iron Lady," former prime minister of England. We have many things in common. We're both pretty much English—my father was born in England and my mother in Canada—we're about the same age, we lived through the Depression, and have always had a love of politics. Most important is that we both grew up in our fathers' stores where we each learned how to wait on customers and make change. We also have the same choleric personality and are born leaders. Where I always wanted to be a queen, Margaret made it to prime minister and had the longest rule of any peace-time prime minister in the twentieth century.

From her emergence on the international scene, I have charted her personality and found her to be a pure, unadulterated choleric. Many people have one personality with a secondary in another, but Margaret has all her strengths in one basket.

She is a born leader—quick, active, in charge, motivational, inspirational, a Powerful Personality. Without this determination to rule, Margaret would never have made it to the top. A woman in politics or business has to be twice as smart as her competition; she has to exhibit strength and at the same time stay feminine. Margaret has managed to use her positives without letting her negatives get in the way. She has always said, "You act on what your mind tells you, not what your heart tells you." This is certainly a choleric comment.

But when carried to extremes, Margaret's strengths became weaknesses and someone who seemed to be an international institution was brought down. An article in *Time* magazine said, "Sometimes history conspires to undo a leader who had so completely embodied the spirit of the times that she seemed destined to go on forever." Forever had an end. As William Powell, Tory M.P. said about Margaret, "She's reached the point where everyone else is wrong and she's right. None of us want it, but there comes a point when simply we have to say, 'Enough.'"[96]

When her own party said "enough," the Powerful Margaret turned to her phlegmatic husband, who has stood silently and supportively behind her for years. He gave simple advice: "Margaret, it is time to go." It was time to go, and I was choked up when I heard the surprise announcement.

I have always been so proud of Margaret as she has stood with the heads of state at international convocations—one woman holding her head high among all those men, a spot of color amidst the drab monotony of navy blue. While others measured each sentence to make sure it sounded good and meant nothing, Margaret just opened her mouth and said what was on her mind. There was never the question, "What did she mean by that?"

It was Margaret's frank expressions and strong opinions that got her elected in the first place and her determination to bring about change in a phlegmatic country that brought it out of the economic dark ages into the light. She never hesitated to do what she thought was right, whether or not it was popular.

One of the great benefits in understanding the personalities is that we can predict in what area a leader will meet opposition and ultimately fall. For each type we can know that their strengths when carried to extremes become weaknesses. When Margaret defended the Falkland Islands, people applauded her fortitude, courage, and strength of convictions. When she pushed for a poll tax, her victory was labeled self-centered, arrogant, and tyrannical. She now had "no heart for the poor working class." When Margaret picked up her country and tried to make England competitive, she was praised. When she opposed the creation of a currency for all of Europe (ECU), actually reflecting the feelings of isolationism among the commoners in her country, the press said she was narrow-minded and with no vision for the future.

Margaret's willingness to state her opinion whether or not people liked it was her greatest strength, but carried to an extreme it became her weakness. The moment a chink in her armor was visible, pretenders to the throne jumped in and the outspoken leader was brought to her reluctant knees.

Former Defense Secretary Michael Heseltine, a flamboyant choleric with a sanguine twinkle, had been sitting in the wings waiting for the Powerful Margaret to exhibit some vulnerability. And when her ratings took a momentary dip, he moved in for the kill. He marshaled the troops of opposition.

Margaret's own party turned in mutiny. From one week to the next, the tide of opinion shifted and Margaret was forced to submit her resignation to the queen. *Newsweek* headlined, "Iron Lady Falls." Margaret didn't fall; she was pulled down and she made her exit with dignity. She didn't go down, however, without a fight. I was proud of her as she met her attackers in Parliament, showed no signs of weakness, and even stated for the cameras, "I'm actually enjoying this." Only a choleric could enjoy a bitter confrontation that had defeat as its ultimate conclusion.

Heseltine, the obvious successor, was smug in bringing Margaret down and was beaming with the flush of victory. Hardly had Heseltine begun the celebration before two other men decided to enter the fray. If we're going to have a fight, let's not give the prize away easily. Joining Heseltine was Foreign Secretary Douglas Hurd and Chancellor of the Exchequer John Major, Margaret's next-door neighbor and personal favorite.

When asked by an interviewer how she'd feel not being in the driver's seat, Margaret answered that if Major won she'd be a backseat driver. Commentators picked this up and the remark was used as a tool against John Major, who had only five days to promote his image and acceptability. There seemed little hope for him, but an amazing change of heart hit the public. One politician stated, "We are suffering from a massive guilt complex. The nation can't believe what we've done to Margaret." On that note came the vote!

John Major drove into a surprise victory with, I assume, Margaret in the back seat. Little was known then about John Major, but his face was immediately on the front page of all the newspapers. We learned quickly that he was the son of a trapeze artist, a person from the lower middle class, a modern Horatio Alger. His family at one point had lived in a two-room flat three floors above the bathroom. He left school at sixteen and never went to college. He was a clerk, he mixed concrete, and he collected fares on a bus before going to work in a bank. At forty-seven, he is the youngest prime minister of the century and the only one without a memory of World War II.

In most cases, whether the politics is in government, business, or the church, the strong choleric leader is replaced by the kinder, gentler phlegmatic. The Peaceful Personality patches up the problems left over from the Powerful. This principle is surely true with John Major. Margaret had recently been referred to as belligerent, abrasive, recalcitrant, and in strident opposition—all choleric descriptions. As Major appeared, the words applied to him have shown him as a phlegmatic. He is not "ideologically rigid." He is "a quiet, considerate man with a ready smile who has not forgotten being hard up." He is "a man of the people" who in eleven years went from obscurity to prime minister under the personal grooming of Margaret Thatcher. I knew he was a true phlegmatic when I read that he wears gray suits and has six identical gray ties.

The *New York Times* says he has a calm demeanor, "a soothing style," and "a reasonable voice." They went on to explain, "In style and manner, John Major and Margaret Thatcher couldn't be more different. A civil servant who has worked with him said that he is never hasty to form a view on a new subject. 'He didn't like being bombarded with five or six issues and decisions all at once,' this official said. 'He would take them one at a time, take the briefing papers home, and come back the next day with his mind made up.'"[97]

No snap decisions here. In his first official statement as prime minister, Major gave a phlegmatic wish, "I want to see us build a country that is at ease with itself." Knowing his need to be at ease and his desire to avoid controversy, we can assume that he will institute no sweeping changes and will aim to unite the party. One commentator called him a Thatcherette, and another said, "If Margaret Thatcher had a political son, he would be John Major."

If John Major were a choleric, he would probably purge the cabinet of any possible opposition in order to insure control, but Major, to keep peace, immediately appointed his two opponents into influential positions. Douglas Hurd, author of seven novels, remained as Foreign Minister and Michael Heseltine became Environment Minister. Heseltine once wrote down his goal for the nineties as "No. 10," meaning to become prime minister. *Time* magazine speaks of choleric Heseltine as a powerful orator and administrator who has been hiding in the wings waiting to pounce on Margaret and gain control. They also refer to his dramatic weaknesses: "A reputation for impetuosity has followed him since an episode in the Commons in 1976, when, irate over a demonstration staged by Labour M.P.s, he seized the ceremonial mace and brandished it over his head."[98]

Considering his quick anger and his desire for power, Heseltine bears close watching by phlegmatic Major. One of the most tenuous positions for a phlegmatic leader is having a roaming lion in supposed submission waiting to take more than a bite out of his superior.

The understanding of the personalities with their strengths and weaknesses gives us all a tool to see beyond the present and into the potentials of the future. We can predict probabilities when we know the personalities.

In my book *Personalities in Power*, I analyze the presidents from Franklin Roosevelt through George Bush and show how they all came in on their strengths and went out on their weaknesses. I show how Bush, a phlegmatic, came in after a sanguine President Reagan, the purveyor of Happy Days and Happier Times. Bush set out to bring unity to the country and peace to the world. Because of his amiable nature and constant calls and letters to world leaders, he was able to encourage communistic nations to release their hold and was also able to marshal support from diverse nations when Iraq's Saddam Hussein quickly conquered the peaceful nation of Kuwait.

What a fascinating point in history when we have two of the most powerful nations in the world led by phlegmatics. They have both come in on their strengths. Will they go out on their weaknesses?

Quick Reference Chart
for the
Personalities in Business

Popular Personality—Sanguine

Best at:
- Initial contact with people
- Creating enthusiasm and excitement
- Encouraging and uplifting others
- Making sure the group has fun

Is apt to be:
- Too easily distracted and forgetful
- Should make presentations that need humor and a light touch

Warning:
- May come on too happy or cute
- Not considered serious or believable
- Don't let them handle the money

Realize they need fun and adventure!

Powerful Personality—Choleric

Best at:
- Motivating people to action
- Controlling the plans and productivity
- Giving quick and clear instructions
- Making sure the group sees the immediate gain

Is apt to be:
- Too impulsive and intimidating
- Should make presentations that need authority and conviction

Warning:
- May come on too overpowering and seem to look down on others
- May threaten less confident people

Realize they need action and excitement!

Perfect Personality—Melancholy

Best at:
- Planning and explaining the details
- Keeping the books in order
- Being sensitive to the needs of others
- Making sure the group sees the long-range goal

Is apt to be:
- Too easily discouraged and critical
- Should make presentations that need accuracy and sincerity

Warning:
- May come across too intellectual and remote
- May make others think, "I'm not smart enough to do this"

Realize they need order and crave understanding!

Peaceful Personality—Phlegmatic

Best at:
- Making sure the group is relaxed and comfortable
- Always finding a middle ground
- Not threatening any of the participants
- Not overreacting to negative situations

Is apt to be:
- Too undisciplined and indecisive
- Should make presentations that need to be believable

Warning:
- May come across too low-key, dull, or lazy
- Appears too unethusiastic and unconvinced
- Don't count on them for motivation

Realize they need rest and some quiet time!

Working Together

Without an understanding of the personalities, few people can ever accept their mates as they are. Some never figure out why they married the only person in the world who doesn't appreciate them. Many know they made a mistake and assume that if they could get a new partner they could live happily ever after. All of these negatives are intensified even more when the two work together, whether it is a family business, the same corporate office, or in network marketing.

In order to use this simple tool in a family situation, it is important to get a feeling for the four personalities. You can improve your relationships instantly by applying these basic truths to your life. These points will help you understand each other even if you don't work together, but it is especially designed for you who are trying to run one business with two different personalities.

The *Popular Personality* is best in people skills and in making others relax and have fun. Their charm, sense of humor, and magnetism draw people to them, and this asset should be appreciated rather than demeaned as lightweight and shallow. They will hug, pat, love, and encourage new people in your business and will make them feel that they are worth something. These are traits you can't go out and buy, so respect them as positive. These Popular Personalities have no innate feeling for schedules, figures, book work, or timing, and it is unfair to expect this person to be able to balance the budget. Pushing them into mathmatical arenas will so unnerve them that their brilliant assets will fade.

I talked with a physician who had a small office where his sanguine wife was the receptionist. She loved the patients and they loved her. At the end of each day he required her to stay until she could balance the books, and she would often be in tears trying to find that last penny. He as a Perfect Personality could have done the job in fifteen minutes, but instead he would sit and read the newspaper while she struggled with each day's accounts. When I asked him why he made her do this, he said that he felt it was good discipline for her and that she needed to learn that all of life is not fun. The fact that they both left the office each night feeling miserable and that she was ready to quit both the job and the marriage didn't dawn on this intelligent man as a problem. When I told him that God had not appointed him to discipline and punish his wife but to love and accept her, he was amazed. He'd never thought that anyone should accept anything or any person that wasn't perfect without constantly trying to change them. When I told him to take her off the bookkeeping and to let her have fun, she threw her arms around my neck and began to cry tears of joy. She had been set free.

Those of you who are the Popular Personality should realize that you need to come in from your extremes. With your cheerful conversation you can be appealing, but realize that too much, even of a good thing, can become annoying. Try to discipline yourself to be ready on time, to make lists to aid your memory, to get your household pulled together. Whether you are a man or woman, use your natural humor, but don't try to outtalk and overshadow the others.

The *Perfect Personality* is the opposite of the Popular Personality, and they usually marry each other. They are attracted to each other's opposite strengths, but they go home to live with their opposite weaknesses. Initially the melancholy man is intrigued by the sanguine woman's charm and ability to tell stories and amuse crowds, but upon marriage he wipes out her charm with criticism, no longer thinks she's funny, and is constantly trying to shut her up.

What happens to this pair when they work together? The results can be dreadful. The perfectionist is always keeping watch, checking the time, and analyzing the productivity of what was once a happy person. Trying to keep this exuberant person under control is like wiping out or beating down all of the bubbles of creativity and producing a robot who is only functional with simple instructions. The melancholy has a way of putting guilt on the sanguine to such a degree that she becomes a chattering basket case. When the perfectionist finds something out of place, even if the two of them have been the only ones in the room for a week, he will have to say, "Who hid the scissors? Who left the door open?" This ridiculous question cripples the sanguine instantly and heaps guilt upon her causing her to cease any productivity for the next hour.

During the years that Perfect Fred did this to me, I learned to accept blame instantly. "I did it," I'd say with a smile and not let the inquisition do me in. When we got so we could talk about it and he realized what his questions did to me, he worked at changing. Now when we're in a hotel room alone and he asks, "Who left the cap off the toothpaste?" I can answer without fear of reprisal, "It was the maid. She was in there brushing her teeth with your toothbrush when I caught her."

Is there any hope for this couple to work together? Not without understanding. The sanguine learns to keep quiet and tries to stay out of trouble and the melancholy is constantly depressed. What was once an emotional relationship becomes stale, dull, and routine because neither one is any longer functioning in their strengths but instead plodding along in their weaknesses.

A new book on Canada's former prime minister Pierre Trudeau portrays him as a melancholy married to a sanguine Margaret Sinclair, twenty-nine years his junior.

I assume he was attracted by her childlike simplicity and bubbling sense of humor, but after marriage he saw her as shallow and unintelligent. The book *Trudeau and Our Times: The Magnificent Obsession* tells how he quickly gave up hope of any intellectual conversation with her and informed important guests to ignore her and speak in French. "Don't worry about her, she wouldn't know what we were saying if we were speaking in English."[99]

Pierre had grown up frail and so sensitive that he cried at anything, but his melancholy nature turned to criticism and cynicism as he was faced with an exuberant young wife who would happily dance on tabletops and humiliate him. She was never tuned in to his feelings and was, according to the authors, "the possessor of a sensibility best described as California North."[100]

According to the text, Trudeau is now searching to find his own personality and analyzing his past. It's a little late for this marriage, but perhaps he can repair his personal dream.

Once there is an understanding that each of us is born with a specific and special personality, that one is not better than the other, that we are to accept each other as we are and not try to change the other one, that our strengths are used to fill in each other's weaknesses, there can be a healthy change. The other person won't transform, but we can look at them differently and focus on their positive attributes. As Philippians 4:8 says, "If there be any virtue, think on these things."

Once these two personalities determine that they will accept each other and not try to straighten each other out, they can divide their responsibilities and function as much as possible in their strengths. No matter which sex is the melancholy, this person should keep the schedules, make travel arrangements, balance the budget, dole out the allowances, send in the orders—anything that has to be done properly. He should not drag out his martyr robe and put it on and wail, "Oh woe is me. I'm the only one who does anything around here."

The Popular Personality should appreciate what the other is doing, lift him up, and thank him ahead of time for doing all the work. This premature praise helps him leave the martyr robe in the closet, and with hope, he will someday give it away to the Salvation Army.

What happens when the sanguine is the man? This flies in the face of conventional wisdom that pictures the man as serious and balanced with a flighty, fluffy wife. When these stereotyped roles are reversed, the woman has to assume the responsibility for the financial records and together they map out the overall plan for their future. This man has always made it through life on his charm and his mother doted on him. He therefore doesn't like his wife to tell him he can't buy a new motorcycle this month. Sometimes just to thwart her, he'll go charge up some big toy for himself and hope she'll figure out how to pay for it. The sanguine male is so in need of attention that he will often pick up the check for the whole table while his melancholy wife sinks under it. When the use of money becomes a manipulative tool, this abuse leads to serious marital problems. But when a couple can see each other's weaknesses and help each other by filling in the gaps, this financial problem can be solved.

A lady came to me after a Personality Plus seminar and told me this story. She is melancholy and her husband is a sanguine. Right off you can anticipate the inherent problems. For years she had balanced the budget, paid the bills, and had put money in the bank. Then she and her husband went to a financial seminar where the male speaker told them that only the man of the house should handle the money. To let the woman get her hands on it was a violation of God's principles of economy. This speaker included no reference to the different personalities and spoke as if his advice was directly from God Himself. Since they had paid to go to this seminar and the man was obviously an expert, they went home and did what he said.

Here before me was a depressed and defeated woman who couldn't figure out why things had gone so wrong when she was doing "God's will." Now that he held the purse strings, the husband had become like a kid in a candy store. He had bought a cabin cruiser, even though they lived in the desert, and he had to drag the boat around looking for a lake. He had all new clothes and was stunned when the electric company turned off the lights and the cable TV was disconnected. She cried to me, "The mortgage is overdue, we have no money left in the bank, and he's running around playing games. Where have we gone wrong?"

I summed up what she'd told me and asked, "If someone came to you and said, 'When we followed Plan A the bills were paid and we had money in the bank and we loved each other, but now with Plan B we're in debt, about to lose the house, and we hate each other,' what would you tell them?"

The response is obvious. Whether man or woman, we should each be functioning in our natural strengths and working to overcome our weaknesses. We should not use our personality as an excuse for poor and irresponsible behavior, but use it as a guideline for household and business management.

The Powerful Personality always has to be in control. When this individual is a male, he has a much easier acceptance factor because we have been taught for years that men are supposed to be in charge. A male with a choleric's Powerful Personality usually reaches his potential, runs everything he touches, and is respected even when he is controlling things that aren't his responsibility. But what happens when the choleric is a woman and she has a passive, phlegmatic husband? Is this some aberration of heredity?

I've learned that in the average church, especially ones that think an understanding of the personalities is too worldly, all men are expected to be Powerful, natural leaders, in firm control of their families, spiritual giants who give godly answers to all of life's problems. And all women are expected to be Peaceful, dear, sweet, gentle-spirited wives who love the sound of the word "submissive" and who have no ambition beyond serving church suppers or washing the communion cups. All children should be Perfect, serious little melancholies who do their homework, love their parents, enjoy long blessings in restaurants, and are happy to be seen and not heard.

The church seems to have no natural spot for the Popular personalities who might attract attention away from the pastor and who probably aren't very deep or spiritual anyway. Such a shallow person might be brought in once a year to speak at the Mother/Daughter Banquet, where amusement is more important than depth.

When we look at these stereotypes, we can more clearly see the hopelessness facing a woman who happens to be born a choleric—or even worse, a choleric/sanguine combination. A woman who is bossy and fluffy at the same time? Surely something is wrong here. Because of the lack of understanding of the personalities, this woman is fighting a losing battle. She has to motivate her husband without appearing to be controlling, she has to do half his work without complaining, and she has to smile when people say, "You are so lucky to be married to such a dear sweet man!"

Even in our enlightened times, traits that are applauded in a man are deplored in a woman. When critics called Margaret Thatcher the Iron Lady—firm in resolve, determined to win—she retorted, "If I were a man you'd be praising these as strengths."

Choleric women in politics such as Margaret Thatcher, Diane Feinstein, and Ann Richards are almost the only ones that make it to the top because they can handle the rebuffs and they have enough confidence to push ahead when others say it can't be done.

In a family business, the Powerful woman has a frustrating role. This combination can only progress where each partner sees the personality differences and is willing to work with them.

Every family needs a Peaceful Personality to balance out the more volatile personalities, to mediate problems, and to say "let's all calm down" when events are rolling toward a crisis situation. When the Powerful Personality wants to make a hasty decision, the Peaceful says, "Let's think it over." When the Popular wants to take a day off and go party, the Peaceful asks, "Have you thought of the consequences?" When the Perfect gets depressed over a deluge of details that won't fall into line, the Peaceful shrugs and says, "It won't make that much difference in the long run."

The controlling choleric needs the moderate phlegmatic, but often they see the Peaceful Personality as lazy, unmotivated, and stubborn. These weaknesses are often accentuated by the fast-paced expectations of the Powerful, and the refusal to jump on demand is often a quiet way of expressing passive resistance.

The Powerful Personality is always the one to get excited by the possibilities, set the goals for productivity, and urge the phlegmatic on. To make the business a team effort, the phlegmatic has to be willing to assume the agreed upon responsibilities and do them. If it is the man who is phlegmatic, he must perform his part on time so that she doesn't have to nag him. Most henpecked husbands wouldn't be so if they had just gotten out of the chair in the first place.

When you pit the choleric, with a high anger level, against the phlegmatic, who tries to outsit the deadlines, you have a volatile situation. The choleric screams disapproval at home but the phlegmatic, hating conflict, waits until in the protection of a group to make snide remarks. The phlegmatic man drops statements like, "There's no point in me doing anything; she'd do it over anyway," and "Living with her is like sleeping with General Patton."

When they get outside, the Powerful wife is ready to beat her Peaceful husband to death for these comments and he dryly says, "Just a touch of humor, my pet."

This scenario would not take place if each of the partners understands the personalities and is willing to perform. The choleric will not be nagging if the phlegmatic is holding up his end of the bargain. The choleric loves work and is willing to do far more than half if the mate will just follow through on time. So often the choleric gives out instructions and the phlegmatic nods in agreement to save confrontation—and then never does the work. This is his silent method of control. "If I sit here long enough, you will have to do it."

Each personality controls in a different way. The *Popular Personality* (sanguine) controls by charm. "Come on over and help me paint the bathroom. We'll have such fun and you'll just love the color."

The *Powerful Personality* (choleric) controls by threat of anger. "If I have to tell you to do that one more time, you're in for trouble." Children of a Powerful Personality definitely know when they're in trouble, and they respond when Mother says, "Don't do anything to upset your father or he'll kill you."

The *Perfect Personality* (melancholy) controls by quiet threat of depression. "It's all right for you to go out and leave me home alone." Which translated means, "If you go out, I will go into a depression that will make you wish you'd never thought of going."

The *Peaceful Personality* (phlegmatic) controls by procrastination. "If I hold off long enough someone else will have to do it. Then I can say sweetly, 'I was just about to do that.'"

Once we can see what we are doing to each other, we can begin to change. Our aim is to be:

- A Popular Personality who is organized and on time.
- A Powerful Personality who is humble and accepting.
- A Perfect Personality who is cheerful and not critical.
- A Peaceful Personality who is motivated and not sarcastic.

We each need to pull in from our extremes and work with each other, not against each other. Two horses pulling in opposite directions can never get the cart to the barn, but when they pull together, they can reach the goal more quickly.

When I first met Roxanne, she came running up to me and said, "Without you we would never have dared to get married." I then heard how Roxanne and Bryan have become quickly successful in network marketing because they understand their personalities and are working with each other and not against each other. She is an extreme of both the Popular and Powerful personalities. She is a charming, magnetic story-teller with the drive and ability to become an executive in an oil company. She quickly rights all wrongs and is a walking seminar.

When Roxanne first dated Peaceful Bryan, he remembers she told him how to cut up his chicken and in what order to eat his vegetables. Their personalities had almost nothing in common and they didn't know why they had even liked each other in the first place. Roxanne was given my *Personality Plus* and she quickly saw why they had such differences of opinion. "We were such a classic case of opposites," Roxanne told me, "that I thought we ought to get married and see if your theories worked." She laughed heartily as she said this and then continued to explain how they had gone into the networking business as a sideline, but everywhere they went they found people who needed help and who were attracted to her confidence and sense of humor. When they set up business meetings, she made everybody feel welcome and excited.

Bryan, who told me he had never thought he could stand up in front of people, presented the plan in a low-key unpressured way that intimidated no one. "His greatest asset," Roxanne added "is his believability factor. He doesn't overstate things as I do and when he says this works, people believe him." As they have used their opposite strengths and worked to overcome their weaknesses, Roxanne and Bryan have become so successful in network marketing that they have both left their former jobs and are living in a style way beyond their past expectations.

Roxanne and Bryan dared to take a risk, they prepared by making a study of their personalities and acting upon the knowledge, and now they are wearing the dream of a lifetime.

Don't Take No for an Answer

Those of us with shy personalities or with victimization backgrounds that make us feel worthless are often relieved when we get no for an answer. It allows us to quit with no responsibility. In sales, accepting a quick no can cripple a career and in business curtail creativity. If we all put the brakes on our ideas with the first negative response, no one would move past the stop sign. Stop signs don't mean "sit here forever" but "pause long enough to assess the situation and move on." No matter what our goal, we need to consider what others say for there is wisdom in the advice of many counselors. But we should pause, weigh the evidence, and then move on.

In the 1990 baseball draft, Todd Van Poppel was considered the number one choice. The draft is arranged to give the poorer teams the first crack at the best talent, but Todd announced that he was unavailable. He and his parents had decided he would go to college before becoming a professional baseball player. The teams that needed him the most took no for an answer; however, Sandy Alderson, general manager of the World Champion Oakland A's, decided to woo the six-foot-five-inch right-hander. Todd's ninety-seven-miles-per-hour throw intrigued Sandy, who already had a stable of winners. He visited Todd, encouraged him, and showed a personal interest in him that no one else had done. Much to the surprise of the teams who might have won young Todd, Alderson came away with the prize. Contrary to the purpose of the draft, number one ended up with number one.

Winners never take no for an answer.

Keep Going

What does it take to wear the dream well, to keep on going and improving as time rushes on? Often when we have somewhat attained the dream, we become satisfied with status quo. We lose the initiative and the hunger to stretch ourselves and to continue the process of growth. Not so in the case of Sir Laurence Olivier, often called the "greatest actor of the century."

When I majored in drama and speech all through college, Laurence Olivier was held up to us as the greatest actor in all the world and if we could only attain to some small measure what he had done, we would be a success.

Olivier himself said to the House of Lords at one time, "I believe in the theatre as the first glamorizer of thought." All of us who knew of him and saw him perform fell in love with the theater and with him. We were under the spell he wove as he plucked written words off the page and hurled them mysteriously toward his audience and engraved them on the slate of our minds forever.

With all of the accomplishments that Olivier obtained over his entire career, many would say that he was always at the height of his career. But if you look at the facts, we can readily see that this is simply not true. In 1929 he was involved in and out of half a dozen different plays when finally Noel Coward cast him in "Private Lives" as the other man. He was fired four years later as Greta Garbo's lover in "Queen Christina." Noel Coward again rescued Olivier by casting him as a dashing man sculpted after John Barrymore, whom Olivier adored. But once again there was disaster as he traveled throughout the U.S. with his wife, Vivien Leigh, in "Romeo and Juliet," which was so poorly received that producers had to refund ticket money to angry audiences. Vivien Leigh sadly lapsed into mental illness in the mid-1950s.

Olivier's dream of being a great actor always rallied him to keep on going, to challenge himself with greater and better roles. He had a burning passion for his work, and it was clear that this was where his heart was at home. And in 1948, Olivier won Oscars for both best picture and best actor in "Hamlet." Laurence Olivier at his best is what everyone has always meant by the phrase "a great actor," said critic Kenneth Tynan in 1966. And upon his death in 1989 at the age of eighty-two, Olivier held the undisputed claim to yet another title: the twentieth century's definitive man of the theater.

Olivier poured over his scripts critically, analytically, and on-stage his performance was always physically energetic, scaling balconies and executing dizzying falls. Olivier went to great lengths to fit his person to the role. To deepen his natural tenor voice for Othello's baritone, Olivier studied with a vocal coach and soon his voice was a full octave lower. In some of the early Shakespearean roles, he would pad his legs so as to look good in tights and he was known to take liberties with the spirit-gum makeup to pull off a role.

A less dedicated and less driven actor would have been tempted to give up during the years in and out of plays and being fired as Garbo's lover in

"Queen Christina." He certainly could have thrown in the towel. He could have rested on his past successes and simply allowed his fans to remember how great he once was. But something within Olivier drove him to be challenged to lunge ahead to prove the critics and directors wrong. And late in his life Olivier again could have retired on his laurels: receiving knighthood in 1946, the "life peerage" in 1970, and the thanks of nations and generations. But in 1974 Olivier was diagnosed with *dermatopolymositis*, a crippling degeneration of skin and muscular tissue. Still Olivier continued to work in a British mini-series and appeared in the movies "The Betsy," "The Boys from Brazil," "Marathon Man," and finally a television production of "King Lear" at the age of seventy-five, which he left for ages to come to see the century's greatest actor—and left us wanting more.

Melancholy Olivier strove for quality, not status quo. He didn't compromise his own standards and he wasn't afraid of failing. He just got back on the horse and rode it again. He paid great attention to detail, to the idea and concept of his characters, and he brought great power—physically and verbally—to his roles as he transformed the written word into living art.

What does it take to wear the dream well? The dream must fit, first of all. It must be of a durable fabric that can stand wear and tear, feast and famine. It must be flexible enough to be stretched and pulled at times, big enough to allow for growth. It must bring out the best in you, and it must offer hope to others. Olivier indeed wore the dream well and he wore it with class!

Try to Fly

Even as a child, she dreamed of flying. Every chance she got she would sit and study the birds as they flapped their wings rhythmically and soared through the air. Her mother warned her many times of the hazards and dangers of climbing fences and perching there as one of the birds she watched. But the child was convinced she could fly—someday by watching and dreaming enough she *would* fly. Heights intrigued her and so it was that she fancied if she could just get to the rooftop of her own home, there she would be able to fly.

One day she did get to that rooftop, and there she stood until all at once, dreams gave way to reality. Madly flailing and flapping her arms as she had seen the birds do, it seemed for a while she would be successful, but all too soon this child's body met the ground below. It was amazing that she had not done more damage, the doctor said, but in the end the child suffered only a broken "wing." And for several decades she put away the fantasy of flight from her mind.

However, at the age of forty her dream was revived as she was harnessed into a flying suit and took wing across the stage as Peter Pan. All of us fell in love with Mary Martin, the girl who wanted to fly, who encouraged us to "only believe and you can too!" Mary often said it was her favorite role because it was so close to her heart. It was a dream come true, a dream that spanned several decades.

Have you had a dream since childhood? Is there an opportunity for you now to see this dream realized? What would it take for you to "only believe" that you can? A little fairy dust? Thinking happy and positive thoughts? Climbing to the top and taking flight doesn't happen overnight. Seeing your dream come true successfully may span a few decades, and occasionally you may even break a "wing." But if it's a worthwhile dream, it will be worth the wait. And I can almost hear Mary Martin say "only believe."

Be Willing to Be Versatile

Tom Jones arrived at a press conference in Sydney "elegant and understated as befits a man of fifty." There was a touch of nostalgia as the journalist wrote, "The mane of dark curls is greyer and closer cropped and the chest that has set a million female hearts pounding was buttoned up in a trendy black shirt. . . . But the Tom Jones magic still casts its spell."[101]

When Tom Jones was asked the secret of his staying power he replied, "I think it's versatility. I like a wide variety of music and I can sing a ballad as well as I can an up-tempo song, which is rare for entertainers." The Voice headed off on a tour of Australia's major cities with the confidence that when you can add enough variety to a basic talent, you can grow old and not lose your touch.

Have a Passion for Your Product

In the competitive world of cosmetics, fragrances come and go, but few last forever. However, Estée Lauder, the company and the creator, seem eternal. For forty years Estée has been "seeing" fragrances. Almost any scene of beauty—a beach, a palm leaf, or a crystal chandelier—gives her inspiration for a new aroma. It was the reflection of two crystal chandeliers on a glass of champagne that stimulated her imagination into inventing the wildly successful Youth Dew in 1953.

Estée dared to dream that she could take a few pots, test tubes, and droppers along with some family fragrance recipes and with hard work and talent turn them into a business that today captures 40 percent of the upscale cosmetics market. How has Estée Lauder continued to wear the dream over these many years? Is her success due to clever advertising and a collection of chemists?

She has both, but her ability to maintain is due to her passion for her profession. She loves fine fragrances and she is excited each day to be part of what she considers an artistic community.

One of the consistencies in people who sustain success is that they have a genuine passion for what they're doing and believe in their product. So often I have people approach me who want to be a speaker. They see the up-front platform presentation and have only a slight idea of the years of preparation and dedication it has taken to put me there. When they ask how they can get into the business of speaking, I present them with two key questions: *What do you have to say? Does anyone need to hear it?* Without a passion for a subject which is so much a part of you that you must share it, whether or not you ever get paid, you can't be successful in any field that demands response from people. Not only must there be personal passion, but there must be a need for what you have to offer. Is there a possibility that people will want to buy it, wear it, smell it, read it, listen to it, or eat it? Even a brilliant idea that nobody wants will probably fail. Conversely, if you have a product that people want and a passion to promote it, you can be a winner.

Estée is a winner, presiding over a private company worth an estimated two billion dollars. She has a passion for her product and people have responded. According to a magazine article, Estée "is a zealous believer in the worth of her own products, and she simply cannot stop spreading the word."

Another reason for her success is that she is willing to work beyond the norm, even when she doesn't have to. In a society where the majority want to work as little as possible for as much as possible so they can get home to their lounge chairs in time to watch their favorite sitcoms, an individual who is willing to sacrifice the personal present for a future possibility is rare. So often when I explain to a would-be author what it takes to write a book, they sigh, "It sounds too much like work." And it is work. Most overnight successes have worked for years without praise waiting for that magic moment when all the preparation pays off.

Estée is still working. No matter where she is, she has a tray of equipment so she can experiment on new aromas. "I"m always working on a fragrance," she says. She tries new ideas out on her friends and watches their reactions. If they get excited, she knows she's headed in the right direction. She personally approves her packaging and she is willing to go into the stores and apply her make-up on the customers herself on occasion. She looks at everyone's face as a project and in her choleric way gives instant advice, whether or not it is asked. Estée, the woman who first thought up "gift with a purchase," is a practical person who wants women to look and smell good without spending a fortune or taking hours to do it. For those who are depressed, her answer is to put on fresh blush and lipstick. For those who want to keep their husbands, she suggests spraying from head to toe before he leaves in the morning so he'll remember your aroma all day!

On the way up the ladder, Estée always aimed to associate with people of creative worth and social value, knowing that your friends can draw you up or pull you down. So many insecure people tend to spend time with those they deem of little worth in order to make themselves feel important, but this is a path to failure. People who want to achieve must surround themselves with others who have made progress. They must listen to tapes of achievers, and read material that will be inspirational. Estée has through the years become friends with the Duchess of Windsor, Princess Grace, and Britain's Charles and Diana. She travels in the company of William and Pat Buckley and dares to tell CZ Guest she needs more blush. Even though you and I will probably never dine at the White House, we can lift our sights from where they've been and observe the patterns of behavior in those who have achieved in our area of interest.

Although Estée has achieved enough success to be included in the *Wall Street Journal* Gallery of the Greatest, she never takes it all for granted. She continues to learn, she works at dressing properly for each occasion, and she is the epitome of what she calls the "elegant achiever."

"Living the American dream has been intense, difficult work," she says. It's hard work, but somebody's got to do it!

> "Dreams come true for those with nerve."
> —Edwin M. Reingold

For twenty-one years, Dick Heinemann has been selling *Time* magazine—not door-to-door to put himself through college, but as sales director on up to vice-president for advertising of Time, Inc. His drive in supervising and motivating others in the sale of magazine advertising for twenty-seven publications is the reason their ad revenues are up when others are down. Why is Dick a success when so few make it to the top in the fiercely competitive advertising business?

First, he has the best natural personality combination for a salesman. He is sanguine—complete with contagious enthusiasm, delightful sense of humor, captivating smile, and obvious love of life—combined with choleric—can hardly wait to get to work, relaxes with "fierce games of golf and tennis," and has "finely honed competitive instincts."

Second, he has a passion for his product. He believes in *Time* and he can sell its services with no apologies or guilt. He says, "I have had the luxury for twenty-one years of always being able to sell something I love and believe in. That is the best of all jobs for a salesman."

What an ideal situation, to love one's occupation so much that work and pleasure blend together as one. Dick's passion for his product may be summed up by his advertising-sales manager, "Making a sales call with Dick is a little like a religious experience. By the time he finishes his delivery, the congregation is on its feet."[102]

Keep Working

"Not a day without a line" was the family motto taken seriously by Paul Klee (1879–1940), world renowned Swiss artist. Klee believed in this choleric never-let-them-rest way of life and the Bern Museum of Fine Arts produced a showing in 1990, fifty years after his death, attesting to Klee's diligent work ethic right to the end.

Entitled "Paul Klee: Creation in the Year of Death," the exhibition displayed only those works of art produced in his last year—numbering around four hundred.

Although some of his works have a similarity to the paintings my daughter Marita did in kindergarten on shirt cardboards and successfully sold to the elderly neighbors, Klee achieved awe and admiration for his squiggles and one-eyed generic people that carried him into the artist's hall of fame. Klee was considered a humanist, master colorist, a minimalist abstractionist, and a surrealist, but one thing he could never be called was lazy. In January of 1940 he produced one hundred fifty-eight separate works and stated, "Never have I drawn so much and with such intensity."

Inspite of ill health, Klee continued painting to the end and his four hundred paintings in that last year proved how prolific one can be when following the credo, "Not a day without a line."

> "Having your dreams fulfilled can
> be far more therapeutic
> than having them analyzed."
> —ad for Hyatt Resorts

In 1936, as an eight-year-old child I remember listening on the radio to the boxing match where Max Schmeling surprised the world by knocking out the unbeatable Joe Louis. Now eighty-five years old, Schmeling, still Germany's most popular sportsman, goes to work each day at his Coca-Cola bottling plant in Hamburg-Bramfeld, continues to play golf, and rides an exercise bike. When asked the secret of his success he replied, "I live in the present and look to the future. If you do nothing, you die earlier."

Stay with What Works

In an era when televangelists have been routinely falling from their pedestals for financial mismanagement, improbable messages from God, or sexual peccadillos, one name stands above the rest—harmless and blameless, the son of God without rebuke—Billy Graham. How has he escaped the inquisitive press and atheistic accusations? How has he sustained fifty years of ministry unblemished and managed to be chosen as one of the "Ten Most Admired Men in the World" thirty-two times? Inquiring minds want to know.

I'm sure that when Billy was growing up on a dairy farm in Charlotte, North Carolina, during the Great Depression he didn't dare to dream that he would one day be considered as the most highly respected religious leader of the twentieth century. At the age of sixteen when he committed his life to Christ at a revival meeting, he had no expectations of even becoming a pastor, yet as his faith grew he decided to prepare his dream by attending Florida Bible Institute, and he later graduated from Wheaton College in 1943. As a young eager graduate, Billy chose to associate with Youth for Christ, where he was encouraged to speak to servicemen during World War II and later to the struggling Europeans as they were recovering from the devastation of the war. Billy never tried to do anything spectacular, he just preached the gospel. He didn't pretend to present secrets of success for people waiting for motivational marvels, he just repeated over and over that the only way to personal change with permanent value was through the power of the Lord Jesus.

Billy set a simple goal. "My one purpose in life is to help people find a personal relationship with God, which, I believe, comes through knowing Christ."

Throughout the years Billy has stayed true to his purpose to preach God's plan of salvation to all who would listen. He doesn't make a grand entrance to a drum roll and cymbals, he doesn't appear in gaudy clothes draped with gold chains, he just emerges quietly in a conservative suit and begins to preach. He doesn't do anything dramatic, play the piano, cry, weep, wail, rant, or rave, he just stays true to his purpose, firm in his belief that if he presents the Word, God will bring the increase.

In 1949, Billy and his team put on their first crusade in Los Angeles. They optimistically planned to stay for three weeks, but overflowing crowds poured in each night for two months. Suddenly the name Billy Graham took on international recognition and his career of Christian crusades was launched. Could he have ever dared to dream that he would become the confidant of presidents, that he would be regarded highly by heads of states in eighty-four foreign countries, that he would be used to preach the gospel to more than one hundred million people— more than anyone else has ever done?

How has Billy been able to wear the mantle of his dream so successfully? By an unusual coincidence I was able to ask that question of George Beverly Shea, longtime friend and associate of Billy Graham and also his crusade soloist who can bring an ardent athiest to his feet with his booming rendition of "How Great Thou Art." In November of 1990, Fred, Marita, and I arrived in Hong Kong on an around-the-world speaking tour and read in the local newspaper that it was Billy Graham's seventy-second birthday and he was celebrating it in Hong Kong in preparation for his Hong Kong Crusade at the stadium. The next morning at breakfast, Marita spotted Larry Ross, director of public relations for the Billy Graham Evangelistic Association. We had all met in the past and as we happily renewed acquaintances, Larry informed us that Billy Graham was staying at our hotel and would be holding a press conference the following day. He invited us to attend and lend prayer support with the team. It was preceding the conference that I had the opportunity to ask George Beverly Shea, "How has Billy remained unscathed over all these years?"

His response was two-fold. "He's never strayed from his purpose and he never allows himself to be alone or unprotected." George Beverly Shea then told me that early in his ministry, Billy had finished a message and walked off the stage when a woman waiting in the wings threw her arms around him in an adoring embrace. Later that day he called his team together and admonished them to never let that happen again, to be sure one of them was always at his side. George Beverly Shea said that Billy explained how easily a ministry could be ruined by even a taint of gossip no matter how innocent the situation might be. From that time on, the team has protected him and he has stayed openly accountable to them. The reward has been a faithful relationship that has kept men like George Beverly Shea, Cliff Barrows, and T. W. Wilson by Graham's side for over forty years. In a day when long term business associations are a rarity, the Billy Graham team is an exciting exception.

That day at the press conference I had the opportunity to observe the man, the men, and the ministry firsthand. Without trying, Billy Graham has a star quality about him that his natural ease and confidence increase. As he approached the platform, tall, tanned, and handsome, it was difficult to believe that he was seventy-two, and when he spoke his voice still had the power and resonance of a young man.

The scene was amusing to me as I looked at Billy Graham standing erect with two Chinese clergymen on each side appearing to be half his height. Billy, the feature attraction, was wearing a conservative dark suit, white shirt, and red tie while his supporters were decked out in full ecclesiastical regalia, white starched suits with black shirts and clerical collars. As Billy Graham stood flanked by these men in costume, I felt they looked like a set of Chinese bookends I'd once had. The oriental chairman never changed his expression or his position throughout the entire proceedings. One of the clergy explained the rules to the press, who didn't seem to be listening and then Billy gave his opening statement. He was warm, engaging and displayed a sense of humor as he explained that his wife had grown up in China, the daughter of a missionary surgeon, and had not come to the United States until she was seventeen. He reaffirmed his purpose of proclaiming the gospel of Christ and shared that he was not here to enter into political discussions of the world crises, "I've come to talk to the hearts of your people. World conflict starts in the hearts of people."

When asked about his opinion of the Persian Gulf situation he replied, "Jesus and Paul both lived in occupied territories and yet never tried to solve political problems. They just preached the Good News to the people who would listen."

"Will you address Hong Kong's problems at your crusades?"

"I will address them from the Bible's perspectives and the Holy Spirit will apply the gospel to the listeners. I don't have the ability or reasoning to solve the problems of Hong Kong."

At that point a disheveled reporter from Sweden walked to the microphone and asked in arrogant tones, "Since you commented about how glad you were to see the Berlin Wall come down, what are you going to say about the wall that will be erected here in 1997?'

Billy Graham answered simply, "I won't comment on that."

"How brave of you," he sneered into the mike. At a point when a put-down would have been expected, Billy said, "How brave of you to walk up here and ask that question."

Several times he restated his purpose to preach the gospel and stay out of political issues, and I suddenly realized that many people put on the firing line don't have a single purpose and are therefore easily led into commenting on issues that get them into trouble.

A representative of the Baptist Press asked, "Have you ever considered changing or updating your methods, and if not, why not?"

"No," Billy answered, "I've not considered changing because my message is the same and the method works." He used as examples the crowds that came out in England, and how in Hungary they had the largest crowds in the history of the country and that thirty thousand people came forward to make commitments to Christ.

Billy Graham knows better than to fix something that's not broken.

One reporter asked him if these commitments made at the Crusades really last or if they are just decisions made at an emotional moment and soon forgotten. Even though the question was given in a sarcastic tone, Billy Graham replied in a kindly manner and explained that in 1959 he had conducted crusades in Australia. Twenty years later, there had been a follow-up study of all the recorded decisions and they found that not only had these been real commitments, but that many of the Christian leaders in Australia today are products of the 1959 crusade.

Billy showed his sense of humor when a young lady wishing to impress the group asked two involved questions. When she started into the second one Billy stopped her and said, "Don't go into your second question. I've already forgotten your first one."

Someone asked why people don't "pick on you more" and Billy replied, "I guess they feel sorry for an old man." Another reporter followed that up with, "When are you going to retire?" Billy's answer brought a slight laugh from the serious, humorless group when he said, "I have no plans to retire. I've searched the Bible and I can't find anyone who retired."

On that day in November, I learned several principles on wearing the dream.

1. Know your purpose and stick to it.
2. Don't fix what isn't broken.
3. Never allow yourself to get in compromising circumstances.
4. Associate with godly people who will keep you accountable.
5. Be knowledgeable about worldly politics, but don't be drawn into taking sides.
6. Don't be impressed with yourself or take yourself too seriously.
7. Keep a sense of humor in serious situations.

The Hong Kong Crusade turned out to be the single largest outreach effort in the forty-year history of Billy Graham's team.

"While overflow audiences jammed two stadiums in Hong Kong, Graham's appearances also were beamed via satellite and video to more than thirty countries in Asia and the Pacific region, reaching about one hundred million people each night of the crusade. The messages were translated into more than forty-five different languages."[103]

In spite of a typhoon and rain for three nights the people sat and stood attentively and thousands had to be turned away. There was no new message, no gimmicks, not even a roof over their heads, just Billy Graham standing in front of a six-thousand-voice choir, preaching the gospel, and giving hope to a troubled world.

We have seen how Ron Chapman has been able to wear the dream successfully and remain the number one DJ in the Dallas-Fort Worth area for twenty years. We along with roving reporters, scandal mongers, and television cameras have noted that he uses his personality strengths to the maximum, that he determined to succeed since childhood and never wavered from his single-minded purpose, that he kept working with a passion even when he had achieved his goal, that he has been willing to pour his life into others and teach all he knows, that he has built a trust with his people because he has always kept his promises, that he has stayed out of trouble when other showbiz personalities have been involved in financial and personal failures, and that he has kept a sense of humor and optimistic view of life through it all.

We have seen how Sandy Alderson wouldn't take no for an answer, how Laurence Olivier, Mary Martin, and Tom Jones persisted to perfect their craft, and how Estée Lauder, Dick Heinemann, Paul Klee, and Max Schmeling still have a passion for their work after above-average achievement.

We've had a personal behind-the-scenes view of Billy Graham and heard the supportive thoughts of his long-time staff. We've seen why, when some of his peers have fallen from their pedastals, Billy Graham has remained above reproach. He has stayed true to his purpose and not diluted his efforts with new diversions. He has not made himself into a mini-god surrounded by fawning groupies, but has remained humble, doing nothing to cause devotion to him but only to the Lord he serves. Although he is a serious student of God's Word, he has maintained an engaging sense of humor about anything that doesn't have eternal value.

Each one of us wants to wear the dream successfully. No one wants to be a failure. But not all of us have succeeded as these people have. Where do some of us go wrong?

Four Steps to Failure

One day as I was studying the book of 1 Samuel, I saw a lesson I had never observed before. The people of Israel were demanding that Samuel the prophet give them a king. Samuel explained that they didn't need a leader when they had God as their Father and he reviewed how God had sent Moses to free them from slavery, to part the Red Sea, and to lead them through the wilderness. He reminded them that God had led them for forty years as a pillar of fire by night and a cloud by day. He had been their King!

After Samuel finished his speech to the rebellious children of Israel they replied, as some of our children might, "We know all that, but we want a king anyway." Samuel cried out "Why? Why?" and they answered, "We want a king

1. so that we can be like other people,
2. so that we can have a leader we can see and touch,
3. so that we can have someone to fight our battles."

As I saw these reasons, I realized they are the same ones you and I use today, the same ones our children will use tomorrow. We want a human leader like everyone else, only better—whether it's a parent, a mate, a mentor, a pastor, or counselor, we want someone to help us. Everybody else has got somebody. Why not me?

We're not content with God's provisions. We don't want to pray to someone afar off; we want someone we can see and touch and feel. We want to look eye to eye and talk to someone and tell them our hurts and pains.

We want someone who will fight our battles for us. We're all a little weary. We don't want to do what it will take to keep our lives together. We'd like to find someone who will do it for us. We want a parent who will kiss the cut and make it well. We want a doctor who will give us a quick shot to good health. We want a counselor who will shape up the other person so we can be happy.

That's what the Israelites wanted and God said "No, no, you've got Me." But the people just sighed and said, "You're a nice fellow and You did part the sea and feed us manna in the wilderness, but don't You see? We want a real live king!"

God finally gave in, as you and I might have done with our pleading children. "All right, you want a king? I'll give you a king." Under His breath He may have said, "And you'll rue the day you ever asked."

The following story shows how God chooses leaders and how, because of their human weaknesses, they often fail.

When Saul was a young man, he had no human reason to believe that he, a commoner, a member of the smallest Hebrew tribe of Benjamin and the smallest clan in that tribe, could ever be a king. He hadn't dared to dream any such thought and he had done nothing to prepare for such an opportunity. Yet when the Israelites demanded a king to rule over them, God reached down and picked out Saul. He had few qualifications except that he stood a head taller than everyone else and he looked like a king. He was so shocked at being chosen that he hid among the baggage in hopes they would pass him by and choose someone else. But Samuel, under God's authority, sought him out and presented him to the people.

Saul's friends were dumbfounded. If Saul's choice as king was a surprise to him, it was a laughable mistake to his friends. Could this be Saul? Son of Kish? One of the boys? Speaking with the prophets? Has Saul got religion? Could this be true?

Some others were so distressed that someone with no training was chosen to be king that they refused to give him any gifts in honor of his coronation. Saul appeared to be an illogical choice and he started out with no great vote of confidence from those who knew him best. However, the opinions of the people didn't really matter because Saul had been clearly called out by God.

Any time God calls a person into any form of leadership and the person doesn't have the natural talent or educational training, God gives him the necessary personal gifts to do the job. Saul was changed by the Spirit, and even his best friends couldn't believe the transformation. Saul was then presented to the people as their new king, their first king, and they received him with shouts of acclamation.

Before sending Saul off to his kingly duties, Samuel reviewed with him the rules of his new royalty.

1. *Obey God's clear commands*—don't second-guess God and go off on your own.
2. *Don't get greedy*—God will provide for your needs so don't take what's not yours.
3. *Don't take yourself too seriously*—remember you were nobody when God found you.
4. *Be responsible and mature*—don't blame other people for your mistakes.

Saul heard the king rules and pledged before the people to obey them.

Saul was *called* out by God, *changed* by the Spirit, *chosen* by the people, and *committed* to obedience.

Saul had not even dared to dream he might be king. He hadn't gone to seminary or King's College. He hadn't even prepared for the dream, but suddenly the mantle had been dropped upon his shoulders. He was wearing the dream.

Wouldn't you think that any one of us visited with such unbelievable good fortune would be able to wear the dream well? Wouldn't we be eternally grateful for our personal promotion, especially when we didn't even deserve it?

In the last few years we've had examples of these same failures in our public life.

We've seen politicians who have been exposed as disobedient to the simple rules of life: ones who have been involved in adultery, seducing a minor, pornography and perversion, excessive favors, and many types of financial mismanagement.

We've seen highly respected Wall Street brokers and junk bond dealers get greedy and reach beyond the law. We've seen young men accused of murdering their parents for a fortune.

We've seen religious leaders who have built themselves monuments, who have named schools, hospitals, and television programs after themselves and then fallen from their pedestals.

We've seen them all rationalize their situations, excuse their behavior, and blame it all on other people.

Human nature is the same now as it was in the time of Saul. If you wish to wear the dream, then stay clean, work hard, and be a role model for those behind you. Heed this call; don't fall like Saul.

Let's ask ourselves a few questions. Were we ever called out by God? To be called out usually means that we were somewhere doing something which hadn't made us a logical choice. When God called Fred and me out to become Christian leaders, we were out in a spiritual wilderness. Because of our two sons born with fatal brain damage, we had given up on God. How could there be a God who would allow bad things to happen to good people like us? We had given up on church leaders. One pastor had visited us once and admitted he didn't know what to say to people in our situation. He never reappeared. A healer in a cult Fred had belonged to said the reason our sons were dying was because of my lack of faith. If I would only believe their church doctrine, the boys would be healed. I couldn't believe what they said and the babies died adding guilt to my lack of faith.

We'd given up on people because in our grief our friends didn't show up. They didn't know what to do or say. There were no books, tapes, or seminars back in the early sixties to help people deal with problems and heartaches. There was no one there to give us encouraging words or help us handle our grief and pain. "Just put it behind you, pretend it never happened, and get on with life." We each tried to follow these admonitions and we did it in different ways. Fred, who had a restaurant business, opened a nightclub to keep him away from home in the evenings and prevent him from looking at his dying sons. I went back into theater work and became the volunteer coordinator for the founding of the Long Wharf Theatre in New Haven, Connecticut.

If God had assigned you to go in search of a logical couple to go into full-time Christian work, would you have chosen us? Would you have looked at us—Fred out every night with the dancing girls in Good Time Charlie's and me out day and night with young actors raising money for a theater? Would you have looked at us and said, "There's a stable spiritual couple—I guess I'll choose them"? Probably not. How grateful I am today that God didn't send a committee to observe us or a reporter to interview us. On His own, without a personnel panel or aptitude tests, God called us out. He reached me at a Christian Women's Club luncheon where I realized my need for a power beyond myself and where I prayed to ask Jesus to come into my life and change me. He reached Fred in a little church we began to attend that met in a school gymnasium. One day soon after, the Lord inspired Fred to close Good Time Charlie's and turn it into a church. So we moved the church from the gym to the nightclub and it was nicknamed St. Charlie's. Fred became the patron saint and I the mother superior!

Doesn't God have a sense of humor to choose Fred and me? To pull us out of the theater and the nightclub and turn us into leaders, speakers, and authors? We were called out by God—this wasn't our idea. We were changed by the Spirit—people muttered, "Are these the same Littauers that had Good Time Charlie's?" We were chosen by the people—within a short time we were on full-time staff at Campus Crusade for

Christ and had moved from Connecticut to Southern California. We were committed to obedience. We were determined to live for a God who had redeemed us.

Fred and I had dared to dream of the happy-ever-after life of personal, business, and social success. We had prepared our dream with education and selfless community service. We had been wearing the dream, living in the big house, driving the fancy cars, wearing the fur coats, and even founding a country club. We had it all, until the tragedy of our sons left us devastated and depressed. We needed to repair the dream. But the Lord didn't just patch us up and put band-aids on our pain; He called us out from the world, changed us by His Spirit, had us chosen by the people, and inspired us to be committed to an obedience we had not even known existed.

We had a new dream—that we would become effective Christian leaders. We were so in awe of the call that we wanted to hide in the baggage, but when Dr. Bill Bright, founder of Campus Crusade for Christ, asked us to come to Arrowhead Springs Hotel and be directors of conference services we emerged from our luggage and quickly prepared the new dream. We studied the Bible in a personal way, we attended every lecture given at headquarters that summer, we listened to tapes and read books, we began to fellowship with other Christian speakers and writers, and the Lord gave us a crash course in Christian leadership.

From that time in 1968 until now, Fred and I have been wearing the new dream.

What happened to Saul when he had the kingship thrust upon him? How well did he wear his new dream? Unfortunately for Saul, he compromised his standards and adjusted God's command.

1. *He disobeyed the rules.* The first rule for Saul—and for us—was to obey what God had called him to do. Saul was told by the prophet Samuel to go to Gilgal and wait seven days, at which time Samuel would arrive, they would build an altar, and Samuel would present the burnt offering to God in praise of His mighty power. King Saul went to Gilgal, but on the seventh day when Samuel didn't appear on time, Saul became impatient. *Why wait for Samuel? Why not do the sacrifice myself? Surely I can do it. I'm the king. Won't it be better for my men to see me as the spiritual leader instead of Samuel? Why shouldn't I be the good guy?*

See how easy it is to become impatient with God's plan and to wonder if it was God who called you out in the first place? Then it's a quick step to rationalizing that you can do it better your way, anyhow. Besides you'll get all the credit for being spiritual if you can display your faith in front of the people who are already restless and bored.

Saul did not spend days in prayer over this question. He didn't seek out godly counsel. He just moved into rationalized disobedience. No sooner had he presented the burnt offering than Samuel appeared—a little later than Saul had expected, but on the seventh day. Saul went out cheerfully to greet Samuel and salute him.

Can you remember as a child when you'd done something wrong and Mother drove up, how you ran out to meet her with hugs and kisses and excess joy in hopes to charm her enough so that she'd overlook your disaster when she fell upon it? That's what Saul did. When Samuel didn't get charmed by Saul's greeting, Saul rationalized again. *I was afraid you weren't coming. My people were leaving. The Philistines were threatening to attack and I said to myself, You'd better call out to God.* "I forced myself . . . and offered a burnt offering" (1 Samuel 13:12).

That sounds like a good enough reason to me. It even seems spiritual, but Samuel wasn't taken in by Saul's excuse, "You have done foolishly by not keeping the commandment. God had intended to establish your kingdom forever, but because of your disobedience He has chosen a man after His own heart to succeed you" (1 Samuel 13:13–14, paraphrased).

Note that God didn't kill Saul or even dethrone him. He just removed the hope of the future. He allowed him to continue on as king, but he took away the power. "The Spirit of the Lord departed from Saul" (1 Samuel 16:14).

Some of us may be like Saul, good people who meant well but who took things into our own hands. Some of us may have been busy doing good works, having charitable thoughts, moving in a positive direction—but not following God's commandments for our life. Some of us may feel God's plan is too slow and we've become impatient. He hasn't killed us off, but we no longer feel His power. We don't know how to keep hope alive.

One of the rules that God put clearly before Fred and me was that we should not enter into business transactions unless there was unity, unless we both felt the venture was a good idea. When we have obeyed this principle we have been blessed, but there were times when Fred felt "led of the Lord" to open a business that I had no heart for and that I could see was doomed from the start. When he became impatient and was going to proceed no matter what I thought, he would resort to rationalizing around my objections. He would present charts and graphs on the promise of the future and then ask me for any opposite proof. I never had statistics to back my opinion. I just didn't "feel" right about it. Remember, men, that women have an uncanny perception and sensitivity that logical men don't possess.

When I couldn't prove him wrong, Fred would consider me an irrational woman and move on. He would even give me verses to convince me he was right. Each venture that he went into without my agreement, without family unity, failed. They not only failed, but they brought with them large financial losses and deep family stress.

2. *He got greedy.* It's easy to dream up new ideas, and even to prepare them logically, but when they violate whatever rules God has made clear to you, it's impossible to wear the dream for very long.

Saul chose to overlook God's second rule when he went into battle and brought back more of the spoils for himself. He was supposed to kill off all the people and take none of the oxen, sheep, camels, or donkeys. The instructions were clear, but when Saul and his men won the battle they spared King Agag and the best of everything. "All that was good they would not utterly destroy: but everything that was vile and refuse, that they destroyed utterly" (1 Samuel 15:9).

What Saul did sounds logical. Why destroy good things? Why not keep them for yourself? Who will ever know if you take a little extra? When you've got all these sheep, how can anyone tell if you add a few more? Here was an intelligent person who made a rational choice to ignore God's word and take some booty for himself.

The Lord spoke to Samuel and told him what Saul had done. Saul's greed so upset Samuel that he cried all night, and when he went to him in the morning, he asked Saul how he had done. "I have performed the commandment of the Lord." This was a half-truth. He had won the battle and destroyed what was of no value, but he had kept what was of worth to him.

Samuel asked him to explain the bleating of the sheep and the lowing of the oxen and Saul, realizing he'd been caught, lied to get around his greed. "We kept the best to use as an offering unto the Lord."

Samuel, discouraged with Saul's refusal to admit his disobedience, explained, "When you were a nobody, we chose you and God anointed you King. Why did you disobey God's clear command and bring back the spoils you were instructed to destroy?" (1 Samuel 15:17, 19, paraphrased).

Then Samuel gave a message that I have heard all my life but didn't understand until I personalized the story of Saul.

"Hath the Lord as great delight in burnt offerings and sacrifices, as in obeying the voice of the Lord? Behold to obey is better than sacrifice, and to hearken than the fat of the rams" (1 Samuel 15:22).

God is not looking for external shows of religion but obedience to His word. He's not interested in our contributions to worthy causes if we cheated to get the money. God wants truth not just on the surface, but in our inward parts.

3. *He built monuments to himself.* How many good people, like Saul, who have achieved success and been put in positions of honor, compromised their standards, became greedy, and lost the dream?

The third area of fault in Saul's life was that he got to believing he was all-powerful. He forgot his roots and where he had come from. He put aside the miracle of God's making him king of the Israelites. He became impressed with his own abilities, authority, and good looks. The appealing humility he once had that caused him to hide in the baggage had been replaced with pride and conceit. When Samuel went looking for him he was told, "Saul's gone to Carmel to make himself a monument" (1 Samuel 15:12).

How many of us who have dared to dream beyond the norm, who have prepared the dream through study, hard work, and prayer have taken ourselves too seriously and not been able to wear the dream with humility? I've learned through experience that the Lord lets us build our monuments, He even lets us enshrine ourselves on pedestals for a period of time, but if we don't remember who gave us the talent, if we don't realize that we were nothing when He found us, He ultimately lets us fall into our own trap. If we disobey, cheat, get greedy, and build monuments to ourselves, it's only a matter of time before we fall off our pedestal.

4. *He blamed other people.* The fourth mistake Saul made was that when he got caught, he blamed other people. When questioned by Samuel about taking the spoils, Saul maintained his innocence and said, "The people took of the spoil, sheep and oxen" (1 Samuel 15:21). *It wasn't my fault. Left to my own, I would have done what's right.*

All of us as children blamed other people for our mistakes, but as we grew up we were to put away childish things and become responsible for our own actions.

Saul was an intelligent young man who made it to the top quite quickly. He was called out by God, changed by the Spirit, chosen by the people and committed to obedience. But once he was king and began to enjoy his position, he compromised his standards.

- He became impatient with God's timing and disobeyed God's plan for his life.
- He got greedy and took what wasn't his, never expecting to get caught.
- He forgot his humble beginnings and built himself a monument.
- He blamed other people for his mistakes.

The Lord repented that He had ever made Saul king over Israel, and He allowed an evil spirit to trouble Saul from that moment on. Saul was often so depressed that he would bring young David in to play the harp and soothe his troubled soul. He sought out diviners and witches to give him peace about his future and he ultimately committed suicide. "He took his sword and fell upon it" (1 Samuel 31:4).

Probably no one reading this today is a king, but we're all leading somebody somewhere.

Although few of us have been placed on a platform before thousands of people and asked to pledge obedience to a set of standards, we all have a knowledge of the difference between right and wrong. We are born with a sense of good and evil, and as children we test out how far we can go in the wrong direction before a parent will pull us back and insist we behave. As we mature, we achieve some kind of balance between being hesitant on one hand or doing our own thing on the other hand, no matter who gets hurt. Maturity is a balancing process that many of us never learn. We swing as if hanging on to the pendulum of some huge clock. We move to one side and then back to the other, never able to compromise or meet others in the middle.

"You don't like this meal? I'll never cook for you again."

"You don't like this suit and tie? It's the last time I'll ever dress up for you!"

"You don't like my advice? From here on you could be standing in the path of a moving train and I wouldn't say a word."

So much of what we do in life is based on the response of other people. *If they like what I say and do, they're fine people. If they reject my ideas, opinions, food, or clothes, they aren't worth working with. Drop them. Who cares?*

One of the hardest lessons I've had to learn is to do what I know to be right whether or not I get a positive response. I've had to learn to obey the rules whether or not anyone is looking. We are all good people who mean well, but when we don't get our "just desserts," as my mother called them, we quit. Or if we have an opportunity to reach beyond the ethical norm when no one is looking, we'll take the chance.

When Judge Kimba M. Wood read the verdict to junk bond king Michael Miliken, she said of this brilliant man who had let his life swing out of balance, "Your crimes show a pattern of skirting the law, stepping just over the wrong side of the law in an apparent effort to get some of the benefits from violating the law without running a substantial risk of being caught. . . . This kind of misuse of your leadership position and enlisting employees whom you supervised to assist you in violating the law are serious crimes warranting serious punishment and the discomfort and opprobrium of being removed from society. . . ."[104]

A writer for the *Los Angeles Times* commented on the trial, "We have learned that financial genius is before the fall. . . . Finally we have learned that brains and ability without integrity can damage our institutions."[105]

To say nothing of our lives, our families, and our reputations!

> "If one advances confidently in the direction
> of his dreams and endeavors to live the life
> which he has imagined, he will meet with
> success unexpected in common hours."
> —Henry David Thoreau

In the excessive eighties we saw preachers, politicians, and stockbrokers lose their grip on life and smash to the floor. The most distressing of these were the televangelists who fell while we were watching and who lowered the faith of faint-hearted believers and became the objects of ridicule for Johnny Carson and Arsenio Hall. "Saturday Night Live" did an interview where a character called the Church Lady questioned the morals of a Jimmy Swaggart look-alike and spanked him on the hand for being a naughty boy. The public waited to see if God was going to call Oral Roberts home, and the *Charlotte Observer* took sadistic pleasure in being the catalyst to the downfall of Jim and Tammy Bakker.

Everywhere I went people asked me, "Were they really Christians in the first place or was it all a sham?" As I look at the life of Saul, I can answer that these fallen leaders were also *called out by God*. They were all initially unlikely candidates for stardom, but they were *changed by the Spirit*. And as they grew in stature they were *chosen by the people* and supported by those whose lives had been positively influenced. I'm sure that initially they all meant well and sincerely spread the faith in the most effective way they knew how. To negate their ministry would be as much of a mistake as to accept their ultimate behavior. Where did they go wrong? How do good people get in trouble?

When Saul stood before the people at his coronation, he committed himself to obedience. He would follow God's rules for religious leaders, he said, but once in a position of power he compromised the standards. He forgot where he had come from, and he took control into his own hands. It's so easy after daring to dream and achieving more than you thought possible to let Pride creep in and say, "You've done a great job!"

Once you decide the rules are for the other people, it's easy to do your own thing and disregard the standards you are setting for others. "I'm the king; I'm in control. I'm the ultimate authority." Whether it's in religion, politics, business, the military, or the family, the people in authority often live a double standard.

Scripture tells us the love of money is the root of all evil. The money itself is not the problem, but the love of it. How easy it is for any one of us to get greedy. We feel it's our right to take a little extra, to give ourselves a bonus. We've worked hard. We deserve it.

If no one complains and money is coming in, why not take a little more. Once the taste for luxuries is established, it's natural to build bigger buildings and better businesses. As I heard John DeLorean say on TV one night, "Once you've been chauffeured in a limousine it's hard to go back to driving a Ford."

Possessions lead to power and people begin to build monuments to themselves as Saul did. They don't take a piece of marble and chip away until it looks like them but they name buildings, schools, ministries and TV programs after themselves. When the Bakkers changed PTL to the Jim and Tammy Show, the show became a monument.

Ultimately, the truth will find us out. The leader who compromises his standards will fall, often putting the blame on other people. I deeply regret the stumblings of our spiritual, social, and political leaders and hope we can learn from these four fatal steps to failure.

Barry Phaelor, former television producer at Jim and Tammy's Heritage USA, wrote me of his feelings about the fall of PTL. He had dared to dream he could go from Clemson University to television production and had prepared for the possibility. He loved the glamor and excitement of working with the Bakkers, but he was helpless as he watched the death of a dream.

> "I did it my way!" These popular lyrics epitomize the way most of us feel about controlling the direction our lives will take. We want to make our own dreams come true. Society, our families, and even our churches encourage us to "go for it!" But many times our ambitious dreams and goals capture control of our heart and become the center attraction in our lives. As our intimacy with Christ slips away, we have nothing left except the all-consuming thrust of the dream itself.
>
> In my years at PTL, I saw the most spectacular dreams fulfilled as the Lord used a man and woman of meager beginnings as instruments tocarry forth spreading the Gospel and bring healing to the desperately hurting body of Christ. Many years of perspiring preparation by Jim and Tammy Bakker brought forth a ministry

founded in a humble furniture store which only a few years later spanned four squaremiles of property near Charlotte, North Carolina. The dream Jim and Tammy had for ministry and for people became a reality as they asked of the Lord, sought His will, and knocked on every door that came their way. The result was obviously a miracle—to those of us who will admit it. Marriage workshops, seminars, television outreaches, and twenty-four hour prayer presented to a hurting, dying world a God who really loved them.

But somehow during the miracle there undoubtedly began the struggle which is in all of us between fulfilling our own inner dreams and following the narrow path of direction set forth for us by the Lord. When we achieve our goals we sometimes decide, maybe even unconsciously, that we have to take it all from there, that we have to carry forth the dream on our own. Of course the Lord has given us the need to strive, to fulfill, to create that which He has placed in each of us. We must do the asking, the seeking, and the knocking, but we must continually depend on the Lord for His will and direction for us no matter what that will may be. We must give all of ourselves and our dreams to the Lord. This requires brokenness and humbleness that many of us do not want to give. We cannot "do it our way" any longer but must submit to the holy hand of the Father and allow Him to order the steps of our lives. Sometimes our dreams must die.

The struggle at PTL, the creeping greed and immorality, saw the destruction of years and years of hopes and dreams not only for Jim and Tammy, but for many others involved, all the way to the viewers and supporters of the ministry itself. Jim and Tammy saw their lives crumble before them as the ministry they had worked so hard to found was taken from their hands and along with it the lifelong dream. As they went down we were taken with them. All of us who worked there lost our own hopes, our dreams, and our contentment as PTL vaporized into only a mirage. I found that during the years, I had developed an unhealthy devotion to Heritage USA. Along with many others, I spent each minute of the day recalling the past, the love, the excitement, the ministry, the very air which surrounded the property, which held so many precious memories for me. The way it used to be. I would not, could not let go of the dream that Jim and Tammy began.

We all tried to keep the ministry alive for the following two years. Amidst more scandal and inner turmoil, we watched each day as one more drop of the lifeblood dripped from what used to be the indestructible PTL. No one seemed to want to give it up, many because of their own personal love for the ministry that used to be and many because of their own selfish motives.

As I struggled within, fantasizing of the day when it would all be the same, the Lord moved me on to another place and another time. I finally had to face the unbelievable fact that the dream was dead! At least for now.

Hours upon hours were spent in nostalgia, wanting only one more minute of a dream that wasn't even mine, the only one I had been blessed enough to see and to experience. I rehearsed in my mind that then was now again. I felt the love; I saw the people; I drank into my very being the glitz and the glamour of a Christian fantasyland where everything was close to heaven. I recalled my old friends; I watched videos of old programs that I had produced and sang along with the music. I read letters from the past and flipped through picture after picture taken in a much happier time when we were all wearing the dream.

One day, I finally realized something that I had already somehow understood many times before—that the dream was dead; it had to die, but through this death came new life for me.

The planting of a seed into the cold and dark ground appears only to be a burial. But in this death, the miracle-working power of God brings forth a new life like no other before it. A fresh, purified creation.

The smell of the death of PTL still lingers on. Most of the former staff members have all gone in different directions around the world as the Lord has provided fresh horizons for each of them. As the memories pass before us and we sometimes long for the past, the Lord gradually brings healing to tired and torn souls. Jim and Tammy along with their family still exist in a world that no one will let them forget. The past for them seems neverending and the present is heavy with regret. But somehow I know for Jim and Tammy and for all of us who were a part of PTL that it's time to have a funeral for the past and begin to repair our dreams.

Few of us realize that when we fail to wear the dream properly ourselves, we bring others down with us and thus necessitate the repair of their dreams, as well.

PART FOUR

Repair
the
Dream

"Into each life comes a time to grow
when dreams must be spoken
and wings must be tried . . .
so reach for your dreams,
spread your new wings . . . and fly."

Repair the Dream

Returning to his homeland of Algiers after a decade in forced exile, former president Ahmed Ben Bella, 73, challenged the long-ruling National Liberation Front with the cry, "I hope I can do something to restore our dreams."

Do you need to repair your dream?

Not everyone has to repair the dream of life. Not everyone has to pick up the pieces especially if they haven't dropped them somewhere along the way. Not everyone has a mid-life crisis.

Ron Chapman has managed to stay out of contentious situations and wear his dream well. In September 1989, Ron's twentieth anniversary at KVIL, the Dallas Press Club sponsored a roast for Ron. Typically these events ridicule and even malign the recipient, but the speakers the Press Club chose gave tributes in humor without a touch of malice. "D" Magazine called the roast a "Three and a half hour Valentine."

Ron has had a few low points in his radio career. When KVIL took a dip in the ratings in 1982, Ron took the whole staff to see Rocky III. They all got the message that if they didn't redouble their efforts another station would deliver the knockout punch. They were up in ratings the next time.

It would be unfair to you readers to let you feel Ron has no detractors and has lived a charmed life of universal kudos. For those who perform at an A+ level, he's their mentor, friend, and inspiration. For those who coast or are less than devoted to their work, Ron can come down so hard that the person lies limp in devastation. Some former employees have said, "Ron Chapman is a genius, but along with the genius comes a dark side. . . . He is good at what he does, but he is also a dictator who can deflate a person's dreams with angry outbursts and criticism."

His staff admits he does lose his temper, but he gives constructive criticism and is always helping them improve.

It is unfortunate that sometimes we carry our attention to work beyond what will sustain a marriage.

"I really don't like talking about my private life," Ron says matter-of-factly. "I was happily married for nineteen years. I'm not real proud of the fact that I'm not married anymore. Frankly, I don't want it known that I have failed at something. One day, by mutual consent, we decided we needed some space between us. And we never got back together. The problem was that she was married to a man who was married to a radio station. Most of what I do is KVIL. I sleep and eat KVIL. I hate to admit it, but it's true."[105]

Ron curtailed his social life at this time and it was several years later that he met and married Nance Murray. She knew before they were married that Ron's work came first so there were no surprises. She is supportive of what he does and has made him a warm and happy home. When Nance came to CLASS she concluded her practice message with the words, "Ron is on center stage and I'm the one who holds the spotlight."

Nance is helping Ron repair the personal part of his dream. He continues to come out on top because he has a passion for his work and he is functioning in his strengths. The *Dallas Morning News* commented on Ron's devotion to his job. "He has had to pay a heavy price for his intense, overwhelming dedication and devotion to KVIL—his marriage. Six years ago, he was divorced from his longtime wife, Marilyn, a former Dallas high school teacher."

If you feel in your heart that your life is on an even keel, that you have dared to dream at least once in your life, that you have prepared the dream by understanding who you really are, that you have been wearing the dream with confident satisfaction, then you may not need to repair the dream. However, you will find in this section inspiring examples of people who have had to overcome a variety of situations, some of which may be similar to your life.

Not all of our problems center on our business, for many successful people have underlying feelings of low self-worth and have difficulty in relationships. In this section we will ask some questions that will help evaluate our lives and repair our dreams.

Is it possible that we can dare to dream, prepare for it and even wear it and still find ourselves a failure? Is it possible that our childhood circumstances led us down the wrong path or that as adults we've made poor choices? Robert Frost, our country's former poet laureate, wrote:

> I shall be telling this with a sigh
> Somewhere ages and ages hence:
> Two roads diverged in a wood, and I—
> I took the one less traveled by,
> And that has made all the difference.[106]

Somewhere along the line we have all made some choices. We have been faced with two paths in the woods of our life and we have had to make a decision which one to follow. At that time we may or may not have had any kind of guidance that helped us see the right way. Some of us took the broad path, the popular path, or the easy path. Some of us were even pushed down the path by a parent who never had that opportunity and wanted us to live it for them. Some of us chose the path that was serene, one where we could see through the woods and out the other side. We could tell where we were going and we knew we would not meet the big bad wolf along the way. Some of us followed paths that others had already cut out and went into the family business— only to find that father was as ferocious as a tiger and frightened us into corners that made life in the forest seem safe by comparison.

Some of us are lost in the woods right now. We've meant well and tried hard, but we seem programmed for failure. Others of us have found our way out of the woods and are standing in the sunshine of success.

Where are you right now? Do you need to review your choices?

Charles had always dreamed of owning his own photography studio. He prepared by studying at Brooks Institute. He then joined the Air Force, where he was in charge of the audio-visual department. As a Perfect Personality he always aimed for perfection and was frustrated because it seemed to him that people were more interested in speed and economy than in the quality of his work. He dreamed that when he got out of the service, he could somehow have his own studio where he could do only things of high quality.

Because of an unexpected inheritance, he received funds to put into a business. He rented a studio in a high-class section of town and he and his wife Mary decorated it perfectly. He bought the best possible equipment, put up his sign, and waited. No one came. A few wanted passport pictures, but he turned these down because he only wanted to do quality work.

Charles was depressed and sat by the hour in the perfect studio staring at the wall. Sanguine Mary was upset over the waste of the inheritance money, "We could have bought a new house or a new car," she told him. This type of comment only made him feel more of a failure. As a true sanguine, Mary mumbled and complained until she got that out of her system and finally accepted the fact that the money was gone, never to return. At that point, she shifted into her happiness mode and tried to cheer Charles up. "It's over. Let's forget it. Close the place down and get on with life." She couldn't understand why he continued to cry over spilt milk. As we talked together we could see that for Charles this was not just a bad business decision—it was the death of a dream. He couldn't forget it and go on because there was nowhere to go. This had been his lifetime dream and it was dead.

Once Mary realized that Charles was grieving over the loss of his dream, she stopped trying to be a cheerleader and waited patiently until he could bring himself to close the studio down, sell off his prized equipment, and look for a new job. He was too disheartened at that time to make a major career change, so he went to work for the city as a photographer.

Like the Air Force, the city was not impressed by his impeccable standards of quality and he was frustrated again. But he dutifully produced training films and low-budget documentaries for three long dull years. Slowly he recovered from the death of his dream and decided he would go to law school. As a melancholy he got deeply into the studies in preparation for a new dream, but after all his preparation he was not accepted into graduate school and his self-worth dropped to a new low.

In seeking answers to his depression, he studied psychology books and self-help tapes. He found he had compassion for others in problem situations, and he was able to analyze and repair his own dreams. As he searched for answers for himself, he realized he loved to analyze case histories and he always seemed to come up with the right solutions. He made a new choice; he took a new path through the woods. He applied to the prestigious program for marriage and family counseling at the University of San Diego and was accepted. He dedicated himself wholeheartedly to his new studies and in the past two years has received all A's. He is now a counseling trainee and shows signs of being a compassionate and intuitive counselor.

Sometimes it's our choices that are wrong. Sometimes our old dreams have to die so we can find the right ones. We have to find a new path out of the woods and into the sunshine.

Do You Feel Uncomfortable with Your Personality?

When we have assessed our personality correctly, we usually feel comfortable with the results. However, I often have people who say, "I just don't think I came out right." *Right* is different for each one us, but trust your intuition if you have questions and aren't sure who you are.

Remember that the study of the personalities is not to pin labels on anyone, but rather to give you a handle on your strengths so that you may function to your fullest potential, and on your weaknesses so that you can see them in black and white and get to work on them. Unfortunately, many people spend their whole lives in jobs where they are struggling through work in their weaknesses and feeling worthless and stupid. If they were using their strengths, their whole career and self-image would improve.

We have also seen amazing repair work in marriages when the partners begin to understand and accept each other and do not let their dreams die unnecessarily.

Pat is a Peaceful Personality who married into a family full of Powerful and Popular people. They had no understanding of the natural differences in people, and they made fun of Pat and her low-key nature. Her husband Jim called her lazy, slow, stupid, unorganized, unexciting, and dreamy. The in-laws not only made Pat the butt of jokes in person, but they wrote letters to her husband telling him what he ought to do about her and fueled his discontent with phone calls and pointed references to how slow and dull she was.

After a number of years of this emotional abuse, Pat felt her own personality had been drained away. And yet no matter how hard she tried to please the family, she couldn't seem to win. Finally, when she was on the verge of suicide, Jim agreed to go to a counselor. At the very first session, the counselor told Jim that if he didn't cease abusing Pat, she would put her in a battered women's shelter. The counselor also told Jim to stop calling his parents and to let them know he would not communicate at all if they continued to insult Pat and try to get him to divorce her.

It was at the beginning of the counseling when Pat found my books *Personality Plus* and *Your Personality Tree* and began to read them. She wrote: "It was the window into my soul which I had been seeking. After years of verbal abuse—horrible names like 'gutless, milksop' I realized I was a perfectly normal Peaceful who had so much going for me. There are other Peacefuls out there, too, living good lives. Happiness, oh happiness! I love being a phlegmatic. How comfortable and right it seems."

What a change in Pat's attitude about herself when she learned it was all right to be a Peaceful Personality.

"Just this year my husband began to study the personalities and it was an eye-opener for him. He began to look at me in a positive, accepting way and is trying not to let things that are just personality differences irritate and confuse him. We love to laugh together now about our own mindsets and feel the future is bright. I'm trying to see he gets plenty of fun and praise and he appreciates my sense of humor and our calm, quiet home. He has realized that my ability to make a real home, a haven for him, no matter where we are in the world, is a real gift. It feels good to be appreciated."

This letter is a sample of the thousands we have received over the years showing how an understanding of the personalities can relieve marital disharmony which often leads to abuse. When each partner accepts the other as he is and doesn't try to remake him (or her), it can be the beginning of repairing a lost dream.

Check Your Scores

If you come out predominantly in one category with a few more traits from the others, read the page on your basic personality.

If you are high in one with a close second in another, read both pages and coordinate. For example, if you are a Popular and Powerful, you want to have fun while doing the work. If you are a Powerful and Perfect, you want to get the work done and have it right. If you are Perfect and Peaceful, you want things to be right, but not if it will cause conflict. If you are a Peaceful and Popular, you want fun, but not if you have to go somewhere to do it.

Any of the above combinations is a natural blend of personalities and perfectly normal.

If your score splits somewhat evenly between two of the opposites (Popular/Perfect or Powerful/Peaceful), this indicates one of several possibilities: You may have taken or scored the profile incorrectly, so go back and check the directions. You may not have a clear view of yourself, so have a close friend or partner discuss it with you. Or you may have had a past problem that caused you to put on a mask over your birth personality. This problem could be childhood abuse, emotional neglect, extreme deprivation, sexual molestation, or being raised by parents who were alcoholics or on drugs. Any of these could have caused a covering of your original personality. Another reason could have been deep insecurities as a teen which caused you to try to be someone you weren't in order to be popular, and thus created a false personality. Another possibility is that you may have married someone who tried to change you and in an effort to be pleasing you wiped out many of your genuine feelings—leaving you somewhat confused about your true identity. Multiple marriages increase this confusion.

If your scores were even all the way across, this may indicate that you had difficulties with the definitions of the words, that you are a Peaceful who has trouble making decisions, or that you have spent your life trying to be all things to all people to such an extreme that you have obliterated your real personality.

If any of these questions arise, try to think back to your childhood desires. Did you always want fun, control, perfection, or peace? Talk with parents or relatives. Try to find your birth personality and begin to function in it. We are never comfortable with ourselves or secure with others when we are playing a role or trying to be what someone else felt we should be.

Read Your Personality Summary

On the following pages I have summarized key points on each personality for your review.

Popular Summary

The sanguine says: "Let's do it the fun way."

Desire:	Have fun
Emotional Needs:	Attention, affection, approval, acceptance
Key Strengths:	Can talk about anything at any time in any place with or without information—has a bubbly personality, optimism, sense of humor, storytelling ability, likes people
Key Weaknesses:	Disorganized, can't remember details or names, exaggerates, not serious about anything, trusts others to do the work, too gullible and naive
Gets Depressed When:	Life is no fun and no one seems to love them

Is Afraid of:	Being unpopular or bored, having to live by the clock or keep a record of money spent
Likes People Who:	Listen and laugh, praise and approve
Dislikes People Who:	Criticize, don't respond to their humor, don't think they are cute
Is Valuable in Work:	For colorful creativity, optimism, light touch, cheering up others, entertaining
Could Improve If:	They got organized, didn't talk so much and learned to tell time
As a Leader They:	Excite, persuade, and inspire others, exude charm and entertain—but are forgetful and poor on follow-through
Tend to Marry:	Perfects who are sensitive and serious, but the Populars quickly tire of having to cheer them up all the time, and of being made to feel inadequate and stupid
Reaction to Stress:	Leave the scene, go shopping, eat more, find a fun group, create excuses, deny reality, blame others
Recognized by:	Constant talking, loud volume, bright eyes, moving hands, colorful clothing, magnetic personality, storytelling ability

Powerful Summary

The Choleric says, "Let's do it my way."

Desire:	Have control
Emotional Needs:	Sense of obedience, appreciation for accomplishments, credit for ability
Key Strengths:	Ability to take charge of anything instantly, make quick, correct judgments
Key Weaknesses:	Too bossy, domineering, autocratic, insensitive, impatient, unwilling to delegate or give credit to others
Gets Depressed When:	Life is out of control and people won't do things their way
Is Afraid of:	Losing control of anything, such as losing job, not being promoted, becoming seriously ill, having rebellious child or unsupportive mate
Likes People Who:	Are supportive and submissive, see things their way, cooperate quickly and let them take credit

Dislikes People Who:	Are lazy and not interested in working constantly, who buck their authority, get independent, or aren't loyal
Is Valuable in Work:	Because they can accomplish more than anyone else in a shorter time and are usually right, but may stir up trouble
Could Improve If:	They allowed others to make decisions, delegated authority, became more patient, didn't expect everyone to produce as they do
As a Leader They:	Have a natural feel for being in charge, a quick sense of what will work, and a sincere belief in their ability to achieve, but may overwhelm less aggressive people
Tend to Marry:	Peacefuls who will quietly obey and not buck their authority, but who never accomplish enough or get excited over their projects
Reaction to Stress:	Tighten control, work harder, exercise more, get rid of offender, stay away from social situations
Recognized by:	Fast-moving approach, quick grab for control, self-confidence, restless and overpowering attitude

Perfect Summary

The melancholy says: "Let's do it the right way."

Desire:	Have it right, make it perfect
Emotional Needs:	Sense of stability, space, silence, sensitivity, and support
Key Strengths:	Ability to organize, set long-range goals, have high standards and ideals, analyze deeply
Key Weaknesses:	Easily depressed, too much time on preparation, too focused on details, remembers negatives, suspicious of others
Gets Depressed When:	Life is out of order, standards aren't met, no one seems to care
Is Afraid of:	No one understanding how they really feel, making a mistake, having to compromise standards

Likes People Who:	Are serious, intellectual, deep, and will carry on a sensible conversation
Dislikes People Who:	Are lightweights, forgetful, late, disorganized, superficial, prevaricating, and unpredictable
Is Valuable in Work:	For sense of details, love of analysis, follow-through, high standards of performance, compassion for the hurting
Could Improve If:	They didn't take life quite so seriously and didn't insist that others be perfectionists
As a Leader They:	Organize well, are sensitive to people's feelings, have deep creativity, want quality performance
Tend to Marry:	Populars for their personalities and social skills, but soon try to shut them up and get them on a schedule, becoming depressed when they don't respond
Reaction to Stress:	Withdraw, get lost in a book, become depressed, give up, recount the problems, go back to college
Recognized by:	Serious and sensitive nature, well-mannered approach, self-deprecating comments, meticulous and well-groomed looks (exceptions are hippie-type intellectuals, musicians, poets, who feel attention to clothes and looks is worldly and detracts from their inner strengths)

Peaceful Summary

The phlegmatic says: "Let's do it the easy way."

Desire:	Have no conflict, keep peace
Emotional Needs:	Sense of respect, feeling of worth, understanding, emotional support
Key Strengths:	Balance, even disposition, dry sense of humor, pleasing personality
Key Weaknesses:	Lack of decisiveness, enthusiasm, and energy, no obvious flaws but a hidden will of iron
Gets Depressed When:	Life is full of conflict, they have to face a personal confrontation, no one wants to help, the buck stops with them

Is Afraid of:	Having to deal with a major personal problem, being left holding the bag, making major changes
Likes People Who:	Will make decisions for them, will recognize their strengths, will not ignore them, will give them respect
Dislikes People Who:	Are too pushy, too loud and expect too much of them
Is Valuable in Work:	Because they cooperate and are a calming influence, keep peace, mediate between contentious people, objectively solve problems
Could Improve If:	They set goals and became self-motivated, they were willing to do more and move faster than expected, and could face their own problems as well as they handle other people's
As a Leader They:	Keep calm, cool and collected, don't make impulsive decisions, are well-liked and inoffensive, won't cause trouble, but don't often come up with brilliant new ideas
Tend to Marry:	Powerfuls because they respect their strength and decisiveness, but later the Peacefuls get tired of being pushed around and looked down upon
Reaction to Stress:	Hide from it, watch television, eat, tune out on life, sleep
Recognized by:	Calm and agreeable approach, relaxed posture, sitting or leaning when possible

Do You Tend to Live through Other People?

Frequently a person who is socially insecure or emotionally unstable will attach himself to a strong personality and live through this new personality. The friend becomes his alter-ego and he feels a vicarious victory as he travels in the friend's shadow.

I first picked up the book *Slim: Memories of a Rich and Imperfect Life* because of the title. It reminded me of the saying I'd seen on the T-shirt of an emaciated teenager, "You can never be too rich or too thin."

Since I'd never been either and had always loved Cinderella stories, I settled onto the sofa to discover how an ordinary girl, Mary Raye Gross, became Lady Slim Keith. Maybe there was still hope for me. Instantly I related to her goals in life as she dreamed, "I lived in palaces, plied the seas in great boats with silken sails and ate mostly grapes. I wore emerald overshoes and diamond wraps, and life was full and rich and perfect."

I plunged into the palaces and seas with her and found that she had been unusually pretty from the start and knew how to intrigue men in high places. I myself failed on both points, but I still had hope that I could relate as she got older, heavier, and less attractive. Alas, in her own words she never aged and stayed slim and rich forever. She tantalized William Powell, who fed her love of luxuries. She married debonaire director Howard Hawks who gave her cars, homes, and yachts as long as she would turn her head from his frequent affairs. When she tired of his philandering, she found and charmed a new man, Leland Hayward, producer of *South Pacific* and other musical hits. She moved on the fast track of show-biz society, attended Broadway openings, and inhaled the glamor and glitter of eternal parties. After ten years of lavish lunches and elegant dinners, Leland left Slim between courses. She had already determined she couldn't live without a man, so she did the obvious thing that any social-climbing American woman would like to do: She captured an Englishman with a title and she became Lady Slim Keith. She fulfilled her dream of the grand life, rich and perfect, but she was bored and empty and never knew who she was, except for her reflection in the mirrors of the men she met and married.

Although few of us achieve her social heights, many of us have her problem. We don't know who we are, only what we are doing and whose we are. So many women I counsel have no personal identity. "I'm Jim's wife—Mary's mother—Bobby's teacher."

What happens to her if Jim dies, Mary leaves home, and Bobby graduates? When the props are pulled out, how many women find they were holding up nothing? If you lost your whole family, would your worth and purpose be gone? Or could you, after a period of mourning, go on and build a new life?

Helen had a handsome husband who provided her with all she had ever wished for in life. He made all the decisions, presented her with cars he'd chosen, and bought the big house he'd always wanted. She raised the children, who went to the schools he selected, and she never went near his business. She asked no questions and he offered no information. When her husband dropped dead at the age of fifty-two, Helen was totally unprepared. She didn't know where anything of importance was kept. She didn't even know if he had a will—she'd meant to ask him one of these days, but he was so young and in good health. She was at the mercy of the managers of his business, and she fell into a dependency relationship with a secretary who knew where everything was and used her knowledge as a control over Helen. By the time she came to me in tears, money had been taken out of the business, the will had not yet appeared, and the secretary had left with the contents of the safe-deposit box. Helen had spent her life in the shadow of her husband and in the role of mother, and at fifty she suddenly found herself alone and lost.

If we as individuals are going to "wear well," we have to do more than live through other people no matter who they may be or how much they have. We must live in knowledge and wisdom, respecting and loving others but not so dependent on individuals for our self-worth that without them our life is over.

Often I've had young women attach themselves to me. Usually they have come from homes where they had a love-hate relationship with their mother and I appear to them to be what their mother should have been. They give me presents, wait on me, write and call me. They smother me and try to possess me. They can't live without a mother-person in charge of their life. Their mother controlled their lives and even though they aren't with her they still need her direction. I discourage this type of relationship because it's unhealthy and always ends up the same. The day comes when I as the "good mother" don't have time to talk on the phone, can't listen to hours of confession, don't answer the last three notes, and forget to thank them for the balloons delivered to my birthday luncheon. This shifts the emotionally needy person into a reverse gear and flashes rejection signals. "My mother never loved me, but I thought you did. Now I see that you don't care either—after all I've done for you."

Are you needy and greedy? Do you have a person you can't function without? Do you need their love and become greedy for their attention? Do you get jealous if they have other friends and feel rejected if they go somewhere without you? These symptoms often come from insecure childhoods, from dysfunctional homes, from domineering parents, or from ones who ignored you or that you could never please.

Do You Feel Emotionally Drained?

So often I have women say to me: "I don't think I can go on another day." "My whole life is falling apart." "I'm an emotional wreck." "I feel like I'm going to have a nervous breakdown."

Men say: "I've never really been a success and I don't know why." "I feel like chucking it all and taking off." "My wife and children have turned against me." "I think I'm having a mid-life crisis."

If you have ever had any of these thoughts or if your personality comes out with opposite splits, there may be some unknown trauma in your childhood that is keeping you emotionally unbalanced today. As we teach *Freeing Your Mind* seminars, we talk with many people who feel as though they had a normal childhood but are a wreck as adults. Many can't remember chunks of their childhood. Some have been in counseling but have not unearthed the root of their uneasiness or insecurities.

To give them a quick survey of their background emotions, Fred developed the following chart. Read over each item and check, if at any time in your life, you had this problem. Then total up your score.

Survey of Emotions and Experience

Please check each word that applies or has ever applied to you. Leave blank any that do not apply or you are not sure of.

— Abortion
— Affairs during marriage
—·· Alcoholic parent
—·· Anorexia or bulimia
—·· Brother or sister molested as a child
—· Childhood "bad houses or rooms"
— Childhood depression
—·· Downcast looks as a child
—· Early childhood anger
—· Early childhood masturbation
— Emotionally abused as a child
— Emotions suppressed in childhood
—·· Fear of being alone
—·· Fear of losing weight
—· Feel unworthy of God's love
—· Feeling "dirty"
—· Fits of rage
— Guilt feelings
—· Hate men
— Hide real feelings
—· Lack of resistance to sexual attack
—·· Lack of trust

— Low self-worth
— Marital sexual disinterest
—· Memory gaps in childhood
—·· Migraine headaches
— Nudity forbidden in childhood family
—· Obsessive fear of rape
—· Panic attacks
— Physically abused as child
—·· PMS
— Poor teenage opposite-sex relations
—·· Recurring bad dreams
— Rejection feelings
—· Same-sex attraction
— Sexually abused or molested as a child
—· Sexual compulsions
— Suicidal feelings
— Teenage promiscuity
—· Temptation to touch children sexually
— Tendency to overreact
—· Uncomfortable with nudity in marriage
—·· Uncontrollable anger
—· Uncontrollable crying
—·· Undiagnosed pains and aches

Total up your score. If you have checked fifteen or more, there is a strong possibility that you have had sufficient emotional pain in your past to influence your present behavior in a negative way.

Now look at the dots beside some of the items. If you marked some of those with two dots, there is a possibility you were a victim of inappropriate sexual interference as a child, even though you do not remember it. If you have marked any of those with one dot, it is almost certain that someone touched you in a sexual manner and you have buried the memory because it was too painful to bear.

By using this survey, we have been able to help thousands find out quickly whether or not there was any type of childhood molestation that is the root of their emotional instability.

Often when intelligent, well-meaning men have a pattern of business failure, we discover some form of sexual abuse in their childhood. If you are at a crossroads and one more thing has fallen apart, consider the possibility that you were tampered with as a child and that your life will not improve until you find the source of your problems. No amount of behavior modification or motivational messages will set you on the right track until you discover the cause.

Oprah Winfrey fascinated the entire country with her impressive weight loss of sixty-seven pounds. People tuned in daily to hear how she was doing, and when she finished her diet she posed for pictures in her tight-fitting designer jeans. Chubby ladies ran for her weight-loss program and her viewers rejoiced in the ultimate self-improvement program.

What went wrong? Two years later the weight was back on, and Oprah publicly admitted that she dealt with the symptoms without digging up the roots. Oprah admitted openly that she was molested as a child and that the weight was not the real problem.

"It's about not being able to say no. It's about not handling stress properly. It's about sexual abuse. It's about all the things that cause other people to become alcoholics and drug addicts."

Oprah described the compulsion that many victims have to overeat, drink, take drugs, shop, or gamble, and she also showed the world that just modifying behavior doesn't cure the disease.

If you have a garden with weeds choking out the good plants you can do one of three things: 1. Leave them alone and let them take over the garden; 2. cut them down, leaving the roots out of sight; or 3. dig up the roots and get rid of them.

Comparing this to our emotional instability or lack of success in life, we, too, have three choices: 1. Do nothing and hope someday we'll get lucky—unfortunately most people choose this because it takes no effort or change, and even though it's not positive, it is miserably comfortable; 2. look at the symptoms of our problems and get counseling to help us cope or medication to lift our spirits—this will bring some measure of relief, but probably not cure our emotional pains; or 3. get to the root of the problem, dig it up, and be done with it. How do you do this? Some counselors are able to lead you into a search of your past—although many can't or won't for different reasons.

Fred and I, seeing the vast numbers of emotionally unbalanced people who are trying their best to be successful, wrote our book *Freeing Your Mind from Memories That Bind*. It contains fifty pages of questions that will lead you into some self-discovery that will make sense out of your insecurities and set you on a path to freedom. You will be able to dig up the roots and burn them.

Our follow-up book, *The Promise of Restoration*, gives additional steps to repairing your dream of success and stability.

For those of you who have family members or employees who never seem to get life together, who have ability but continue to fail, who

repeatedly make wrong choices, who have a history of broken relationships, become alert to the possibility that they were abused in some
way as children and may never get better until the root is dug up.

In the past, Fred and I poured our lives into certain dysfunctional
people who never improved in spite of all our efforts. We now look back
and realize we were only putting band-aids over deep wounds. Don't waste
too much time patching up problems when the patient needs surgery.

Some people will always say, "Isn't it better to leave well enough
alone?" Only if "well enough" is well enough. But if "well enough" is
barely existing, then it's time to take some steps to uncover the pains
of the past.

Cyndi had tried to leave well enough alone, but her life displayed
the pattern of the typical victim. She writes:

> I grew up the oldest child of three. My father had been a welder
> in a local steel mill, but due to an accident, was reduced to plant
> guard. Needless to say, the salary was next-to-nothing. So I grew
> up in a home where money was scarce.
>
> My choleric mother and my phlegmatic father did not make
> for a peaceful household. I was awkward, skinny, and had short
> straight dull-brown hair. My sister, six years younger than I, was a
> curly-haired blonde with blue eyes—the child my mother had al-
> ways wanted. My brother, the only son of the only son, was also
> blonde and blue eyed. They were smarter than I, better looking—
> well, you can guess the rest.
>
> Everything that happened was my fault. I was the difficult one,
> the dumber, one etc.
>
> When I was about tqelve, I was sexually molested by my minis-
> ter. I told no one. Shortly afterwards, he had a "nervous break-
> down" and left the church. It was not until four years ago that I
> finally told my parents. You see, all those years, I thought they
> would blame me. I found out that the man had been run out of the
> church because he had molested two other little girls—that they
> knew of. My father, however, said that it wasn't bad since there
> had not been penetration.
>
> Who cares how far it went physically? I trusted him. The man
> raped my soul and my spirit. I have spent years in poor self-worth,
> not only from his actions, but theirs. I grew up with so much criti-
> cism and condemnation, besides self-condemnation, that I was a
> victim. I chose friends, jobs, and situations that intensified myself
> as a victim.
>
> Until your book. On New Year's Day I sat at the dining room
> table with a cup of tea and opened *Freeing Your Mind*. I spent the

entire day, working my way through it, praying, crying, laughing, rejoicing. On the inside cover of the book I wrote page numbers and references for things that stood out, or that I never wanted to forget. Oh, yes, on Appendix D, the list of 100 possible symptoms— I checked off 47.

Oh, I still have problems. I am still overweight and I still hate housecleaning and money is a problem. But I am basically free. I have a long road yet, but now I know it is possible for me to be a whole woman.

We have found that when people will read *Freeing Your Mind* and will follow the steps of restoration, there will be major changes. But if, like Oprah, they don't continue the program, they will slip back. You can go to the best doctor in the world, but if you don't do what he says and take your medicine you will not get well.

Some victims feel that if they can only get away from the abuser their life will become normal, but unfortunately they often marry abusers. Onalee writes:

As a child, one of my sisters and I were sexually abused by our neighbor and all of us children were verbally and physically abused by our dad. When I got married things were going to be different; however, I married a man much like my father. After twenty years of married life, our home was a battleground—he trying to make me like him, me trying to make him like me, and each of us trying to make our children into the "perfect" people we were!

Since your seminar, I have borrowed and bought and read several of your books. Your book *Freeing Your Mind* has been a big help to my sister and me. We have needed help for so long. I want things to be different, but now we have some tools and some directions to help us. I have been studying and praying almost daily, and my family has been having a worship time together, morning and evening.

True, our home is not perfect, but it is improving, albeit ever so slow! But at least now we have a better understanding of and more flexibility with each other. Now we have renewed hope, thanks to your ministry and to the Lord.

Did You Feel Unloved or Rejected As a Child?

"I've never felt anyone really loved me." How often I hear tales of rejection coming from people who never felt loved, people whose parents were too busy to nurture them properly, people who suffered early losses of loved ones, people who were abused physically, sexually, or emotionally. Any of these background problems equals rejection in the heart of a child. If you add to any of these negatives a portion of poverty, physical abnormalities, lack of education, alcoholic parents, or any other manifestation of a dysfunctional home, you breed a feeling of loneliness and rejection that tells the child "I'm no good. Nobody will ever love me. I'm not like those other people. No one understands me."

There have been many books and articles written on rejection, but because these words of advice approach the problem as if everyone had the same universal personality, much of what is stated falls upon deaf ears. The rejected person who reads cures for rejection that don't work in his or her personal and unique situation ends up feeling even more rejected.

Reactions to Abuse: Melancholy/Phlegmatic

We tend to think of rejections as a suppressive ailment that debilitates its victims into a lifetime of emotional misery—and this is true in about half of the cases. Using the personalities as a basis, we can begin to understand that our reaction to rejection or abuse of any kind varies with our inborn personality. The melancholy and phlegmatic who tend to be introverted have a low motivation and a tendency to a poor self-image. They respond to a negative childhood by withdrawal, reading, watching television, and feelings of worthlessness. They often become loners, have emotional problems, function below their ability, and meet any obstacle with the shrug of "what's the use." They put low expectations upon themselves and unintentionally set themselves up for repeated rejections. They tend to marry domineering mates who will add to their insecurities and feelings of hopelessness. Their apparent refusal to get up, set goals, and move on in life so disturbs their partner that this aggressive person will cry out "there's no hope for you!" This comment, a repeat of what they heard as a child, triggers feelings of rejection and reaffirms their self-image of worthlessness. Reading motivational books and attending high-powered seminars only cripples the passive person who already feels insecure. He says to himself, "Everyone is a success but me."

One young man named Tim came to my husband for counsel. He had a high IQ but he had failed at everything he'd touched, including his marriage. He had taken self-improvement courses and read the right books, but he had no understanding of why he didn't succeed. When Fred probed into his childhood, he found a melancholy boy who had doted on his adorable sanguine mother and had lived off the excesses of her personality. When he was thirteen, his mother fell in love with a flashy actor and ran off with him. Tim was devastated that his idol who could do no wrong had done him wrong. Tim was left alone with a melancholy father who withdrew into his books to blot out his feelings of abandonment. Tim was visibly rejected by his mother and emotionally rejected by his father. Within a year of his mother's departure Tim came home from school to find his father dead on the living room couch. His despondency had led him to suicide. Tim felt it was somehow his fault. If only he had been a better son, if only he had realized how depressed his father was, if only he hadn't gone to school that day.

Tim's double rejection turned to confusion when his mother appeared at the funeral dressed in a dramatic black mourning ensemble and played the role of the grieving widow. The next day she moved back into the home and took up where she'd left off as if she'd never been gone. She became happily loving to Tim, never discussing the father's death and never mentioning what had happened to the dashing actor she had left with the year before. Tim grieved silently over his father and developed a love-hate relationship with his mother. He loved having a mother again, but he hated her for leaving him and then returning without any explanation. When he tried to discuss her past she would reply in a jovial tone, "Let bygones be bygones." He had no assurance that she wouldn't run off again, and he hardly dared to get close to her for fear he would be rejected again.

After college Tim married an outgoing girl whose personality was sanguine like his mother's and who had earned her way through college singing in a local nightclub. By the time their son was a year old, Tina was bored with being a wife and mother and she went back to singing on weekends. A new man in town bought the club and soon he and Tina were having an affair. When Tina packed her things and the baby and walked out, Tim was distraught. How could this happen to him again? What was wrong with him that everyone he loved left him? He'd lost his mother, his father, his wife, and his son. His whole life was one rejection after another.

Reaction to Abuse: Sanguine/Choleric

The sanguines and cholerics who are by nature outgoing and optimistic react to abuse and rejection by denying the problem exists, putting a cover over the pain, and moving on. Even though they feel guilty underneath for what was done to them, they decide to overcome their emotions, push them under, and set high goals. They often become workaholics because they think if they keep busy enough, they won't have time to think about themselves. This personality is most able to move into denial and tell themselves, "It's no big deal." They have little compassion for victims who can't pick themselves up and get on with it. Some of them, to cover their childhood rejection and loneliness, begin to fabricate a life as they wish it were.

Sue had wealthy parents who went on frequent trips, leaving her feeling lost and lonely. They brought home brochures and Sue remembers taking them to "Show and Tell" and creating stories about what she did in each place. As she got older she would make excuses for her parents' frequent absence, even though no one was asking her. When she came to me as an adult in constant depression, it was difficult to make her see that her parents' traveling communicated feelings of rejection to her as a child and to cover this up she had created a false life for herself. As a wife she had expected her husband to give his full attention to her, and when he took a position traveling she fell apart emotionally. We had to go back into her hidden feelings of rejection that she denied having and show her how these were affecting her adult emotions. She had to accept that her glamorous, exciting parents had caused her to feel like an orphan. And while they hadn't meant to, they had rejected her.

Do You Look the Other Way to Avoid Problems?

There are some parents who carry the expression "What you don't know won't hurt you" to extremes. Their children soon learn that if they lie convincingly, their parents won't check up on the truth. They have bigger and better things to do, and besides, all children fib a little now and then. This casual attitude provides a fertile ground for seeds of untruth to grow.

Dee came to me first as a teenager. The daughter of a pastor, she had the appearance of holiness about her. She knew all the right words to say, she could quote whole chunks of Scripture, and she could play hymns on the organ with a spiritual passion. When out of church and parental sight, however, Dee was drinking with her school buddies in order to prove she wasn't too religious. She had been so drunk in class one day that the counselor had called her mother. When questioned, Dee lied and said she'd been drowsy from some cold medication and the matter had been dropped.

"Didn't your mother check any further?" I asked.

""She never checks. She'd rather believe a lie than to be upset by the truth."

From childhood Dee had learned that her mother didn't want to hear bad news, so if there was any she and her sisters just lied about it. This way Mother was able to believe she had perfect, godly children who knew the rules and obeyed them. Little did she seem to know or care what they did behind her back. It became somewhat of a game of how wild the story could be before mother would even give it a faint question.

I pointed out the fallacy of this pattern and admonished Dee to set herself straight before she got in serious trouble. On my next visit to their church, I was pulled aside by Dee. She was now nineteen and was still living at home, but having a secret sexual relationship with one of the married elders in the church. The man's wife had complained to Dee's parents that she seemed to be chasing him and they had done the closest they'd ever come to a confrontation. They asked her one night as she was walking out the door if there was any truth to what the wife had said.

She had laughed, stated that she didn't even like the man, and had left to go meet him at a motel. As she told me this story she was almost proud of what she'd been able to pull off, but underneath was the hurt that her parents had never checked and had never brought up the subject again. "It would shatter their image of themselves if they had to face reality. Besides if they caught me, they'd have to do something about me. They'd just rather look the other way."

Are You Living in a State of Denial?

When we were children, we learned that certain mistakes brought punishment. Being both wise and immature, we tried to avoid the consequences of our actions by lying. "I didn't do it." If we had mature, balanced parents, they didn't let us get away with lying and punished us more for the lying than for the original act. As this pattern of discipline was repeated, we learned that lying only postponed a punishment that would be worse than telling the truth. With some degree of consistency, our parents were able to teach us that instant truth brought about long-range benefits.

As Fred and I were raising our own children, we let them know that we would not discipline them harshly if they immediately admitted their part in any problem. This freedom to be truthful often brought notes of confession before we'd even discovered the crime. One night Marita put a note on our dresser, "Gee Dad, I'm really sorry. Please pray with me that I will not be tempted to disobey the rules. Love, Marita"

I wanted to wake her up immediately and find out what she had done, but Fred made me wait until morning to hear the tale. She had driven her mini-bike up into the hills past the sign that said "No trespassing during fire season." No one had seen her and we might never have known, but she had learned it was better to tell the truth than take the chance on the consequences.

Later I overheard her telling her brother, "When are you going to learn, Fred, that the sooner you tell them the truth the less you'll be punished." Then she added soulfully, "I've learned this from bitter experience."

The important thing was that she had learned.

Since this simple law of truth or consequences is so basic in life and so essential for mature adult behavior, how did some of us escape learning it? Did we have parents who didn't know the truth themselves or who didn't want to know the truth?

Children brought up in a dysfunctional home where there was any type of denial or deception learned that the truth was not only unnecessary but often too much to bear. Joe grew up with an abusive alcoholic father and a pitiful mother who constantly denied that his father was drinking. She fed Joe lies, "Your father's not drunk, he's got an upset stomach." "He didn't mean to hit me; I just got in his way."

Joe heard her tell the boss, "He's got the flu" and the pastor "He's too busy to come tonight."

As a teenager Joe followed his mother's pattern of denial, and by the time he got married he hardly knew the truth from a lie. When he came to talk with me, his wife had caught him in several lies that he had no reason to tell. He had told her he was at one friend's house when he had been at another. He had implied that he received a promotion when he hadn't. He told her he had purchased a present and was having it wrapped when in reality he had totally forgotten to buy it.

No one of these was a terrible lie, but each was a lie nonetheless. By the time Joe talked to me, his wife felt she could never trust him again and he was devastated. He considered himself to be an honest man because he'd never stolen a penny. As we inched back over his childhood, he could see for the first time that he had no clear-cut view of truth. Life had been so full of denial, half-truths, and cover-ups that he had never learned what the truth was. He came up with whatever creative answer seemed to fit the situation.

Only because his wife was sick of his fabrication and told him so did he begin to look at his pattern of behavior as destructive.

My husband grew up in a home where there was no drinking, drugs, or any apparent dysfunction. The family was a model of proper behavior, and I thought I was marrying into the fairy-tale family. What I didn't realize was that their moralistic church denied the presence of any type of illness. This quirk had not been apparent to me as I'd never been sick in their home, but on our honeymoon as we boarded the Ocean Monarch to sail home from Bermuda, Fred got queasy before the ship had even left the dock. I asked the ship's doctor what to do and he gave me some pills for Fred. When I happily produced them, Fred refused to take them. "I'm just fine," he assured me. I was dumbfounded that this intelligent man I had married denied he had a problem and instead of taking the pills was reciting some statement that was telling him he was not sick. By the time the dockhands released the ship and it made its first lurch toward sea, Fred was deathly ill. By then it was too late for any help and he lay for three days crying out, "I wish I were dead."

Not only was I upset over his refusal to take the medication that would have helped him, but I was doubly distressed when I mentioned his days of seasickness to the family and he glared at me and said, "It was really nothing."

I learned to cover up any illness I had short of imminent death, but I soon found that his denial spread beyond sickness. When his business was losing money, he wouldn't act upon the problems. Instead he denied there were any until it was too late to correct them.

As I look back on it, many of our business and marriage problems were based on his family's pattern of denying anything negative and keeping a purely utopian attitude toward life. Positive thinking is a plus, but denial is a form of dishonesty that is difficult to deal with because it sounds so good.

It was years before honest Fred could see his denial for what it really was: a refusal to face the truth and act upon it.

Is Your Life an Act?

As I finished giving my life story at a church service in Auckland, New Zealand, a lady said to me, "I can't believe how honest you are. We aren't used to that here. We always cover up how we really feel."

A man in California stated, "You and Fred are the first honest Christian speakers we've ever heard."

A lady in Texas approached me in tears, "I cried through much of your message. It wasn't that it was sad, but that it made me feel some emotion that I'd kept stuffed inside for years."

These comments represent hundreds of people who have shared with us that they are surprised and often touched by our willingness to be honest and transparent before others. It's a sad commentary on current relationships that transparency is rare and cover-up is the norm. It is constantly of amazement to us that honesty is so unusual as to deserve comment.

We seem to be acting in some gigantic play. We get up in the morning and tell ourselves who we are today. We put on our make-up and our plastic smile. We add a look of determination and power. We practice our lines on the way to work, and we try not to show displeasure when the rest of the cast feeds us the wrong lines. We push down any inappropriate feelings, keep our masks in place, dance to the beat of the daily drummer, and exit exhausted. No wonder! It's difficult and draining to play a role each day and not step out of character—and yet that's where we find so many people, working to be what they aren't, afraid to utter a real thought.

Like many of us, Liz set out to be real. With her Powerful Personality, Liz never liked phony people and always wanted to cut through the trivia and get down to the bottom line. Liz was always a super achiever, and it was her dream to marry the young man she loved. He was preparing to be a pastor, and she dreamed of helping him minister to those in need. She prepared her dream by developing her talents and studying everything she could find to help her become the perfect pastor's wife.

Liz wrote, "I had worked very hard. I had attended classes to know how to entertain, lead Bible studies, and with my piano and organ talents, I thought I was qualified to be a wife to a pastor of a church. I had a genuine love for people and tried to be the perfect pastor's wife. I purchased many books and I read one, *How to Be a Preacher's Wife and Like It*, until it was nearly memorized. I knew in most circumstances what page had the answer I needed. I began to 'act' the role of the preacher's wife. I tried hard."

Although Liz never intended to be a phony since she had such disdain for pretentious people, she found herself playing an unreal part. As time went on, she developed severe migraine headaches and lost touch with who she really was. Her sparkling personality began to vanish. She states, "No one had done this to me. We had wonderful people in our congregations. My pastor-husband was loving and supportive. He never expected service in our church from me. I had put the pressure on myself by trying to be the 'perfect' pastor's wife. My husband was an effective pastor. For fourteen years, emotionally I slid downhill. I lost touch with myself. At church I was kind and at home I was tense, angry, and unhappy. I became very sick. I began to act strangely. I cried all night and cut paper into tiny squares. I wanted to throw a large rock through the sliding glass door of our bedroom. Our wonderful teenage son was the only reason I didn't take all of my bottle of sleeping pills. After all, my husband would be so much better off without me. Could I disappear to a foreign country?"

These thoughts felt so good to Liz because she was desperate. On Sundays she gathered enough strength to go to church, smile, and try to be the perfect pastor's wife. She continued to hide her problems, but her dream had ended, and her role as the perfect pastor's wife had closed.

Liz had to admit she was living a lie. She was trying to be the spiritual giant but she was a suicidal failure in her own eyes. She admitted she needed help.

On a bright sunny California afternoon, she found herself in her car driving across the city. Her heart was pounding and tears were slipping from the corners of her eyes. "A pastor's wife shouldn't need help," she thought. Liz wondered what a psychiatrist's office was really like, and as she stepped slowly through the front door she expected to see strange people doing some weird things. Two or three people were sitting and reading magazines. They looked very calm. Liz gave her name to the nurse at the desk and joined those leafing through the magazines. Just turning the pages seemed to relieve some of her tension, but perfect pastor's wife Liz couldn't believe she was actually about to pour her troubles out to an unknown psychiatrist.

A lady in white said, "Next, please," and Liz walked in to see the psychiatrist for the first time. "He did not shake my hand, but he made me feel comfortable. Over the next months with private therapy, God began the emotional healing process. The doctor helped me uncover the reasons for my illness and showed me that I had been living a lie. I had programmed myself for perfection and couldn't meet my own standards." Powerful Personalities don't like to play games they can't win, and that's what Liz had been trying to do. She went back to her real personality and threw away her melancholy mask of perfection. "The doctor helped me get in touch with myself and again become a happy and genuine person. I asked my family to forgive me for my abuse to them. Today I'm the wife of the same husband. God has helped me repair my dream. I spend much of my time teaching pastor's wives the value of being yourself and not a phony. Like the Velveteen Rabbit, I have become real."

Are You Willing to Face the Truth?

Even those of us who are genuine and are living in our personality strengths don't like to face the truth of an unpleasant situation.

When Jane Fonda's daughter was arrested on charges of loitering for the purpose of purchasing drugs, disorderly conduct, and obstructing governmental administration, Jane commented, "They should have arrested me, too—for failure to be a good mother. I've been so self-centered that when Vanessa needed a mother, no one was home."

Is there hope when our families fall apart? Can the dreams be repaired? First, we must acknowledge our involvement in the problem and face the truth. Jane stated, "By destroying our family unit, I drove my daughter to seek the same sense of belonging with a pack of drug-infested sleazeballs!"

Second, we must also recognize our limitations in repairing someone else's dream, even if we have caused the original damage. Jane's daughter Vanessa has to determine how she will grow through this incident and what difference it will make in her life. Vanessa said, "I wasn't trying to get attention when this incident happened, but maybe it will bring Mom and me closer together for the first time in our lives."

How much better it would have been if Jane could have looked at what she was doing to her family before it was too late to fix it. Few of us are in Jane's star position, but many of us are so busy in our own pursuits, positive as they may be, that we have too little time to observe what is really going on with our children.

Judy and Jim never expected to have any serious problems with their children. Jim is a pastor and they have lived a positive and moral life. Obviously, church activities have usurped much of their energies and church "emergencies" have often pulled them from family time.

Judy is not a suspicious person and had no serious doubts about her children until some friends stopped by and told Judy they had just put their son in a drug treatment center. "Suddenly bells went off inside me," Judy writes. "Instantly I wondered if what we were seeing in our son's life was also drug related, even though we had checked his room, vehicle, locker at school, and had taken him to a counselor. We found nothing except we saw such drastic changes in him which told us there had to be something going on. Jimmy had changed almost overnight from a fun-loving young man to a somber, moody, angry young man. From being an excellent student, Jimmy was skipping school and his grades had dropped to an all time low. No longer did we see his happy disposition at home."

Judy and Jim decided they had to face the awful truth, so they waited until the weekend was over, picked Jimmy up at work, and took him straight to the hospital for a urinalysis. They knew the answer before they even got there because Jimmy was furious when he found where they were taking him. The tests revealed that Jimmy was heavily involved in cocaine and speed.

"Our dreams for Jimmy seemed to die, and in their place came panic, fearing for his very life and future." Judy writes, "We placed him in drug treatment and the days ahead were filled with anguish, fear, and compassion for our child. We were pastors and we not only had to work to see that Jimmy had a chance to get well, but we had to meet with our board of elders, sharing with them the truth we were facing, and asking them if they felt we should resign. Not only did they not want us to resign, but with gentle arms of compassion, the Lord used them to start repairing the dream for our son's life. They loved us through the trauma to the triumph."

Judy and her husband tried all the positive approaches, and soon Jimmy's problems obsessed their time and sapped their strength. At one point it came clear to Judy that Jimmy had become the lord of her life. Every waking hour was spent trying to make Jimmy better so they could get to the end of this nightmare and be happy once again. Once Judy saw that her life was at a standstill because of Jimmy's mistakes, she realized how impossible it was for one person to remake another's life. She asked the Lord for His plan and not for hers.

"You see," Judy said, "There is a difference in doing a work for God and doing God's work."

The family stopped their compulsive behavior to get Jimmy back to normal, read James Dobson's *Love Must Be Tough*, and began to live by these principles of putting the responsibility for recovery where it belonged—on Jimmy. It was difficult to pull back, but it was necessary for Jimmy's rebuilding.

Judy concludes: "When that happened, Jimmy began walking out of the shadows of drugs back into our hearts and lives. And now we are rebuilding the dream in our family, taking time to really hear each other and realizing that though painful, we have come through. We not only want to be a healthy Christian family ourselves, but reach out in encouragement to other parents who face trauma in their family."

To repair broken family dreams, we must face the problem and move to action.

Can You Start All Over Again?

Some of us begin our careers straight out of school and continue along the same career until retirement. Others of us run into an obstacle that causes us to rethink our dream. As I grew up I wanted to be a teacher. I prepared for my dream and wore it well for four years before marriage. Then my focus changed and I desired to be a wife, mother, socialite, club president, and civic leader. When I lost my two sons, nothing seemed to matter anymore. I had it all and yet I had nothing. My dreams had died.

In my search for meaning, I studied Scripture and began research on the four personalities. Soon people asked me to share the personalities, and what I had started as a parlor game became a speaking ministry. People asked if I had any books on the subject and I dared to dream that I could become a writer. A miracle took place when a publisher heard me speak and offered me a contract for two books before I had written a paragraph. I encourage those of you who may think it's too late to start a new career. I didn't write my first book until I was almost fifty, and this is my eighteenth!

Marilyn Heavilin went back to college when she was forty, got her degree, and thought she was set for life as a high school counselor and English teacher. She was so excited when her son Nathan came to the same school because they could ride together and enjoy quick fun moments between classes. In his junior year on the way home from playing basketball, Nathan's car was struck by a drunk driver and he was killed. As Marilyn tried to pick herself up from this tragedy, she continued to work at the school, but everywhere she turned she saw the memories of Nathan. What could she do? Did she have to leave her job? Was she supposed to waste her training?

At that point in Marilyn's life, I challenged her to come to our CLASS seminar for speakers and learn how to share her touching story of hope and recovery with other people in need of encouragement.

Marilyn dared to dream that she could shift her career and begin to minister to others. She prepared by putting her message on paper and delivering her story whenever someone needed a speaker. She had her "colors" done, learned to dress stylishly, and even shed thirty-five pounds to help her feel better about herself.

After a year of taking every opportunity that was given her to speak, Marilyn was relieved to resign her position at the school and pursue her dream of becoming a professional speaker. In six years, Marilyn did become a nationally known speaker and author of four books. She has spoken for MADD and at the national convention of The Compassionate Friends. Marilyn also utilizes her training as an English teacher as the CLASS editorial director, plus she types and edits most of my manuscripts. Marilyn did not let her circumstances confine her. She built new dreams from fragments of the old dreams and has now put her experiences in a new book, *When Your Dreams Die*.

Are you being controlled by your circumstances? Did your dream become damaged along the way and now you're afraid to try to repair it? Take a chance and ask God to show you one step you could take even today to start to repair your damaged dream.

Many of us, as Marilyn did, prepare for specific vocations. We study hard. We compete for the best positions in our field. But then when we attain our goals, we may feel like we're in a rut. Perhaps we spend hours on the freeway when we should be selling a product or could be enjoying extra time with our families.

Perhaps you weren't able to achieve your desired goal. You were detained along the way in a job that is not satisfying. Do you have to stay in this situation for the rest of your life? Can you repair your dream?

Newsweek magazine reported, "Millions of workers want out of their offices. They hate taking the highways and the subways to get there and dislike the interruptions and wasted time once they arrive. Many fear their demanding jobs will make them strangers to their kids."

According to the article, over fourteen million people have decided to change their unpleasant working situations and have found alternate workplaces, including their homes, motorhomes, and cars, which are fitted with all sorts of technological equipment. These people have not let their circumstances confine them—and you don't need to, either.

Several years ago, at the age of thirty-nine, Bob needed to make a career change. He had worked for a utility company for eleven years, for a construction firm for five years, and had been involved with a sports ministry that had not made it off the ground financially.

Bob prayed for direction and made a list of career options, sending out numerous resumés without much response. Bob had talked about his desire to be a policeman after high school and college, and it became clear that the Lord closed other doors and left the sheriff's department open.

He began the lengthy process of background checks, testing, and fingerprinting, and almost one year later Bob was hired on the contingency that he'd pass the Sheriff's Academy. Once his friends heard of his new dream they began making judgments. Many people thought they had been given the *gift of discouragement*. They told Bob he was crazy, ignorant, too nice to be a cop, wasting precious time, and doomed to failure. Few came with words of *encouragement* and acts of friendship. The most important asset was the unqualified support of his wife and daughters.

Together they learned to spit-polish boots and shine belt buckles until their reflection nearly shone in them. Each day they counted out seventy-five sit-ups, sixty mountain climbers, fifty push-ups, and twenty pull-ups, each in two-minute periods, until they were all exhausted. Hours were spent at the high school track timing the mile and a half, 220-yard dashes, and windsprints. For a thirty-nine-year-old to compete with twenty-one to twenty-four-year-olds was strenuous. In the process, Bob lost twenty-five pounds and many inches, looked great, and felt good about himself. His wife Pam made audio tapes of over one thousand spelling words to speed his learning on the four-hour roundtrip to the academy every day. Flash cards with radio calls, vehicle codes, and California penal codes were given as quizzes each night.

The whole family learned together the difference between a burglary and robbery, legal and illegal searches, and how to check a female for weapons without violating her person! They learned how to defuse arguments and violent situations and how to defend with a baton or wrestling move.

No evening was complete without Pam doing three loads of laundry; white underclothes, jogging suits, gym clothes, towel, and the uniform, which had to be starched lightly and ironed to a military press.

Weekends were not exempt either. Pam quizzed Bob for tests and spent time at the firing range where she learned the power of a .38 Special police revolver. By evening each day, Bob was ready to calm nerves disquieted from a sergeant's commands and from the pressure to perform above average. The emotions and memories of the day's homicide photos and audio tapes of actual murders haunted his mind. Bob's confrontation with the stark reality of life caused him to pray as he never had before for God's protection and strength.

Pam recalls, "All of us went through the academy that summer; we pulled together on the rope of encouragement. God was the central cord of the rope, our family and friends were entwined around Him, and we all were strengthened by the experience. I must say there were times when there were some frayed ends of frustration, fear, and fatigue; there were times when we thought we were losing our grip, times when we felt at the end of our rope. But God always gave us a little more slack or a knot to hold on to for a little while longer. There were friends who seemed to come at just the right time to strengthen us in our determination. They became knots of hope in the rope of encouragement. When situations and struggles seemed never-ending, our good friends were optimistic and hopeful. When we were tired and doubtful, they reminded us to trust a God bigger than a drill instructor or commanding officer."

Bob did graduate from the academy and he turned forty that same week! Bob's graduation was the realization of a dream, a shared victory of a repaired dream.

Ex-president Jimmy Carter dared to dream he could achieve the top honor in the United States. He prepared as governor of Georgia and studied politics and history so that he could be a perfect president; however, world events turned against him and the Iran hostage crisis defeated him. Carter had to repair his dream and he did. He dedicated his time to helping the poor through Habitat for Humanity building low-cost housing, he and Rosalyn teach Sunday School, and they have written six books since 1981.

Rosalyn wrote, "If we have not achieved our early dreams, we must either find new ones or see what we can salvage from the old. If we have accomplished what we set out to do in our youth, then we need not weep like Alexander the Great that we have no more worlds to conquer. There is clearly much left to be done, and whatever else we are going to do, we had better get on with it."

Is Your Spiritual Life in Balance?

So far we have asked questions to encourage you to evaluate your life and see if you need to repair your dreams. These questions were intended to bring you to a realistic appraisal of your present situation and to motivate you to look at your past for possible clues to any negative behavior patterns in your life.

Many positive changes can take place when any one of us is willing to face the truth, but what if you can't put your finger on your problem? What if you've tried to improve and it hasn't worked?

Perhaps it is time for you to see if your spiritual life is in balance. Whether we believe in God or attend church, we have to realize that we are born with a spiritual nature. We usually take care of our bodies and our minds, but many of us ignore our spirit, our need for something beyond ourselves. We aren't aware that we have a desire to worship and so we tend to revere things such as money, cars, houses, clothes, jewelry, people, positions, degrees, and even success itself.

God seems so far away, and like the people of Israel we want to worship something we can see and touch and hear.

The *Atlantic Monthly* had a cover article entitled, "Can We Be Good without God?" The summation of it was that if we do not have a personal belief in God, we have no reason to be honest. If there are no eternal judgments, then why not take what you can get and not worry about the consequences?

Many people live self-centered lives with no spiritual relationship. Some win and some lose. Those who are successful may go through their whole human existence without coming face to face with God, but those of us who need to repair our dream may seek some divine guidance.

How do you find it? Do you have to go to church? Do you have to become sad and saintly? Do you have to be a religious fanatic and run around saying, "Praise the Lord"?

As we deal with people who have problems beyond their ability to repair, we always ask if they have ever made a simple commitment to the Lord. Some respond, "Well, I try to be good," or "I live by the Golden Rule,' but we want to know if you have ever paused in your life and asked the Lord Jesus to come into your heart and change you. If not, it doesn't cost a thing to make that request and you then can know—not guess or hope—but *know* that the power of the Lord lives in you and that you can call upon this strength in time of need.

For those of us who are the Popular Personalities, we may question, "If I ask the Lord into my life, will He send some old man in a white robe like Moses to tell me, 'Thou shalt not have any fun any more'?"

The Perfect Personalities want to analyze, study, and meditate before making a life-changing decision, and the Peacefuls wonder, "Will being religious take a lot of work?" Because of their inborn appetite for control, the Powerful Personality is difficult to reach on a spiritual level because giving one's heart to the Lord means giving up control of one's life to an intangible force that can't be seen, touched, or heard. Often this Powerful Personality has to come to the end of his ability to run his life before he is open to a power beyond himself. When some part of his dream needs to be repaired, he suddenly seeks some supernatural touch and can overnight become a Christian leader.

I look back on my life and realize Fred and I—two Powerful Personalities—were content to be nice church goers until we went through the tragedy of losing our two sons. We and the doctors did all that we could to save our boys and only when we had exhausted all possibilities did we open our hearts and minds to the control of the Lord Jesus. I was so unsure of any real help from the Lord that I remember ending my commitment prayer with "...and if you can do anything with me Lord, good luck." Hardly a spiritual phrase, but a representation of how I felt at the time.

Within a few months of my dedication Fred got to the end of his ability to control. He realized that he had been successful in business and in civic leadership but he saw himself as a failure in the home. When this concept came to his mind, he was willing to give up control and hope the Lord could achieve what he couldn't.

Although our sons both died and there were no miraculous resurrections, the tension, anger, and grief began to subside. As the Lord repaired our dream that had been twice shattered, we started sharing our life story with others and within two years we were on full time staff of Campus Crusade for Christ International.

We are typical representatives of the Power Personalities, who don't go seeking a spiritual relationship with the Lord until all else fails and who then jump in whole heartedly and become Christian leaders.

Former Motown record producer and song writer Frank Wilson shares how he, at the crest of his career faced something over which he had no control. In 1974, having sold over thirty-five million records, he found himself in a nasty custody struggle over his young son Franko. He claims he had tried everything on the boy's mother, "psychology, money, my influence with her friends, and nothing worked."8 Desperate for any kind of a solution after a confrontation with the Los Angeles police and the prospects of a lengthy court battle, Frank gave up control of his life. The Lord showed him how to handle the situation and Frank recalls, "Having looked at my life, then, at that point in time, I realized I had been deceiving myself, and there was little I was actually controlling. He offered to take care of the situation for me.

"It was the most difficult thing I'd ever done—to leave the situation in the hands of God, but He came in and by His power resolved it. I thought if God can do what I had tried to do for five years without success, then what would the rest of my life be like if I had the guts to turn it over to Him?"[112]

Frank did "turn it over to Him." He took a year off from Motown, grounded himself in his new faith and returned to share his repaired dream with others in the record business including Stevie Wonder, Smokey Robinson and Marilyn McCoo who all gave their hearts to the Lord because of his witness.

Frank "had the guts" as a Power Personality to give over the control of his life to the Lord and today he and his wife Bunny travel internationally helping third world leaders to put their ability to control in the right hands.

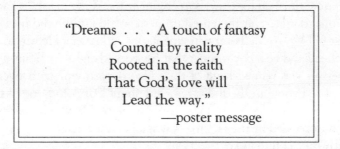

"Dreams . . . A touch of fantasy
Counted by reality
Rooted in the faith
That God's love will
Lead the way."
—poster message

I first met Daryl Lloyd as the Operational Services Director for Advanc Life Foods in Australia when I arrived to speak at their annual convention. I was impressed by his engaging sanguine personality, bright sparkling eyes, and ebullient sense of confidence. He was sharply dressed and carried his cellular phone to lunch.

Daryl was wearing his dream with style. He coordinated the convention complete with multi-media effects, and encouraged every presenter personally. Later we met his model-perfect wife, owner of a high class beauty salon, and we found Trish to have all the strengths of the melancholy. They understood their personalities and had learned to accept each other without trying to make each other over.

As we two couples became acquainted and we continued to return to Australia to speak for the conventions, Daryl shared his life story with us.

Daryl was the result of a chance meeting of an Australian girl and an American G. I. on leave during World War II. He was adopted by a farming couple who raised him with much affection but little money. When his birth mother found she couldn't ever have any more children, she decided to try to get him back. She challenged his adoptive parents in a court struggle that took three years and even threatened to kidnap him. She sent him birthday cards and notes to torment the family, but his mother intercepted them for stability's sake and on his twenty-first birthday she told him about the problems and threats and gave him a brown paper bag full of the birthday cards. At that point Daryl made a choice not to read the messages and to thank his adoptive mother for protecting him.

During his high school years Daryl had become the ringleader of the rebellious teens and thought school was a place for fun not for learning. At fourteen he was expelled and found himself with no education, training or skills and with very unhappy parents.

Daryl dared to dream that he could work in television and earn enough money that he could keep himself and his parents from poverty. He got a job with Telecom at fifteen and decided to go back to school at night. He could now see a purpose in studying because he had a goal in mind and at eighteen he finished his courses in engineering. With his ability and drive he set out to take over the entertainment world and he did find employment at GTV 9 in Melbourne in videotape production. He was so eager to surge ahead and be a boy wonder that he worked eighteen hours a day and at nineteen was named head of the video department with twenty staff under him. People in the industry heard about Daryl and one of those he met was Bruce Gyngell, president of 9 Network. Daryl admired this man and was impressed by the fact that Gyngell could walk into any group and instantly take command of the room.

By the time Daryl was twenty he was so stressed out by overwork that he had a physical and emotional collapse. As he was recovering he received a phone call from Bruce Gyngell who was then at 7 Network. He offered him a three year contract as program manager and Daryl, then twenty-one, began to repair his dream. Gyngell's custom was to choose one young man in each city where he had business to be his observer for a year. He chose Daryl, who looks back now with wonder at the opportunity he had. Each time Gyngell was in town Daryl met him at the airport, stayed at his side, drove him around, and learned by observation. Daryl told me, "I was what was called the 'Briefcase Carrier.'"

This experience gave Daryl a personal education he couldn't have received in school from a successful man who was willing to be a mentor for someone with potential.

At twenty-five Daryl went into the advertising business with a man he knew little about. Daryl was to sell accounts while his partner took care of the office. This appeared to be a positive blending and Daryl brought in so much business there was exceptional growth. His reward was a lavish townhouse, two Mercedes and a reputation that enabled him to walk into any restaurant and be greeted and seated immediately.

Daryl had dared to dream that he might be a success, he had prepared the dream with such fervor his life had fallen apart and at twenty he'd started all over again repairing his dream. By thirty he had achieved everything he'd ever wanted. He'd never have to live in poverty again.

What Daryl didn't know as he was out building business was that his partner was not handling the money correctly and suddenly without warning to Daryl, the creditors swooped into the business and shut it down. Daryl was pursued personally and he lost everything he had gained.

"I'd done nothing wrong," Daryl told me, "but in an instant it was over. I wad thirty-one years old and through no fault of my own my dream was over."

Daryl suffered what many of us have been through. Some of the people who loved you when you were on top hardly speak to you anymore. Some that were beneath you in rank suddenly rise above you. People you've helped don't seem to remember your favors. Daryl was lost and didn't know where to turn.

"Out of all the people I knew only one called me to express sympathy," Daryl told me. "Mrs. Crosson, the mother of a former employee, offered her concern and said, 'Maybe you'll learn to rely upon the Lord instead of on youself.'"

Daryl didn't know what she meant, but since he was out of work he began to search for answers. "I had to face the reality that what I'd been doing for thirty-one years had amounted to zero." Daryl didn't want to admit defeat, but Mrs. Crosson's challenge stayed with him. For six months he read, analyzed and studied everything about success including the Bible. As he worked through it he determined to prove the Bible wrong, but as so many others before him, he was finally convicted that there was some strange power in the scriptures. "One day I realized" Daryl told me wide-eyed, "that either Jesus Christ is who he says he is or he's a poached egg."

As he was trying to get a handle on his new spiritual perspective, Daryl was embarrassed to let his girlfriend Trish see how broke he was and how depressed he'd become. He'd always been in charge of life and been happy. How could she respect him now? One day Trish said, "I'm glad you've lost all your money. You didn't need it and now you'll have more time for me." Daryl was stunned. "I couldn't believe anyone could love me when I had nothing to give. "Her ability to love me for myself and not for my money gave me the boost I needed to get moving again."

Daryl got a job selling kitchen equipment and he was instantly successful. Daryl could sell anything! One day he got a phone call from Ivan Bennett in London, "I've observed your ability and I'd like to offer you a position with my company Infrapulse Limited. You would be Market and Export Manager for all of Australia and the Southern Pacific Rim."

Daryl told me, "It took me thirty-one years to lose it and three years to get it all back." Daryl and Trish got married and he said, "I figured that any woman who could love me when I had nothing would stick with me for life." And she has. Daryl, after years of traveling, has settled into his executive position with Advanced Life Foods, Trish has her beauty salon, and they have together developed a computer program for hairdressers which is being marketed world wide.

When I asked Daryl for his advice to others trying to make it in the business world, he gave me three points.

1. *Your spiritual life must be in order.* "A lot of people think a man is weak if he's a Christian, but it takes a strong person to give up his control to the Lord. Don't tell people that when you accept the Lord in your life it's some magic trick and you don't have to work anymore. You have to do your part, but at least you know the source of your power and where to turn for direction."

2. *There must be harmony in your home.* "There's no way you can live with problems at home and be a success at your job. They either work for or against each other."

3. *You must be committed to your job and your family.* "Too many of us want to do our own thing without regard for those around us. This only leads to frustration. We need to be faithful to our calling and accountable for our actions."

Daryl Lloyd has repaired his dream and he now shares openly in public what struggles he's been through and what answers he has found.

Can the Lord Sustain You in Times of Trouble?

As Daryl Lloyd said, "Don't expect the Lord to do your work for you, but do know that he can lift you above your problems and give you the ability to weather the crisis." In I Corinthians 10:13 it says "There hath no temptation taken you but such as is common to man; but God is faithful, who will not suffer you to be tempted above that ye are able; but will with the temptation also make a way to escape, that ye may be able to bear it."

When I was losing my two sons, I thought I was the only mother to have gone through such a tragedy but I learned that others had similar problems. I also learned through this verse that God wouldn't necessarily change my circumstances but he would give me a way of escape.

One of the most amazing stories of endurance in extreme situations is that of Janet. I first met her at CLASS when my daughter Marita called me into her room during the small group sessions. "You've got to hear this story," she said. The speaker was an attractive Dallas matron with an obvious sense of humor, but her story was not humorous.

Janet's husband had been a successful businessman who had died several years before and she had begun working with her family in a thriving brokerage business. She enjoyed her work and did her job well, and she was stunned when she was suddenly arrested for improperly handling securities. She had no idea that anything was wrong, but immediately her world changed. She was forced to defend herself in a well-publicized trial and she appeared on the stand as an accused criminal. Her sons were also arrested and her life became a nightmare.

"I couldn't believe I was on trial. I'd always been an honest pillar of the community. How did I get into this?"

Because of Janet's reputation she knew the charges would be dropped but they were not and she was declared guilty. Worse than the verdict was the sentence: Two years in a women's maximum security prison in California. As Janet told her story we listened with tears running down our faces.

Most of us had never thought of a nice normal lady being sent to prison and we were aghast as she told us how she prayed each day that she would not be beaten up or killed.

On her second Christmas in prison Janet wrote a letter to her friends and family giving a glimpse of her grief and a testimony to God's sustaining power.

> "It's nearly Christmas and 2,300 of us women will be huddled in here together. Christmas will be here, and tears will be flowing for children out there with no mama at home, and Dear God—it's Christmas!
>
> "Husbands are at home and no mother in the group at the Christmas tree, and often here tears are choked back. Instead, the grief comes out in pushing and shoving and fists flying and curses screamed out. Grief and frustration is so painful at this time of year. It's like a time-bomb.
>
> "Through the grapevine we hear that the riot squads in their camouflage clothes are getting practiced up for possible big time trouble on this prison ground this holiday season as this heavy grief settles over the women on this crowded prison yard, but a few of us know the true joy of Christmas—and we're practicing too! Singing louder the melody of hope and peace and loveliness of our blessed Savior Jesus' birth. So, it's a contest here—increasingly tense—at this holiday season. I know because this is not my first Christmas behind the barbed wire fences with those menacing old gun towers and guards' eyes on us. But I proclaim that Christ's love song will win out and drown out again the cries of anguish and hatred from this terribly over-crowded prison, filled with lonely, aching women.

"I send out my wishes of Christmas peace and good will to all of you that I love. It's all OK—God is well able to keep us all as we "come to adore Him."

As her friends on the outside decorated their beautiful homes for the holidays a fellow prisoner gave Janet a tiny styrofoam coffee cup from the prison commissary which had been turned upside down to make her tiny version of a Christmas tree. She decorated it with dots of lipstick and put an earring on top for the star. Janet was a witness to the other women as she gathered them around her make-shift tree to sing Christmas carols.

Janet has that tree on her mantle each Christmas as a reminder to the truth that God can sustain us in times of trouble. She also treasures a card from a seven year old girl included in a care package from the Crystal Cathedral and good wishes written on scraps of paper and given to her in gratitude as fellow prisoners passed her in the hall.

Janet had a choice. Now that she is released, she could be bitter, but instead she has chosen to appreciate everything about life: hearing a dog bark or a bird sing; watching a mother nurse a baby; enjoying a sunset; breathing in the beauty all around her. Janet is currently going into prisons to minister to inmates and, because of her experience, she is having an impact on the lives of many other former and current inmates. Janet shares her story with everyone who will listen and she shares the story of Christ— the Jesus who can even walk through your prison and repair your dreams.

Can You Forgive Unforgivable People?

When Fred and I talk with discouraged people who have been rejected or abused, they often ask, "Do I have to forgive him?" Forgiveness is not the first step of restoration, but it is ultimately necessary for a complete healing from victimization. If we say we forgive before we're ready to mean it, the lip service is a fraud, but if we pray daily for God to make us willing to forgive the perpetrator we will know when the time is right.

One Sunday morning as I sat in the front row of a business convention waiting to be called on to speak, the owner of the company walked to the platform to deliver what turned out to be an impromptu message of his own. Holding his seven year old son in his arms, Craig Holiday delivered an opening line I'll never forget.

"When I was the age of my little son, my father walked out the door never to return again." With a catch in his voice he continued, "I hated my father. I wondered why he'd left me. When other boys brought their dads to Boy Scouts I went alone. Sometimes I made up stories about how busy my father was and why he couldn't attend, but inside I was alone and ashamed."

With his son resting comfortably on his hip, Craig gave a stirring summary of his life. Craig had achieved some degree of success until the real estate market in Southern California took a plunge. Caught in a financial crunch Craig saw the end of his dream before him. He and Carol lost faith in each other and needed help. At that point, a friend took Craig to a network marketing meeting and in desperation he signed up. Craig dared to dream again. His business grew quickly and soon Craig was on top again. He expected to be happy. He had the house and the cars and his precious son, Taylor. Each time he looked at Taylor he thought of his father and the hostility rose up inside him. "Anger was eating me up and I couldn't seem to get away from it." Craig knew that he should forgive his father, but the man didn't deserve to be forgiven. One day when Taylor was close to seven Craig looked at him and began to sob. "That's how old I was when he left me." Desperate for relief from this crippling memory, Craig was finally ready to forgive. He called to the Lord and said "I'm willing. Take this burden from me."

In the following months as Craig felt release from his anger, he decided to make contact with his father. For the first time Craig wanted to see him. They had a reunion and his father met his grandson for the first time.

As we in the audience relaxed from the tension of this emotional tale, Craig stunned us all as he added, "And my father is here today. Come up and share with us, will you Dad." We all gasped as a pleasant looking man got up from the front row near me and walked toward the stage. We had all pictured Craig's dad as an evil, uncaring person, but as he went up the steps, little Taylor jumped down and ran toward his grandpa with arms outstretched. As they hugged and cried, Craig threw his arms around them both and all three of them sobbed softly together.

We were all in a state of shock and many in the audience were crying over their own broken relationships. A few began to applaud and soon we were all standing, clapping, and cheering at the power of forgiveness and the proof of restoration. As we settled back in our seats drained of any emotional strength we once had, Mr. Holiday moved to the mike and began to speak.

"It's my fault. I got married too young and in my early twenties I found myself with three children and not enough money. I was immature and I couldn't handle the responsibility. One day it all overwhelmed me and I walked out on it. I knew it was wrong and once I'd done it, I was always too ashamed to go back."

Suddenly our sympathies went to this nice man who wasn't wicked and who had lived a lonely life not knowing how to repair his dream. Craig hadn't known either, but when he was willing to release his anger and forgive his father, he had taken the first giant step toward restoration.

At this point with the audience in both tears and cheers, Craig called me forth to give the Sunday morning message that he in fact had already presented. All that was left for me to do was review the drama we had witnessed and give the conventioneers time to cool down before heading home.

Craig had dared to dream as a child that even without a father he could become a success. He had prepared for his future and had achieved a level of satisfaction until his finances failed and he needed to repair his dream. He went into a new business, put his marriage back together, and forgave his father. Even though his father never came back to raise Craig, he is now allowed to enjoy his grandson from seven years old on and pick up where he left off in a new generation.

> "Dreaming about a thing in order to do
> it properly is right; but dreaming about
> it when we should be doing it is wrong."
> —Oswald Chambers

Josie was a victim of sexual and physical abuse in her childhood and she suffered with the emotional pain for years. She remembers one specific night in her teen years.

> "My sister was sobbing in the bed next to me. With all my heart I wanted to comfort her, but I didn't know how. Life for us was constant violence in one form or another, but tonight it was a particularly brutal attack which left her bruised over her entire body. She was fourteen and I was sixteen at the time. I made a determination to try to do what would keep me from any further brutality by staying in the shadows . . . by retreating to my room . . . by being quiet . . . by being as perfect as I knew how. It didn't always work, but it helped me to survive until the day I could finally leave home.
>
> "As a teenager I went to church for the very first time other than very special occasions. For the first time in my entire life, I felt the touch of love and the voice of love through those pastors and people. I had never heard the words, "I love you" . . . but the

people in this small church loved me to Jesus. I don't remember one sermon, I don't remember one Bible Study, but I do remember their love that told me of a God who loved me and wanted to live in my heart. At that time, I received the Lord . . . and though I didn't understand it all, I knew that He was real.

"The Pastor tried to get me out of the home when he discovered the abuse, but my Dad wouldn't consider it, and abuse laws were seldom enforced at that time.

"There was one older man, Mr. Smith, a jolly old guy, who used to let a bunch of us kids pass through his yard on our way to school. Every day he would be waiting for us outside his house with a hug and a special treat of candy. We all loved Mr. Smith. But one day, I walked through his yard by myself. He asked me come in, but that day it wasn't for a treat, and I would be forever changed. I begged him to let me go and he finally did. I told no one except to let my friends know they should never go through his yard again. I buried it, trying not to think about it. It would be years later when I finally told my husband.

"The day finally came when I could leave home. By that time I had seen or experienced violence of all kinds. My grandfather had tried to rape my mother (his daughter-in-law). This same grandfather had threatened to murder my grandmother on two occasions when I was staying with them, once with a knife and once with a gun. My Dad tried to kill my brother with a hammer, and the only thing that saved my brother was running away from my Dad. I had been beaten, thrown into walls, clothes torn, but I could forget all of that. But what I couldn't forget and what I still try to defeat in my life were the words from him to me, 'You are such a slob.'

"When I left home to attend college, life suddenly opened up for me. I was free and I began enjoying living for the very first time. I was happy, cheerful, gregarious and determined to succeed in life to show my father I wasn't a slob. I met and fell in love with a wonderful young man and after dating a year, he asked me to marry him. The only problem was, he was going to be a pastor. I barely knew where Genesis was, did not know how to play the piano that well (which was considered a pre-requisite for a pastor's wife at that time), and certainly didn't know the first thing about being a pastor's wife. The fear of failure, even though I loved him more than I could even understand, led me to tell him "no". I mean it was one thing if you ruined a plumber or a lawyer, but I knew God would really get me if I ruined a minister. For the next five years, I tried to forget him, but never could. Thankfully, he couldn't stop loving me either. He would never know the reason I said no until long after we were married. Finally the Lord asked me one day if I would be willing to let Him make me adequate for the ministry and something changed. For the first time I dared to dream. In November 1967, I became a pastors' wife and I determined in my heart I would not fail. My husband fell in love with an outgoing, gregarious sanguine, but after the wedding, overnight I changed. Gone was the gregarious young woman he fell in love with and I was back in a self-imposed prison of pain of trying to become what I perceived a pastor's wife should be—serious, perfect, hard working, religious. For the next years fear of failure chased me. I was nice, but I was not happy."

One night all alone, I took inventory. I had a wonderful, husband who always treated me with respect and honor, two beautiful children, a church who loved us, but I hated myself and I hated life. That night I knew I had to forgive and release my dad, and I did. Then something very dramatic happened. I no longer hated him, but at the same time I didn't have any love for him either. It was as if it were a blank slate. The Lord told me, 'Now it's up to you to decide what you're going to put on the slate of your heart.' I chose that night to love my dad and to always plant seeds of love in his heart. That was eighteen years ago, and now one by one my entire family has come to know the Lord, except for one brother, one nephew and my dad.

"This year we asked my dad and stepmother to come stay with us for awhile. We as a family purposed in our hearts that this would make a difference for eternity in my dad. We took him back to his old hometown. As we went I asked him about his past, about his relationship with his father, mother, sister, aunts, uncles and grandparents. He had always been a very private person, never sharing feelings, but this day he started sharing and what unfolded was a life of pain and abuse that he had never shared. As he shared, I prayed that my love and the love of God would begin the healing process in his life. When it was time for him to go home, he hugged me and for the first time in my life that I can recall, he told me he was proud of me. We shared Jesus with him during that time, and he said he wasn't quite ready to make that step, but he was very close.

"No, I haven't seen all I want to see happen, but I believe the curse of abuse through the generations is broken in this family and that the dream of freedom will go on through our children.

Can You Repair Your Dream?

What makes the difference between the hurting person who falls apart and the one who keeps going and seems to rise above adversity? Over the years I have had many tough times myself and have counselled thousands of depressed women and some men. The National Institute of Mental Health gave out new figures in January 1991 that estimate 5.8 percent of adult Americans—about 10 million—suffer from depression annually. Cost to the nation: more than twenty-seven billion dollars in 1989 in lost productivity, seventeen billion just from lost workdays."[10] Why do some people get overwhelmed and some keep going?

1. *Look again to your personality differences.* In tough times the Popular Personality is by nature the most apt to bounce back. Being the eternal optimist and the one most easily able to deny reality, the sanguine can live through almost anything short of a disaster that is so big they can't step around it. Once they face reality and move to repair the dream, they can cheer up quickly and give hope to others.

The Powerful Personality will never get depressed as long as he is in control, but if he were to lose his job, find his wife having an affair, have a pregnant teen-ager and learn he has terminal cancer, he would be the fastest to drop into depression and the most likely to resort to suicide, the ultimate control. All cholerics are programmed to succeed and they can usually grab bad circumstances by the throat and move on.

The Perfect Personalities, because of their long term goal of getting themselves and their surroundings into perfect order, are more apt to be depressed than other personalities. They frequently have chronic feelings of discouragement because nothing is going quite right. Given a few days to think the troubles over, the melancholy can develop a sensible plan of repair.

The Peaceful Personality tends to stay out of trouble and tries to look the other way when problems arise. While their partner is screaming for attention, they may be watching a football game and trying not to get involved. Since their emotional pattern is low key and unexcitable it is often hard to discern if they are depressed. Their strong will of iron will usually hold them in balance until circumstances improve.

When I first met Kay Self in 1983 she was an unemployed psych nurse with emotional and marital problems. She came to CLASS and told me she wasn't sure why she was there because she'd been a failure at many things and would never be a speaker. As I conversed with her and tried to encourage her, she told me of her childhood background where she never heard an encouraging word. Recently she put this story in her own words.

On May 5, 1962, I was a highschool senior candidate for All-School queen. Every class had a representative for King and Queen. I have never forgotten that special honor and Saturday in my life. It has been a bittersweet memory because of the unacceptance of my family and the satisfaction of the visibility at school. I'll never forget that Saturday because I worked hard all day for my angry mother, hoping I could leave for the coronation on a half-way civil, pain-free note. Even being selected by my class was too much of a burden on my mother....she had no time or interest to buy me a dress. I borrowed a pink frock with matching, too-tight slippers from a neighbor girl which she'd worn as a bridesmaid at a wedding several years previously. As the evening approached, I could tell my mom was getting more agitated and I fretted myself terribly about leaving to go "pleasure myself" at her expense. I remember thinking, "I'm not going. She has depressed me to the point of giving up—forever—anything I'd ever want." And then, alas, at 10:00 p.m., the 'ol choleric, sanguine head raised up in me and I was off in a cloud of pink. It was six miles from our farm to my high school. By the time I got there, there was much concern about my welfare. Someone had called my parents after I left, wondering if I was in a ditch....I, being too proud to tell the truth, said I'd had a date (I'd never had a date in my life) and he didn't bring me home on time. Fifteen minutes after arrival, I was crowned Queen. I had one dance with the King to "Babes In Toyland" and speeded home. I had six miles to enjoy my status. There was not a positive word uttered in my behalf on the home front. My younger sibs, seven and ten, I'm sure were impressed but I was made to feel unworthy by my mom and older brother.

Isn't it amazing how damaging the negative words of a parent can be and how long these demeaning thoughts stay with us keeping us from achieving as an adult. In spite of her background, Kay did press on and get an education but even in her successes she could still hear her mother's voice telling her she was worthless. Kay was emotionally crippled when we met and she had given up on a career for which she was uniquely gifted because she felt so insecure. She had chosen psychiatric nursing because of her own "personal interest, experience, observation, and pain," and she had been a success, but by the time we talked in 1983 she writes, "I felt finished after ten years of work and I was sworn off forever."

Kay had dared to dream even when growing up in a negative discouraging family, she had prepared her dream by the correct schooling, and yet she had not worn the dream well. She had given up and it was time to repair the dream. I encouraged Kay to spend a day of counsel and prayer with Lana Bateman, one of our CLASS staff and founder of Philippian Ministries. During this time they went together to Kay's childhood and saw the constant pain and rejection she had been put through. As they prayed over each hurt, Kay began to see a light of hope and a feeling that God loved her as she was. She was not hopeless.

Kay began to study my personality books and found that she was not a melancholy perfectionist but a depressed sanguine trying her best to be perfect so her mother would praise her. As she read the chapter on masking in Your Personality Tree she was able to take off her mask of pain and become for the first time in her life the outgoing, optimistic person she was born to be. As Kay got a new feeling of self-worth and began to recognize her own strengths she went back to work in psych nursing where her new found joy brightened and lightened her patients.

Some people in repairing their dreams change careers in mid-life, but Kay continued in her original direction with renewed strength and resolve. Once she had dealt with her own inner hurts from childhood, she was able to give hope to others, a hope that she'd never had to offer before. When our book Freeing Your Mind From Memories That Bind came out, Kay devoured it, did the prescribed journalizing, and began passing it on to others.

Kay also returned to CLASS and saw the material presented from a new perspective. This time she was not dealing with the trauma and tears that had been present on our first meeting and she took seriously the instructions on how to speak. Each time I come to her area, Kay is in the audience supporting me. She brings her friends and those she is ministering to that they may also receive help. Kay wrote me, "I'm always aware that I came back to work *after* meeting you and Lana. When you talk of restoration, think of me, before and after you came my way. My return and how it happened is a joy. I am where I want and need to be. It is great. I have never taken my turn-around for granted. The Lord worked it all out for good and I praise and thank him and you!"

The next time Kay wrote me her words were like a school girl. "This news is hot off the press! Last week was National Nurse Association Week and I was selected as the winner of the "Excellence in Nursing Award." As the first psych nurse to ever receive this award I am still dazzled by the professional boost and the great recognition by my Lord for my faithful service."

Kay went on to tell how she was honored at a buffet reception where her picture was mounted on an easel under a spotlight. She was ushered through an archway of balloons as the orchestra played. "At any moment I expected Jack Bailey to come out and announce I'd won a Maytag washer-dryer set." What she did receive besides the award was VIP parking for a year, subscription to a professional magazine, membership to the nursing organization, dinner for two in any restaurant in town plus TV and newspaper interviews. By the time the presentation had been made Kay was ecstatic. They asked if she had anything she would like to say. How often these moments are filled with inane statements of thanks such as made by the winners for Best Film Editing at the Academy Awards. "I thank my mother for giving birth to me and my first grade teacher Miss McGuire. . . ." But Kay was ready!

When called up she stood with choleric confidence and sanguine charm and gave an organized message of appreciation. She reviewed what the people at the hospital had meant to her and concluded with "I thrive here and I am thankful for an atmosphere and attitude of positiveness that is so rewarding to me and for the protection of the security guards as I leave each night at 12:30. I am amazed to be the recipient of this award because this past year has probably been the most difficult on a personal level for me. Yet because of you I have maintained my dignity and self-worth. For all that this award means in my heart, I give it back to you. This is to you from me." Kay then held up the plaque and later told me, "I was an Olympic champion as I saluted my comrades! I felt as if the Lord had prepared a table before me and I remembered when I was that lonely winner at seventeen years old and no one seemed to care. Here I was with a genuine ovation and on that platform I traded in the pain of twenty-eight years. I repaired my dream."

2. Review your background problems. We have found that those who were victimized in any way as children find it most difficult to pick themselves up and make the most out of bad situations. Those who have been sexually molested or physically beaten have had their natural defenses so destroyed that they have little fight left. People with feelings of rejection accept difficulties as one more disaster that is getting too much to bear. The victim personality becomes the born losers, expects the worst and often becomes the co-dependent. An adult who is emotionally healthy, has been well nurtured by loving parents, or has successfully overcome adverse conditions can go on to face disappointment with courage.

Fourteen years ago Sandra had a dream that someday she would be a speaker. She had no idea on what subject, but she could picture herself on a platform giving words of encouragement to others.

Though the newly planted dream did not come to immediate fruition, it never left; it only rested at the back of her mind for a number of years. It was during this time of waiting that Sandra prepared her dream. The opportunities and roles of responsibility Sandra found were all a training ground . . . teaching in public school, conducting adult Sunday School classes and Bible studies, and accepting leadership roles in Women's Ministries.

As the dream began to ignite within her heart, Sandra felt a great frustration because she had just had a "surprise baby" after thinking her eleven and eight year old girls were the finish. This choleric was out of control! As far as Sandra was concerned this event had destroyed her dream. During this period she read from my book It Takes So Little to Be Above Average, "Don't let your mind wander out to pasture . . . know that God will give you a ministry when He feels you are ready . . . use every available mental moment to prepare today for God's call tomorrow."

But nothing new happened. Sandra felt surely she had misunderstood that call so many years before. Her prayer was in the form of a request—"If You truly have planted the dream in my heart, please confirm it by opening at least one door for wearing the dream." The call did come! Not just a speaking engagement, but a weekend retreat! Sandra had not quite bargained for something that big, but she accepted with a mixture of excitement and fear. She now was on her way!

The long hours of study and prayer in preparation for the South Texas Retreat only brought Sandra to a clearer realization that she was the one in need. Who was Sandra anyway? As an adopted child, she really didn't know. Thus began her search for self-identity. Since attending CLASS she has examined her own personality as the first step on a journey to wholeness. "I have discovered I was wearing a melancholy mask and I am really sanguine/choleric. What a freedom to be real!

Next she became willing to forgive her birth mother for giving her up for adoption. She read over and over the verses found in Psalm 139:13–16, "For you created my inmost being; you knit me together in my mother's womb. I praise you because I am fearfully and wonderfully made; your works are wonderful, I know that full well. My frame was not hidden from you when I was made in the secret place. When I was woven together in the depths of the earth, your eyes saw my unformed body. All the days ordained for me were written in your book before one of them came to be." (NIV). Through these verses, the Lord healed her emotions of anger and rejection, replacing there a peace, acceptance and feeling of self-worth.

As Sandra prepared to teach others she realized she had not dealt with a sexual abuse in her childhood and that because of this her marriage had little meaning. She saw then that her dream had not come true because she was not healed herself. One day as she was reading Oswald Chambers' My Utmost for His Highest, she was struck by his words: "The outstanding characteristic of a Christian is this unveiled frankness before God so that the life becomes a mirror for other lives."

Sandra saw she could not be a mirror for others until she was clean herself.

Sandra recalls, "Circumstances have literally brought me to the bottom, but as I released every plan and dream, the Lord began giving back my dream only in different ways. Restoration has begun in marriage and restoration of my dream of fourteen years has come as well through the repairs of this past year. A new direction for ministry is being revealed as six different friends have come across my path in these recent weeks—each having a story of sexual abuse. The Lord is placing within me a compassion and burning desire to be their support partner, offering them hope as each one is looking for freedom from the heavy baggage they carry.

"There is hope for a hurting and scarred world. I'm now ready to be a mirror for others lives; offering hope that they too can 'confidently and joyfully look forward to actually becoming all that God has had in mind for them to be' (Romans 5:2 TLB)."

Sandra has faced her background problems. She dared to dream, she prepared her dream for fourteen years, she had to search out the cause of her failures and repair the dream. Now Sandra is speaking and supporting others in need. Sandra has turned her miseries of the past into a ministry of the present.

3. *Call on the God of comfort.* God is not a big bad ogre sitting in the sky waiting to zap all the Ziggys in life as so many people believe. God is not the designer of disaster but he can make beauty out of ashes when we believe in his power and come to him in prayer. If we are in daily communion with the Lord, we will have the confidence that he can make the tough times count. He can comfort us in trouble and use us to minister to others.

Nancy has a Popular Personality and comes from feelings of rejection as a child. Her family has not handled problems well in the past and her victim personality led her to marry a man who also has heavy burdens from his past. Gratefully she has a desire to help others and she is spiritually in tune.

When Nancy first attended CLASS, she started her introduction in her small group by asking, "Have you ever wanted to run away with the circus?" As I watched this beautiful sanguine girl with the dancing brown eyes and the turned up nose tell of the night she was a clown with the circus, I could envision what a perfect clown she would be. Bubbly, exciting, funny—those are words to describe her, but as we listened to her story, we realized there was much sadness behind those sanguine eyes.

From my earliest childhood I was a dreamer—in fact my main playmates were make-believe—at least to adults. To me, they were very real—Leethy, Lorgi and Mary Ann. Only my special Grandma Engler understood their importance and treated them as if they were alive. Every dream and every dreamer needs nurturing. Grandma knew this and applied generous amounts of encouragement. While I was yet in grade school she became ill, and she died when I was fifteen. There was no one to take her place.

Sadly, my parents did not understand the needs of a sanguine child and though I now know it was unintentional, their words smashed some precious, fragile, beautiful dreams into millions of pieces.

Obviously as a sanguine I wanted to be the most beautiful, charming, smartest and most talented little girl I could be. How disappointed I was to hear my mother say to my sisters and me, "Not one of you girls is really pretty." I wanted to be beautiful, and to my own mother, I was not even pretty. To this day I become uneasy when someone tells me I am attractive. I tend to wonder if an ulterior motive lurks behind the comment.

In high school I considered trying out for a solo in our school musical. I planned to sing "Canadian Sunset." My father's comment was, "When are you going to stop hitting your head against a stone wall?" I never did try out. I settled to sing in the chorus. Under duress, my father attended a performance and afterward he told my mother he was most surprised. He could pick out my voice, and I was good. Even though I did have the voice—my dream had been crushed. As each dream was destroyed, my confidence and self-esteem diminished.

I was sure marriage would change that, but the person I married had many needs of his own as well as a suitcase of broken dreams. He was unable to give me the acceptance, approval and nurturing I so desperately needed. While I had hoped for the "happy ever after," I found myself face to face with what looked like "happy never after."

By the time I met Florence at CLASS I had faced the reality of my problems and had begun the healing process. I knew there was some "good stuff" out there. I was just not quite sure how to reach it. Life seemed to be sliding downhill and out of control.

At this point Nancy decided to take charge of her choices and not let the feelings of hurt and rejection ruin her life. She began attending meetings of Al-Anon where she found women from all walks of life, but with one thing in common: they all were co-dependents trying to overcome their pain of the past and the misery of the present. Nancy wanted to help those who had no spiritual values and give them hope, but she realized that humanly speaking she didn't even want to go to the meetings. Nancy prayed for a willing spirit and asked the Lord to show her the real reasons why she was uncomfortable in the group.

As she prayed, the answers came.

Pride: I did not want to be associated with alcoholism in any way, nor did any of my Christian friends. I certainly did not want to lose their approval.

Fear: Al-Anon and AA are secular organizations. While it was all right for someone to refer to God as "good orderly direction" or a tree, the name of my Jesus was most unwelcome. I was afraid I would be rejected if I shared my faith.

Then the Lord asked me, "What are pride and fear?"

By now I was crying and my tears had a repentant flavor as I responded, "Pride and fear are sins, Lord. Please forgive me. Then I remembered that several years before I made a commitment to go wherever, whenever, to do whatever the Lord asked of me even if it meant going to Al-Anon.. Today I look forward to attending each meeting in joyful obedience.

While making the fifteen-minute drive from my home to the meeting, I pray. I ask for a sensitive heart and ears to hear cries for help. I pray that all who attend will see the love of Christ in my eyes, and that God will give me His eyes to see just who needs special hugs and love. I ask for wisdom in choosing my words carefully to give hope to hurting hearts.

One after another, women have come to me to tell me they too are believers. My boldness for the Lord, worded very carefully, has been contagious. Others are becoming braver. In a recent conversation with another believer in our group, we came to the conclusion that God is about to do something wonderful and we will be right in the middle of the action. I love it! It is like being "backstage" with the Lord just before the curtain goes up!

I have cried with women in my group. Sometimes the tears are from sadness and sometimes for joy. Each woman is searching for genuine love and because of Jesus, I am able to offer the "real thing."

One Christian friend in Al-Anon told me with tear-filled eyes that she had been ministered to in a deeper way by her friends in Al-Anon than by the members of her church where she has attended and been in leadership for years! How I would like to take all those from Al-Anon and AA and all the Christians and put them into one giant size bag. For while those in Al-Anon and AA are not afraid to be real, many do not have the true source of power through Christ. On the other hand, Christians have the true source of power, but most are afraid to be real. If I could just shake them up together so all could have Jesus and the ability to be real, the potential would be explosive. So much could be accomplished in evangelizing the world!

I often suggest Florence's books on the personalities to help them in relationships, an area in which co-dependents are so weak. Another bonus is that they *love* me. Just last month I was one of three invited to sit at the head table for our twentieth anniversary banquet. And they are really after me to become assistant group representative. From the pain of broken dreams has emerged this exciting opportunity to minister to other women in need.

After reading Marilyn Heavilin's book *When Your Dreams Die*, suddenly it was clear to me. I am healthy enough to begin to dream once more. However, my approach to dreaming has been altered.

1. I've asked the God of Comfort to place within me the dreams He would choose for me. They will have a better opportunity to survive. Based on Psalm 37:4, I believe God delights in fulfilling His dreams for us.

2. I choose not to dream dreams that depend on the actions of other people, especially people close to me such as my own family.

3. Even if I am the only one who believes in my dream, if it is truly from the Lord, it can come true.

4. While nurturing and encouragement from others would always be welcome, I am now healthy enough to nurture and encourage myself.

Nancy is not only working to repair her dream, but she is repairing her ability to dream.

Dianna wrote me that finding out she was sexually abused as a child was a "bombshell in my life. My life exploded into thousands of jagged fragments. I gathered as many pieces as I could carry and did what I knew had to be done—I read Freeing Your Mind and sought professional care. After six months I am now a success in process . . . I have become not a 'broken vessel' but a sieve. A sieve that has allowed the Lord's love and His healing wash through me."

4. *Examine your family pattern of problem solving.* If you come from a defeated family who looked upon every disappointment as unfair, settled in under the black cloud, and accepted negatives as inevitable, you are apt to do the same, but if your family stood up in the face of invasion and fought off the dragons you will find it natural to do so. Stop and think. Even if you grew up in negatives, you can make a conscious effort

to change your attitude and your actions will follow after. Don't let the unkind words of the past ruin your future.

Paul Lewis was born without a left arm. As a child he heard comments such as "He'll have to be smart . . . he can't do manual work." "He'll never ride a motor bike." He remembers being called "The one armed bandit" and "Captain Hook."

Paul had little support from his family. He lived with his father as a child, but went to live with his mother when he was fourteen. His father had been divorced twice, and Paul hoped for a better situation when he lived with his mother in India. However, he felt he was in the way there, too, so after attending boarding school in India for two years, he left home at sixteen and went to Australia.

All of his life, in spite of the negative comments, Paul was determined he could do anything anyone else could do. He got his first motor bike at the age of ten and rode it successfully.

When he came to Australia, he had difficulty getting a job, but he was eventually hired by Advanced Life Foods. When we met Paul, he had just been promoted to foreman of the warehouse. His goal is to be promoted to leadership within the company.

Paul admits it is hard to trust those who give him compliments since most comments he received in childhod were cynical or given in jest.

Paul commented, "My handicap is not that I only have one arm; my handicap is the person I have to convince that I'm the same as everyone else." Paul is in the process of repairing his dream.

Do you have a handicap that you have allowed to hold you back? Have people's unkind comments discouraged you or have you used these comments to build rungs of determination on the ladder to success?

5. *Decide to help others.* Much of my teaching time is spent in CLASS showing others how to take their tragedies and use them to help those in similar situations. Only someone who has lost a child can comfort a grieving mother. Only an incest victim can say to another "I know how you feel" and be convincing. Only someone who has battled cancer can feel the pain with another victim.

Actress Jill Ireland experienced many broken dreams. When she was told she had breast cancer, she didn't let her illness keep her down for long. As soon as she was physically able, she became a spokesman for the National Cancer Society and wrote the book *Life Wish*. She kept her marriage intact and with her husband Charles Bronson she continued to raise their seven children.

Soon after finishing *Life Wish*, Jill learned that her adopted son Jason was a heroin addict and that her elderly father was unable to speak due to a series of strokes. She felt shattered. Jason's problem must be her fault. "For years I'd covered up his willfulness, refusing to hear a word against him. I thrashed myself terribly about what I did wrong and what somebody else did wrong and what I could have done."

Jason was adopted as an infant and Jill knew little about his background—certainly nothing that would explain his extreme irritability in the first months. Later, when he entered school, he was diagnosed as a hyperactive child—a doctor prescribed drugs to calm him down. As a teenager, Jason got into marijuana and cocaine. Heroin was next. Jill stood by Jason, subsidizing many hospitalizations over the years, but there seemed no end in sight—until two years ago, when Jill and her son finally met Jason's birth mother. That's when they found out that his natural father had died of a drug overdose. Jill believed that the birth mother may have been using drugs when she was pregnant with Jason. "I'm pretty sure I brought home a drug-addicted baby," she said.

This information was enough to loosen a huge emotional knot. Jill told this story in her book *Life Lines*.

Jill had to face another dream in need of repair when her cancer returned. While facing eight hours of cancer treatment per day, Jill still managed to start her third book, *Life Time*, about the important women in her life.

Have you had setback after setback like Jill Ireland? What have you done to repair your dreams? Broken dreams can be pivotal points in our lives if we choose to pick up the broken pieces and repair our dreams. Or we can just gather our perplexing problems around us and retreat into our own little shells where we hope we will never have to hurt again. Jill Ireland wrote books that will help others survive their own broken dreams and in the writing process gave purpose and promise to her own life.

6. *Evaluate your expectations*. So often when one marriage fails, the tendency is for each partner to rush right out and get married again. We think we have learned from our mistakes and since the last dream can't be repaired, we'll just build a smarter and wiser dream. It all sounds good, but unfortunately we seldom take time to retrain ourselves in new patterns or evaluate our former behaviours before we marry again. When the second marriage starts to crumble, we have to ask, "Is there any hope? Can we repair this new dream?

In an article by Dr. Daniel Brick, he shares the dreams he had for his own second marriage.

> I guess most people have an idealistic picture of what marriage
> will be like. Marilyn and I were no exception. Despite the fact
> that we had both come out of difficult prior marriages, we had an
> idyllic vision of our life together: We'd build our dream house, raise
> a big family, enjoy the good life. It never occurred to us to discuss
> our expectations more specifically.[113]

It didn't take long for Daniel and Marilyn to realize that in spite of
all of their wonderful expectations something was wrong.

Somewhere along the way, we stopped having fun. And we discovered
that instead of a common dream for our marriage, we each had very
different expectations.

The Bricks were going separate ways in their marriage and it took a
great deal of effort and commitment to repair their dream.

> We realized that we had spent infinitely more time and effort
> planning and building our home than we had our
> relationship. . . . Just as there is no one way to build a house, per-
> haps there was no one way to structure a marriage. We decided to
> step back and try to come up with a plan that would work for us.[114]

Do you have a "dream" marriage that has turned into a nightmare?
Is it possible to repair your dream? Take time to sit down with your
spouse and discuss your expectations of your marriage and your partner.
You each may be surprised what the other's expectations really are. Do
your expectations fit reality, are they reachable? If not, cut them down
to size and determine to work together to repair your dream.

7. *Develop a sense of humor*. When I look back over almost forty years
of marriage, I realize that without a sense of humor we would not have
made it. In times of trouble we were able to see the funny side of life and
know that someday we would look back on these circumstances and laugh.
If I had never walked through troubled waters I would have little compassion for others. If I had not been able to look at difficulties as growth
opportunities I would have quit in despair. If I had not developed a
sense of humor in tense times, I would have no books to write. In CLASS
we teach "Every bad experience is a good example"

Recent research shows us that a hearty laugh now and then is good
for our health and our self-image.

> "When we laugh at our flaws and failures, we put them in perspec-
> tive," says women's humor specialist Regina Barreca, Ph.D., professor
> of English at the University of Connecticut and author of *They Used
> To Call Me Snow White (But Then I Drifted)*. "I compare it to see-
> ing a monster on a movie screen. It looks huge until the camera

pulls back and you suddenly see that the monster is nothing but a hand puppet.' Laughter works the same way, she says. 'If you can laugh at a vexing situation, you cut it down to size."

"Humor can even help minimize our errors to begin with. Experts say people make more mistakes and have more accidents when they're tense. But by laughing at ourselves, we release some of that tension and reduce our risk of failure.[115]

Humor can defuse the destruction of anger. A study of doctors and lawyers done at Duke University showed that those who scored high on the hostility scale on personality tests were four times more likely to die primarily of heart attacks, by the age of fifty. "Being angry is bad for your health," the study states. "It's hard to stay angry when you're laughing." [116]

I once watched columnist Art Buchwald on television and observed a phlegmatic heaped happily and heavily in a large over-stuffed chair, relaxed and ruminating over his life with interviewer Bob Costas. His dry wit and sly smile give the impression of a man content with himself and without a care in the world; however, as he talked he pulled himself up from the pillows and shared about his childhood spent in a series of foster homes. The emotional abuse and rejection of the past have given Buchwald a feeling for the pain in people and he explains that humor is anger vented in a satirical vein. "I've spent my life getting even," he said "and my great joy is saying, 'See, I told you' to those who said I wouldn't make it."

Humor can also relieve pain. When Norman Cousins was given little hope for a cure of the severe inflammation of his spine and joints, he determined not to just curl up into a crippled ball and die. He started his own search for relief so that he could go on with his own dream of living a long, healthy life.

He discovered that ten minutes of solid belly laughter would give him two hours of pain-free sleep, and laughter became a significant feature of his treatment. He programmed laughter into his life. Norman's condition began to improve, but he wasn't willing to leave it there. He had to share his discovery with others so that they could dream of a healthy life also.

As he shared the results of his personal experiment with health care facilities, hospitals began to set up facilities for patients to enjoy humor and be creative. St. Joseph's Hospital in Houston has established the Living Room, the cancer floor which has been redesigned to accommodate a large room furnished with easy chairs, hi-fi equipment, an art corner, video and audio sets and a library. Both the ambulatory and wheelchair patients kept the videotape machine busy viewing comedy films obtained from film companies free of charge. Now more than two dozen similar programs have been developed throughout the country.

Norman Cousins once said, "Any battle with serious illness involves two elements. One is the ability of physicians to give patients the best that medical science has to offer. The other is the ability of patients to summon all their physical and spiritual resources and put them to work fighting their disease."

Quoting Russian novelist Fyodor Dostoyevski he added, "If you wish to glimpse inside a human soul and get to know a man, don't bother analyzing his ways of being silent, of talking, of weeping, or seeing how much he is moved by noble ideas; you'll get better results if you just watch him laugh. If he laughs well, he's a good man. . . . All I claim to know, is that laughter is the most reliable guage of human nature."[117]

As long as Norman Cousins lived, he shared his dream by helping himself and thousands of others use laughter as a vehicle to relieve pain and offer hope.

8. *Give words of encouragement to others*. When I wrote my book *Silver Boxes, the Gift of Encouragement*, I had no idea how this message would motivate others to give out positive words. I paraphrased Ephesians 4:29, "We should say no unkind words to others. We should use words that build up other people and do them a favor, offer them a gift, present them with a little silver box with a bow on top." People began to give each other silver boxes as reminders and I received mail about the value of encouraging words. Many schools have used the ideas to help the students improve their language and build each other up.

Donna wrote:

> Our son graduated from eighth grade this year, and the speaker for graduation had attended your seminar. She spoke about the Silver Boxes. After the service she presented each eighth grader with a silver box—a box so they could remember the value of en-couraging words. But it wasn't just an empty box wrapped in silver paper. Inside each box was a message written for that student. She had been their seventh-grade teacher and she knew each child well enough to give him or her the words that would help when they became discouraged or felt overwhelmed.

When we are disheartened how grateful we become to the person who lifts us up by encouraging words. When we use kind words to cheer up another person we soon feel better about ourselves. It's true that when we purpose to lift up others we are lifted up ourselves.

Maxine wrote:

> "Something I've been doing since I read your book, *Silver Boxes*, is each day look for someone that I come in contact with (at the store, doctor's office, etc.) to compliment or encourage in some way. It has been *so rewarding to me* to do this. The smile and response I get from them has blessed me much more than I have been able to help them. Thank you, Florence, for motivating me to take another step in my recovery process."

For any of us that are in the process of repairing our dreams, giving words of encouragement to anyone we see will pick up our own attitudes. "It is more blessed to give than to receive" (Acts 20:35).

9. *Never give up.* It was Winston Churchill who spoke the words "Never, never, never give up" during the darkest days of World War II. When England had lost hope, Churchill inspired the nation. "Lift up your hearts. All will come right. Out of the depths of sorrow and sacrifice will be born again the glory of mankind."

Some of us are in times of sorrow today. Some of us may have to cut back on our luxuries or move to smaller homes for a season, but we must never give up.

Some of us have small losses compared to those who lose their lives for their country. Some of us can't even imagine what we'd do if faced with physical disability or extreme handicaps.

Chucky Mullins watched his dream die when he was permanently injured while playing football. This has not deterred him. He is repairing his dream.

When Chucky Mullins, University of Mississippi football cornerback, was hit on the back while intercepting a pass, a vertebra exploded. Doctors said he should have been dead, but he lived in spite of all odds against him. Paralyzed and confined to a specially built wheelchair Chucky has won the hearts of the people in Oxford, Mississippi. His buoyant spirit and engaging smile have encouraged those who have come to encourage him. The town donated land and raised money to build him a custom home to accommodate his needs. Over a million dollars came in from all over the country and Chucky could have settled into his newly donated security. People with far fewer problems than Chucky often use minor handicaps to keep them from having to work, but Chucky has faithfully taken his therapy and is determined to improve.

When interviewed on television he stated that he was going back to
school, get his degree and become a football coach. Surrounded by young
supporters who were in awe of his courage, Chucky called out, "Pray
for me and never, never, never give up."

What a testimony for those of us who quit when the going gets tough.
We may have to repair our dream but never, never, never give up.

When Noni Joy Tari attended CLASS, she sent me this note:

> Because God loves us so much, He only uses two alternatives
> in how He ministers to us regarding our dreams:
>
> He turns them into Fertilizer or He brings them to Fruition.
>
> When people have broken dreams or dreams die, it is one of
> the most painful experiences in a person's life. But God never
> simply buries our dead and broken dreams because He'd be bury-
> ing our hearts along with our dreams. Instead, He creatively turns
> our failures into fertilizer for an even more wonderful dream, a
> dream with even more potential to come to fruition.
>
> In my own life I have learned that I never need to be afraid to
> wish and hope and desire and dream big. Because when I honestly
> tell the Lord about my dreams, one of two positive things will
> happen.
>
> Either the dream will become fertilizer for something even bet-
> ter, or the Lord will give me the gumption and oomph to bring my
> dream to fruition. I can't lose either way!

It Couldn't Be Done
by Edgar A. Guest

Somebody said that it couldn't be done,
But he with a chuckle replied
That "maybe it couldn't," but he would be one
Who wouldn't say so till he'd tried.
So he buckled right in with the trace of a grin
On his face. If he worried he hid it.
He started to sing as he tackled the thing
That couldn't be done, and he did it.

Somebody scoffed: "Oh, you'll never do that;
At least no one ever has done it;"
And the first thing we knew he'd begun it.
With a lift of his chin and a bit of a grin,
Without any doubting or quiddit,
He started to sing as he tackled the thing
That couldn't be done, and he did it.

There are thousands to tell you it cannot be done
There are thousands to prophesy failure;
There are thousands to point out to you, one by one
The dangers that wait to assail you.
But just buckle in with a bit of a grin,
Just take off your coat and go to it;
Just start to sing as you tackle the thing
That "cannot be done," and you'll do it!

PART FIVE

Share
the
Dream

"Wise leaders of the people will share their wisdom with many" (Daniel 11:33,TLB).

The Dreamer Shares the Dream

Mark Twain once said, "Biographies are but the clothes and buttons of the man—the biography of the man himself cannot be written."

As the sister of Ron Chapman I know the clothes, the buttons, and the man himself. When as children we lived in those three rooms behind our father's store, who would have dreamed that Ron would one day be named the "Personality of the Year" at the 1989 National Association of Broadcasters convention and that his station would win "Station of the Year for Adult Contemporary" and be designated as a "Legendary Station"?

When asked to comment on his victories Ron said, "Nothing we have ever done at KVIL has ever been designed to win awards. We simply do what we do for the sake of the listener. But what this award means to me is that other people in the industry think we've been doing some things very well."[118]

And they have.

Many people know Ron Chapman as the inspiration for KVIL's success, as the entertainer who encourages his listeners each day, as the comedian whose humor never quits. Dallas-Fort Worth commuters have viewed his face on billboards along the highways. "Ron Chapman—top of the morning for twenty years!"

Nationally he is known for motivating his listeners to send him checks for twenty dollars that turned into a pool of money—nearly a quarter of a million. Everybody knows the clothes and buttons, but few know the man. Few know that he formed a Twenty Dollar Club for all those who contributed and he keeps in touch with them and offers them special privileges. "If one of them calls me," he told me recently, "and says they're a Twenty Dollar Club member, I'll put their needs right up front. They come first with me."

Few know what he did with the money and some even think he kept it for himself. When asked initially what would be done with the money, he responded that he would do something big for the communities, something that no one could do alone.

"Together we can do something which individually none of us would be able to accomplish. Pool the funds and then it doesn't hurt anybody and we've really made a difference and that's what we're looking at right now."

The Big Question provided subject matter for Ron Chapman and his listeners for many mornings until the decisions were made.

The Salvation Army received one hundred thousand dollars to rebuild the inside of a warehouse in North Dallas. It is now a medical center where street people can receive attention.

A Fort Worth shelter for women and children who are victims of domestic violence was given sixteen thousand to buy a van to transport those in need. This shelter also found that the children had to get to their schools in different parts of town, so the van delivers them each day and picks them up.

The Tarrant County Food Bank got fifty-six thousand to buy a heavy duty refrigerated truck with a power lift tailgate. This makes it possible for them to deliver food safely to those in need. On the side of the truck it says, "Contributed by KVIL."

Money was also donated to refurbish classrooms at the East Dallas Community School for underprivileged children.

The remaining funds were given to a group called Common Ground. Ron was impressed with the work they are doing in restoring abandoned homes in Dallas. They find houses in the inner city and buy them for a token fifty dollars. They get the neighbors to help repair them, and then they rent them to local people who only have to pay twenty percent of their income—whatever that is. In return, the renters must keep the property up and help Common Ground restore the next house. By working with the needy people, the staff has discovered many skilled workers who are unemployed and they have found them jobs. The group found that one deterrent to finding employment was the person's lack of a home address. For street people who wanted to be self-supporting, this dilemma created an endless circle of hopelessness. Common Ground fixed up a condemned hotel so that the sincere seekers could have an address.

All of these charities are obviously worthy of the contributions made by KVIL, Ron Chapman, and the Twenty Dollar Club as they shared their money to give dreams to others.

As Ron was giving away money in Dallas-Fort Worth, our brother Jim was getting ready for his annual stewardship drive at his church in Bath, Ohio.

The Rev. James W. Chapman needed to raise $253,000 to meet the 1988 budget, almost the same amount as Ron had just received. Just a few days after Ron's news hit national media exposure, Jim used the material for his Sunday morning message.

"I opened my sermon by saying that I came from a family of expert fundraisers."

Then he told them about Ron's exploits. "Ron's listeners trusted him," Jim said. "He's been on the air in Dallas for thirty years, twenty at that station. And they know he wouldn't let them down."

He continued, "I said I hated to inject sibling rivalry into the issue, but if my brother can raise more than $240,000 in a week with no purpose at all, how will I be able to face my family if I can't raise that much in a year for a very good purpose?"

Jim was confident his congregation would meet the church's budget needs, "But we will accept twenty dollar checks from anyone in the community who wants to contribute," he said with a laugh. "Make them payable to Bath Church."

Jim sent a tape of this sermon to Ron, who played some of the most humorous sections on his show. Not only did Ron have fun with the sermon, but Jim was rewarded when one man from Dallas felt sorry for him and mailed him a check for five dollars.

Many of Ron's contributions to others are not so visible as the twenty dollar game. He is very giving with the staff at the station and is willing to spend time with those who are eager to learn.

"He's a teacher," says one DJ. "And obviously if you're going to teach, you teach your way. He has very strong beliefs in the way things ought to be done. I'm sure he has crossed paths with some people. But he's always fair. He's always out there hustling."

Ron is also the first to help a friend in need. Suzie Humphreys was once a local anchorwoman who was replaced and disappeared from view for six months. Ron heard she had fallen on hard times and he called to see if he could help her. She hated to say that she was freelancing and doing dinner theatre. "There's not many jobs for ex-TV-hostesses," she told him. She would go to the unemployment office and stand in line in her lizard shoes and designer dresses. When she'd get to the front she'd be so embarrassed when the girl would say loudly, "There are no television jobs today, honey."

Ron was shocked to find that a person with her sanguine strengths in communications was unemployed. He felt so bad about Suzie's situation that he brought her on KVIL staff and put her in a helicopter doing traffic reports. Everyone loved her personality, but Ron soon found she couldn't tell one street from another. Her descriptions of traffic were so hilarious that the reports were soon comedy routines. Ron would ask her questions on the air and she would respond with descriptions of traffic tie-ups that had little to do with the truth but were so amusing that people listened just to hear Suzie's reports.

One morning, a pregnant Suzie felt air-sick in the churning helicopter. She asked the pilot to take her down. He let her out, took off, and four minutes later the helicopter crashed and he was killed. Suzie knows that the good Lord had His hand on her that day. The following Tuesday, gutsy Suzie was back in the air and she continued her humorous sky view of the Dallas traffic for over a year. When she finally decided she'd flown enough, Ron had to find a new place for her.

Ron didn't know what to do with Suzie. The people loved her so much he brought her into the studio with him. "Somehow it never clicked," he explained to me. "We had amazing chemistry talking on the phone, but looking at each other across a turntable took away all the excitement."

When I asked Suzie why it didn't work she replied, "When I was away from Ron I could be irreverent, but when his big eyes were across from me I didn't dare insult him."

Since Ron didn't want to lose Suzie, he bought her a Dodge van, equipped it for reporting, and sent her out to the highways and byways of life. She had a wreck the first day. Suzie made fun of the van and kept complaining about it so finally Ron got her a new "KVIL Yellow Van." She drives around each morning, stops for coffee at a convenience store, carpools her children, and takes the dog to the vet. She stops in parking lots and people run to have a party with her. Whatever Suzie calls in to report is funny. She represents the women listeners and is the only staff member who dares to top Ron Chapman's lines. "He tells everyone on the station 'No surprises,' but with me he laughs and says, 'Give me surprises.'" And Suzie does!

One year she and Ron had a contest called Suzie's Run Away. It was an adult pajama party and the winners were going to Cancun with Suzie.

The day of the departure she took all the ladies to the beauty shop for a makeover before their trip. A few minutes before the plane was to leave, Ron got a call from the airlines to say that Suzie and her group had not arrived. Ron asked them to hold the plane and he'd find Suzie somewhere. He located her in the Yellow Van and told her the plane was waiting for her. About a half hour later he got a call from the airport police asking if he owned a yellow van. When he said yes they told him, "Well, it's parked here at the curb and you'd better send someone to get it."

"I'll try to locate a set of keys," Ron replied.

"Don't bother," the officer said, "They're in the ignition."

Sanguine Suzie had abandoned the Yellow Van with the motor running and had happily flown off to Mexico.

When I asked Suzie her feelings about Ron, she said, "He helps anyone in need and he's the squishiest person I know. People don't realize that you can do all that he does and be a Teddy Bear—but that's his real personality."

Well-known Dallas broker Billy Bob Harris was convicted on some SEC charges and sent to the federal prison at Big Spring, Texas. As you can imagine, many of his friends and people he had helped forgot who he was once the gates shut behind him. Not so with Ron Chapman. He maintained contact and often drove to Big Spring to visit Billy Bob. When he got out and wanted to re-enter the mainstream of life, Ron gave him a job in the traffic-copter as he'd done for Suzie. When I was in Dallas one day, I tuned into KVIL and heard Billy Bob giving tips on the stock market. I asked Ron, "Isn't it a little risky to have Billy Bob broadcasting stock advice?"

"Not at all," Ron replied, "What better person to have telling people how to do it right than a man who served time for doing it wrong!"

I had to agree.

Ron is not only generous, an exceptional role model, and a faithful friend, but he also is willing to share his talent to be master of ceremonies at charity events and serve on philanthropic committees. He is on the board of Dallas Friends of the Police, an organization that gives out awards for outstanding police activity. Ron was chosen to introduce President Ronald Reagan when he spoke in Dallas, and his favorite picture is the one with him standing behind the lectern bearing the presidential shield.

Ron and his wife Nance heard about a place called Brian's House that was founded to care for children who had AIDS. They realized there were many needs the children had that were not being met, so

Nance founded Brian's Friends and motivated women to give time to the children in addition to items such as soap, diapers, and other sundries.

There are few people today who are willing to even touch a person with AIDS, especially when they aren't related and don't have to participate, but Nance has been able to motivate society ladies to cuddle and love these little ones who have no hope of a normal life. The amazing results of maternal care have surprised everyone involved. Instead of dying quickly as the estimates showed, these babies are doing so well that they are living beyond any expectations and living longer than those in care centers where there is little touching and tenderness. Ron explained to me, "We've all found the value of love in extending life in terminal patients. The new problem is arranging schooling for those who are of kindergarten age. No one ever thought they'd live this long."

What a blessing it is to any one of us when we can share our love with those in need and be able to extend and enrich the lives of others.

When Ron feels there are civic problems that need to be confronted, he brings them up on the radio and evaluates their importance by the response of his listeners. After the 1988 Cotton Bowl Parade, Ron asked his people to comment on the television coverage and the calls were entirely critical of what had transpired. Soon the Cotton Bowl Council called to ask him to join the parade committee.

In one of their meetings, a network producer challenged him, "If you can deliver us a spirited crowd on New Year's morning, we'll do a better broadcast." Ron's choleric nature rose to the bait and he began to plan the 1989 Cotton Bowl festivities. He knew he could count on his people to show up; they had rallied many times before. "It's not an easy thing to get thousands of people up at 7:30 on New Year's morning when they've been out partying half the night," Ron told me.

With the Powerful Personality, the impossible only takes a little extra effort and on the following New Year's Day, one hundred and fifty thousand people were cheering in a carnival atmosphere at 7:30 in the morning for the television cameras. The festivities were so successful that teh committee wanted Ron to serve again. But Ron always felt constrained by committees, so he passed the position to his more diplomatic wife Nance, who did a sensational performance for 1990.

Many of Ron's KVIL listeners have grown up with him. He started out with them as teenagers on his Sump'n Else dance stand. They grew to love him, and many of those who looked at him as their teen idol would today as adults do whatever he asked. They know him, admire him, and trust him, and he puts himself out personally for them.

"This is going to sound very corny, but it's true," he said. "It is very rare in your life that you get a chance to create something that is very special. I got that shot at KVIL, and there's so much of my blood, sweat and tears in KVIL that my goal is to keep what I call this 'Camelot of radio' alive. Even in markets like Chicago and Los Angeles, nobody has what we have. We have a love affair with a community. It's a two-way street. It's a family and it's unique. And I just want to keep it alive as long as I can."[119]

With a lucrative contract that keeps Ron and Dallas happy well into the nineties, he should be able to share his love affair and keep fun alive.

It is rare in the entertainment world today that anyone could become enough of a legend that the call letters of his station could become an argot of his trade. When stations coast to coast consider a change, they list the possibilities: "We could go country, talk show, or KVIL."

Ron admits he's had two scoops of everything and that he's not expecting to leave any monuments around.

"But if anyone were to remember me, I would hope it would be as someone who took radio disc jockeying and maybe gave it a little respect. We've become Kleenex. We've become Coke. I haven't done it all alone, but in this company, I've been the thread that has taken the spirit of it through twenty years, and I think I've done it rather well. So if anyone were to remember me, I would hope it would be as someone who elevated the art."[120]

Ron Chapman is more than a DJ; he has become an artist. As I wrote for him at his roast:

> Dear Ron, You may not have received high grades for
> Trying out the tongue twisters as a tot
> Taunting the typing teacher a lot
> Tooting the trumpet for no wage
> Tampering with the tuba in the cage
> Telling the teacher lies that caused no harm
> Toting in tomatoes from Miss Lil's farm
> Taking it easy on deck and below
> Training the troops for the talent show
> Taking the trophy when sent your way
> Talking and taping in the trailer each day
> Tutoring and teaching at the University
> Titillating the translators on TV
> But as your speech teacher I give you A
> For your talent, your taste, and your triumph today!

Dolly Shares the Dream

There are many of us who wish someone would give us an A in Life. Dolly Parton received her A from the Carson-Newman College in Jefferson City, Tennessee. On October 21, 1990, Dolly was given an honorary doctorate in recognition of her personal contribution to the people in her area. She started out in a three-room cabin and has risen to fame and fortune, but she has never forgotten where she came from and she has always been willing to share what she's earned with others. In addition to her gold and platinum records, Dolly has built a theme park called Dollywood in Pigeon Forge, Tennessee, easing the unemployment rate and bringing plenty of tourist dollars to a deprived area. Dolly is not afraid of hard work and has never become too important to share with others. All she has ever wanted is to make other people happy.

In 1988, Dolly formed the Dollywood Foundation, an organization that encourages young people to stay in school.

"A lot of my family members dropped out of school, and I often wonder about all the great things they would have done if they'd had an education," she says. "So when I decided to get involved in a charity, I wanted it to be beneficial—but also have personal meaning. I want to help kids get that high school diploma."[121]

Dolly is a typical Popular-Powerful Personality whose favorite verse is "a merry heart doeth good like a medicine." She loves her work and says, "Tell me you love me and I'll work that much harder." She believes that with hard work and a positive attitude nothing is impossible, but she also feels responsible to give back to others from what she has received.

"There's no greater gift than to be able to share those things. The only thing that's better is dreaming. If anyone is looking for a New Year's resolution, my advice is to start dreamin' and wishin'. Dreams do come true. You've just got to believe."[122]

In the past, people who had wealth and education were taught that they had to serve the community in some way to repay the country for their blessings. Franklin Roosevelt, our only four-term president, went into local politics to serve the people. Even though his background was the opposite of Dolly Parton, he wanted to share with others. He had been brought up as an only child with a governess and tutors to care for him and teach him, and he felt obligated to give back some of what he had received. George Bush had a similar background and was so willing to share what he had that his childhood nickname was Have-Half. He made a career of government service doing what he was called to do whether or not he received credit.

Many of us were taught to give to others and to share our talents and abilities with those less fortunate. Scripture tells us, "For unto whomsoever much is given of him shall be much required and to whom men have committed much of him they will ask the more" (Luke 12:48). A basic principle is that if we've received we should freely give; yet through the Me Generation and the eighties, the Age of Greed, we have somehow developed a "me first" attitude that is in contrast to our biblical and patriotic background. Because of this, people who are genuinely generous and looking for no credit become novelties and catch our attention.

"KJ" Shares the Dream

Kevin Johnson, "KJ" of the Phoenix Suns, at twenty-four years old is one of the finest guards in the National Basketball Association. Even though he is short and light by basketball standards, he averages over twenty points and ten assists in each game. Former Los Angeles Lakers coach Pat Riley said of "KJ" in 1989 when the Suns were eliminating the Lakers from the playoffs, "Other than Magic, he's the most unique player in the league."

With all the praise and attention "KJ" has received, plus his salary of more than two million dollars a year, it would be natural for him to settle in, enjoy himself, live it up, or get into drugs as so many star athletes have done. But "KJ" is unique. He remembers what life was like when he had nothing and he wants to give even where he didn't receive. In speaking of his old tough neighborhood in Sacramento, California, he says, "Out of all my friends I grew up with, only a couple of them aren't in jail or are involved in something legitimate. It's very sad."

Because he truly cares, "KJ" has decided to do something for the kids that he sees headed for trouble. He wants to prevent problems, not wait until it's too late. Kevin Johnson had a dream that he could make a difference. He spent time talking with people who had done similar projects, he researched what worked in other poor neighborhoods, and he created St. Hope Academy, an after-school support program which currently uses the facility of Sacramento High School.

"We're trying to develop a home-like environment in the inner city for a lot of kids who are disadvantaged or don't have parental guidance," he said. "It's not to replace the home, but to supplement the home. We're creating an environment where adults and mentors love these kids unconditionally and help them with whatever they need, whether it's their homework, reading skills, or problems they may be having in their lives. It's time for people in their communities to take a responsibility and say, 'I have to do something about our community, our kids.'"[123]

"KJ" is doing something about poverty and neglect in his old hometown. As Ron and Nance are doing with childhood AIDS patients in Dallas, "KJ" is going beyond financial donations to personal action. When he can he drops by to encourage and motivate the children and to show them, "You can make something of your life. There is hope."

The administrator of St. Hope feels that the community has responded in a positive way and has begun to contribute financially. But more important is the presence of "KJ" and his willingness to give his time to save others.

The kids at St. Hope, she said, "look up to Kevin as a big brother or father figure, not because he's a basketball player, but because of all the time he spends with them in the summer. They know he really cares. And if they're doing something wrong, and I say I'm going to tell Kevin, they get nervous and straighten up."

"KJ" was brought up in an unusual family situation. His white grandfather married his white grandmother when she was already pregnant by a black man. His mother was the product and he was born when she was seventeen and single. He was raised by his white grandparents along with his mother, and they all taught him that giving to others was a part of life. They instilled moral principles into him that have kept him out of trouble and have made him the unique person he is today.

"My mother taught me that to be successful, I had to be different," he said. "That had a lot of meaning to me when it came to my peers. If you do what they're doing that's wrong, you're going to end up just like them. If you want to be different, you might have to stand alone. It might be lonely, but it will be right, and in the long run, you'll be rewarded."[124]

"KJ" has been rewarded financially and with great personal satisfaction. He has achieved his goals and surpassed his dreams. Now he's sharing his dreams with others that he might give them hope—St. Hope!

Dexter Manley Shares the Dream

Kevin Johnson and Dexter Manley have much in common. They both grew up in tough neighborhoods and they both used their athletic ability to rise above their circumstances. They both have made millions of dollars, in basketball for Kevin and football for Dexter, and they have achieved the highest acclaim for their unique gifts. The difference is that "KJ" has behaved himself and stayed clean and Dexter has let success go to his head. Growing up in Houston, Dexter was a slow learner and was put in special education classes that made him feel stupid. He wanted desperately to be somebody and to show his friends he wasn't dumb. He vented his anger on the football field and his inner rage compelled him to be the best. In high school he could barely read and write, but when he stepped out on the football field he was king. Dexter says, "Texas has high school programs bigger than some colleges and universities. Playing Texas high school football is almost as big as God. You wanna be a part of it. I had nothing else going."[125]

Dexter did all the right things to get ahead. He prepared his dream and by his senior year in high school he was all-county, all-state, and all-American. Suddenly he was a hot property, and even though he was a functional illiterate he was pursued by three teams out of the Big Eight. Dexter chose Oklahoma State University and says of his recruiting time, "They'd do whatever I asked. It spoiled me. I convinced myself that they owed this to me. I used my talent and my ability to get what I wanted."[126]

Even though he only got six out of thirty-six on the American College testing, Dexter Manley was accepted at OSU and he began a life of denial and fear. He admits, "I was a real fake. It was a real denial thing." The school allowed him to take simple subjects and pass as long as he was performing on the field, but he was always afraid he'd be caught. He wasn't.

In 1981 the Washington Redskins made Dexter their third-round draft pick and suddenly he had money, more than he'd ever dreamed of. He let loose and began to drink and get cocky. For eight years, Dexter Manley was involved in a series of problem situations. He was arrested for impersonating a policeman and for altering the registration on his Mercedes. He missed four training camps, came to games while intoxicated, and failed two drug tests.

None of Dexter's escapades seemed to teach him any lesson. He had dared to dream and prepared his dream, but he didn't feel comfortable wearing his dream. Even the warning from his coach didn't move him: "Dex, you're throwing your life away. You're gonna blow it all, you're gonna wind up in the gutter."

Inside of Dexter was that childhood hurt of being poor and slow in school. He'd never gotten beyond his pain; he'd just covered it up, denied it, and hoped it wouldn't pop up again. He said, "My defense mechanism is self-destructive. It always wants to tear me down, instead of build me up."

For a year and a half, Dexter stayed away from drugs, although the longing was still there. He had the feeling that he had become invincible and he bought two grams of cocaine knowing the possible consequences. "I was having a great season," he says, "so I rewarded myself." When the test came back positive, Dexter claimed innocence. "Cocaine makes you a liar. It makes you cheat." Dexter at thirty-one years old was banned for life from the NFL. He had to repair his dream. He entered the John Lucas Rehabilitation Center in Houston and now claims to be cured. In order to repay society for the bad example he's been, he is sharing with others by voluntarily counseling addicts and speaking to children about the danger of drugs. He tells them, "I thought there was a short-cut, that I could beat the system by doing drugs, not getting caught."[127]

The lesson is you can't take a chance on any drugs and Dexter Manley is his own visual aid. Dexter has grown up after seeing what life was like at the bottom. He is willing to teach others from his mistakes. "People in recovery have to have hopes to cling to. I have high hopes. I made a bad decision to do cocaine. But I have to believe I will get another chance."[128] He did. Dexter Manley was reinstated one year after he was banned for life and he was sent to Phoenix. I hope he will continue to repair and share his dream.

Milton Shares the Dream

Young Milton doesn't have much of an outlook on the future. He lives in a government housing project in Chicago where drugs and crime are accepted as normal. Like "KJ" and Dexter, Milton doesn't seem to have a hold on the American Dream, but Milton has a new hope because some local music teachers are willing to share some of their time and talent with underprivileged children. Under the auspices of the Chicago Housing Authority, dedicated teachers are giving violin lessons to youngsters who would be on the streets after school. The talent of the group was obvious to those of us viewing the performance on television and I was touched personally with the difference these teachers had made in some bright children who were born into poverty situations. Because these adults are willing to share their abilities with those less fortunate, their sacrifice enables these young people to dare to dream. One girl looked up proudly and said, "I am going to be a professional violinist." And Milton, with his big brown eyes sparkling, summed up the assets when he added, "This teaches us to concentrate on something good."

So often I talk with people who are still holding grudges against those who wronged them years and years ago—a parent who preferred one sibling over another, a teacher who gave an unfair mark, an employer who paid below-minimum wage and wasn't caught, a friend who turned against them and broke confidences never given out before. Somehow the negatives of life are etched deeply in our hearts like the markings on a tombstone while the positives get trampled like the pebbles on our pathway.

Many people who are high achievers in their personal pursuits take pleasure in pushing down those who gave them trouble in the past and have no thought of rewarding those who helped. The sign of a truly successful person is the willingness, even eagerness, to share the results of the dream with others—to never forget the good.

The People of Chambon Share the Dream

In the early forties during the Nazi occupation of France, the dream of any Jew was to live until tomorrow. They dared not think of a future as they watched friend after friend disappear as if whisked up a magician's sleeve. Whole villages lived in terror of the moment the Nazis would sweep in and swoop up every Jew they could find—but not the tiny mountain community of Le Chambon-sur-Lignon. There the three thousand devout Huguenots, led by their pastor André Trocmé, united in a passive resistance to protect any Jews fleeing persecution. The villagers hid the transient Jews in their houses, small hostels, and barns and when the word came that the Germans were approaching, the Jews would be sent into the forest to hide. They stayed quietly invisible until their rescuers sang lustily, letting them know the troopers had moved on and they could come out again. The people provided schooling for the children and homes for those who had been orphaned along the way. They organized an underground network to help the refugees escape to Switzerland or Spain, and they provided food and clothing even though they had little themselves.

Marie Brottes was a quiet initiator of the movement to keep the Jews from being hustled off to concentration camps. As a believing Christian, she went from house to house encouraging her friends to take part in the protection. One of those willing to help was Henri Heritier. Somewhat like the birth of the Christ child in the stable was the birth of Pierre Sauvage on Henri's farm in 1944. Born to refugee Jewish parents sheltered by the Heritiers, Pierre had little chance to dream, but without the family's help he would have had little chance to even live.

At the end of the war, the Sauvages and the other refugees moved on and Chambon returned to normal. "Many of these people must have thought we flew away like birds from a tree and forgot the welcome we found here," said Joseph Atlas, a Paris engineer who spent three years in Chambon. "Ours is a culture that never forgets. But the horror of the war had to be digested before we could return to our memories."[129]

Almost fifty years have passed since Atlas and Sauvage left Chambon, but they never forgot the good. Pierre is now a filmmaker and he produced "Weapons of the Spirit" to honor what he calls Chambon's "conspiracy of goodness." In October of 1990, a delegation from Israel came to Chambon to award the forty villagers who are still alive from the war years with the Medal of Righteousness. This honor is bestowed upon individuals who risked their lives to save the Jews from extinction and is given by the Holocaust Martyrs and Heroes Remembrance Authority centered in Jerusalem.

"Almost all the people of the plateau were involved in saving these Jews, and no one said a word."[130]

For their selfless sacrificial service, the Huguenots of Chambon were finally recognized. Pierre Sauvage returned to show his film and to share the culmination of his impossible dream. Old friends met for the first time since the war and some found loved ones they thought had been killed. Pastor Alain Arnoux hosted a service bringing together Christians and Jews under one roof worshiping the one God who saved them.

When her name was called, Marie Brottes, with her snow-white hair showing out from under her flowered kerchief, walked across the platform wondering what she'd ever done to deserve recognition. Henri Heritier remembered the day Pierre Sauvage was born and was grateful Pierre cared enough to come back to this place of mixed memories.

After the ceremony, as the returned refugees reminisced and the villagers stood holding their belated awards, one man summed up the spirit of the Chambonnais: "We didn't protect the Jews because we were moral or heroic people. We helped them because it was the human thing to do."[131]

Let us always strive to do the right thing. Let us share our dream. Let us never forget the good.

Robert Penn Warren Shares the Dream

At his death, Robert Penn Warren was hailed as "the most distinguished American writer of the last forty years." A native of Kentucky, he came from a very simple home, but it was one where potential could thrive. His father read to the family almost every night. Warren recalled, "After supper, he made us sit in a little circle, and he'd read to us—Roman history, Greek history, poems, things like that."

Warren's father had really wanted to be a poet, but he was discouraged by those who felt he couldn't make a living writing verses so he went on to become a banker. Warren once said he felt as if he'd "stolen my father's life."

"Once, when I was around twelve, I found a red book in the house. *Poets of America*, it was called. I opened it and found his picture—it had been taken years earlier—with four or five of his poems. I showed it to him with great pleasure . . . but he took it away from me without a word, and I never saw it again. I think he destroyed it. It was a reminder that he had failed at what he really wanted to do." Although Warren's father felt his own personal dream had died, he was willing to help develop his son's inborn talents by reading to him and providing a breeding place for creativity. He was willing to share his dream.

Warren went on to become a three-time Pulitzer Prize winner and the poet laureate of the United States in 1986. He was also the author of ten novels, fourteen volumes of poetry, a volume of short stories, a play, and many other works. He lived out his father's dream, but beyond publishing his works for us to read and enjoy, he spent much of his adult time encouraging other aspiring writers. He was known as "a good friend to writers—constantly generous and giving." Robert Penn Warren not only wore his dream, he shared his dream with the entire world. He has multiplied his talents.

As my father encouraged Ron, Jim, and me to study, read, improve our vocabulary, speak clearly, and share our gifts with others, we all have dedicated ourselves to sharing our dreams that we might not have passed this way in vain. For the ten years I have spent in training potential writers and speakers, my reward has not been a financial one but a feeling of satisfaction in sharing what I have learned with those who want to know and grow. I've taken what I experienced the hard way and given it to others to save them time and prevent them from making some of my mistakes.

Every time I get a request to write the forward for a book written by a CLASS graduate, I agree. These books are my literary grandchildren. I want to continue to encourage others and do as it says in Romans 12:8, "Whoever shares with others should do it generously" (TEV).

Perhaps someday, perhaps after I'm gone, these books will multiply and I'll have literary great-grandchildren.

Terri Shares the Dream

Terri had dared to dream that she could grow up, get married, have children, and live happily ever after. Much of her life went as she had hoped until that day when she received a call to say that her husband who had been riding his motorcycle on the freeway had been in an accident and was crushed under a semi-truck. Her prayer was, "Let him live, Lord, let him live." And he did live, but she no longer has the happy husband she dreamed of. Rather, she takes care of a husband who is a quadrapelegic and needs constant attention.

As Terri worked to repair her dream, she came to CLASS to find ways to share what she had learned with others. She wrote me later:

> I had let a number of obstacles discourage me from believing that God was interested in using me and my story to help someone else. To make a long story short, your message convicted me into action and I did the only thing I knew to do. I wrote an article, "Coping When I Couldn't" and sent it into *Today's Christian Woman.* They accepted it!
>
> I sincerely feel God used you and your message at CLASS to motivate me and minister to me so I would move out, take some risks and be ready for what God has for me to do in the future— ready for the Call, that is. Thank you for plugging away so faithfully for the sake of so many of us out there who for some reason have felt disqualified.

Terri has continued to write and she has a book underway—another literary grandchild for me.

Vince Shares the Dream

When Fred, Marita, and I arrived at the Charlotte Airport to speak at the coliseum for Free Enterprise Weekend, we were met by Vince and Beth. They escorted us to our hotel in a chaufferued limousine and established us in a lavish suite of rooms. They were our guides for the weekend and we became well acquainted. They were dressed attractively and conservatively and appeared to be a typical business couple. They stayed at my side as I waited backstage to speak to twenty-four thousand people at the coliseum, and then drove me to address the overflow crowd of seven thousand in another arena.

During these exciting times, Vince and Beth were supportive and faithful and on the third day Beth asked me if I'd be interested in hearing Vince's life story. Since I am always eager to gather new examples, I took them both to my suite and asked Vince to share his life with me. As I listened to this successful businessman in his three-piece suit with his well-styled hair graying at the temples, I couldn't believe what I heard.

Vince grew up in Utah in what we would call today a dysfunctional family. His father was an angry alcoholic and his mother a legalistic religious fanatic who kept Vince in church singing hymns and praising the Lord. Because his father was abusive and ridiculed Vince, the boy sided with his mother. His father thought he reported to his mother each time he took a drink, but that wasn't so. She always knew. His father nicknamed him "Snitch" and made fun of him in front of his friends. Vince was ashamed to bring his buddies home and he hid alone in his bedroom to protect himself from his father's rage.

Vince always dreaded Christmas, and while his friends got excited over the holidays, he was in fear of what his father would do to ruin the season. Vince wanted a normal Christmas so badly that he would save up his allowance to buy Christmas lights and decorate their tiny house the best he could. One year his father went on a rampage, grabbed the tree Vince had trimmed, and heaved it out the window. If he cried, his father would rave at him and call him a sissy, so Vince learned to stuff his feelings inside and try not to get hurt.

Once when his father was drunk, he was punching the windows out with his fist. He cut his finger in the process and bled all over Vince's library books. Vince was too ashamed to tell his schoolteacher the truth, so he took the blame himself and worked hard to pay for the damaged books.

Vince became a loner with repressed emotions and a pattern of deception, then tried suicide by cutting his wrists. He was terrified of his father and tired of his mother's air of saintly martyrdom. At seventeen he rebelled against the whole sick scene, dropped out of high school, and married his friend, Beth, who came from an equally dysfunctional background. Neither one knew how to love or nurture the other, and Vince was so desperate for someone to accept him that he joined a motorcycle gang who welcomed him and even seemed to respect him. Up to that point Vince had no goals in life, but as he observed the hierarchy of the gang he desired to be like the toughest of them all. No one had ever motivated him to look ahead, but this group offered excitement and brotherhood. They became his family. Desiring a new challenge, Vince states, "My dream was to become a Hell's Angel."

In order to fit into his new family, he began to smoke pot and use drugs, even though he was morally against drugs and had spoken out against them while in high school. Vince became a trucker because he liked the feeling of being free from any restrictions or hourly requirements. As he met with fellow truckers they introduced him to "speed," a drug that increased alertness and extended the number of hours the truckers could drive. Vince says, "I found when I took speed I could get six hours of sleep in just two. When I got tired I'd pull over, pop some speed into my mouth and go to sleep. As it would get through my system I'd wake up and be ready to go."

One night in California, Vince and thirteen members of his club got high while partying at another gang's clubhouse. For Vince, the evening is a drug-crazed blur. He was asleep in his tent in the yard, and when he

woke up there was a .45 caliber pistol is his face. A police officer informed him he was under arrest. Vince spent the summer in jail awaiting trial. He was charged with fifteen felony counts, and was facing a
sentence of twenty-one years to life in prison. He was in jail with several
Hell's Angels, and soon the dream to be like them wore thin. "Life in
jail was miserable and I saw my heroes ending up dead or in prison for
life. I didn't like the odds and decided if I ever got out I'd go straight."

Vince was acquitted for lack of evidence, but it was not so easy to
change his lifestyle. He began dealing in drugs and fencing merchandise
that he trained young boys to steal for him. By the time he was caught,
he was accused of even more felonies. This time he was convicted and
sentenced to jail. By this time, he and Beth had already started a family. This was the environment they were raising their two boys in.

During this time his mother kept praying for him and her church
prayer chain was constantly active. One night his mother woke up,
sensing Vince was in trouble. As she prayed, God laid on her heart,
"Don't worry, he's in training for leadership."

In jail Vince plotted how he could escape, and he pictured himself
as a hero somehow getting killed in a blaze of glory. After a long incar-
ceration, Vince was paroled early and wondered what to do with the
rest of his life. He knew his record didn't fit him for any normal career
and yet he knew a return to crime and drugs would ultimately put him
in prison for life. With his long hair, outlaw outfits, and no marketable
skills, he seemed doomed to repeat his past mistakes. He hesitated to
apply for jobs assuming he'd be rejected. One day a friend suggested
Vince go with him to an Amway business meeting, where he was amazed
that people seemed to accept him as he was. On Sunday morning he
went to the worship service and heard that God loved him and would
forgive him. Vince didn't believe this and felt he was too bad and dirty
for God to care about him. While at the convention he bought a tape
of Sammy Hall, a rock and roll singer who had been on drugs and had
an amazing testimony of how the Lord Jesus had transformed him. Vince
thought he might be able to relate to Sammy since they both had lived
in similar circumstances.

Driving down the highway in his semi, Vince turned on Sammy's
tape and listened to him tell what a wasted life he'd had. Then Sammy
sang "Amazing Grace." When it got to the line "to save a wretch like
me" Vince was overwhelmed. In tears he called out, as if on his CB,
"Lord, if You're speaking to me, come in." He knew the Lord was
speaking to him and he could hardly drive any longer. He got emotional
and had to pull his truck over to the side of the road under a bridge. As

he got out, he remembered the altar calls of his youth. He thought, "If I'm going to give my life to the Lord, I'll have to kneel."

Vince knelt down beside his truck in the roadside gravel and prayed. Feelings of guilt, shame, unworthiness, and repentence swept over him as he asked the Lord Jesus to take him in and change him. When Vince went home and told Beth what had happened, she responded that she had dedicated her life to the Lord that weekend at the Amway convention, but had not dared to tell him. As new believers in the power of the Lord, they both started attending a church. Vince expressed to me, "That fall I went forward in church four times. I wanted to make sure I really got it!"

He and Beth also began going to the local Amway meetings. An Amway distributor named Don later told me, "When I first saw the two of them in their biker outfits at our meetings and Vince with his long hair and beard, I must confess I didn't think there was any hope for either of them. They'd raised their two sons on their backs on motorcycles and they lived in an old trailer. I was sure I was wasting my time working with them, but I felt led to do it any way."

As he showed them how they could pull their lives together and make some money in a legitimate way, they agreed to try. With low expectations he taught them and encouraged them and he was stunned the night Vince walked in with his hair cut and his beard shaved off. "I didn't know who it was at first," he told me later. "He looked like a totally different person."

Shortly thereafter, Vince brought him a brown paper bag and handed it to him. Inside were all his drugs and paraphernalia. He showed the contents to his business leaders later that evening, and Vince explained that handing this over was his way of making a commitment to the Lord and putting an end to his old life. The group was shocked and emotionally touched by Vince's demonstration of his new dedication to the Lord.

The man who had introduced Vince to the business slipped out of the meeting and returned shortly with a brown bag of his own. He gave it to Don and mentioned how he had more things at home that he was ashamed of. They went to his house and he showed them his collection of satanic albums. Don suggested he get rid of them and Vince listened as his friend explained that these records cost too much to throw out even though he knew they were bad to have around. Don asked him how much the whole collection was worth and he bought them for the asking price and took them to the trash.

The next day another man in the group brought Don a brown bag full of drugs, the third bag in one weekend. Soon Vince found himself encouraging others to give up whatever was keeping them from living a successful life. Vince worked hard at building his networking business, and as his life changed, others in the business asked him to share his story for their group. At first he didn't think he had a story, but as he told what happened to him people were touched. He would show pictures of Beth and him in their outlaw outfits and he always used a brown bag as a visual aid. After his talk people would present him with their own brown bag. Some left them on his doorstep and once he went to his car and found a big box full of brown bags sitting on his hood. Soon Vince, called "Snitch" as a boy, was known as the "Brown Bag Man."

One day a young man came to Vince after a meeting. He was both a junkie and an alcoholic and he wanted Vince to help him turn his life around. He had no job and no money and the tiny house he lived in had no heat. He owed everyone he knew and he looked as hopeless as Vince had three years before. Vince was willing to help him if he'd give him the check-book, get a job, and live on five dollars a week spending money. Vince made up a budget and had the bank set up an account with two signatures required on each check. As Vince worked with this man day by day, he could see what he'd been like himself and how irresponsible and immature he'd been.

As Vince concluded his story, he added, "I can hardly believe what has happened to me and how the Lord is using a person like me to change others. My mother's prayers came true. I was in training for leadership."

Vince grew up in a family with no dreams but with a praying mother. As a boy he saw no future until he got into the motorcycle club. He dared to dream that he could be a Hell's Angel. Slight of stature and inexperienced in the ways of the world, he toughened himself up and prepared to live the excitingly dangerous life of an outlaw biker. After several terms in jail he knew his dream was not wearing well and he set out to repair his dream. He prayed for help, turned in his drugs, and got down to serious business. Today he has a large home in Utah, has bought a home for his parents, and is sharing the results of his new dream with others helping them to turn in their own brown bags. His father and his two sons, because of his example, now have a relationship of their own with the Lord.

As Vince grew up he had a mother who loved him and prayed for him but a father who gave him converse signals.

In a recent newspaper article, a columnist asked the question, why have so many youngsters not learned the values espoused by their elders? His answer, "They haven't been taught."

"They haven't been taught by the institutions (home, school, and church) traditionally responsible for direct ethical instruction. And they haven't been taught by the example of their elders. Yet much of our talk about values consists of exhortations to our children to 'return' to where they've never been."[132]

To see a dream come to fruition takes dedication, determination, and hard work. If our children haven't learned these values, their ability to dream is warped. Michael Josephson, president founder of the Josephson Institute of Ethics located in Marina del Rey, California, labels a large segment of the young adult population as the "I-Deserve-Its," or "IDIs."

The columnist continues: "We have to set good examples. No amount of talking about honest and decent behavior will suffice when our children see us subordinating integrity to expediency, cutting ethical corners, or cheating on our taxes or on our spouses.

It's not enough to mourn the good old days, when neighborhoods were safe and when people cared about their neighbors. We have to do what we can to restore the values of the good old days, or the days ahead will be worse than anything we can now imagine.[133]

To teach our children to dream, we must give them a moral and spiritual foundation on which to build their dreams. We must practice what we preach.

Louise Shares the Dream

There are some people who are still holding to old-fashioned values and sharing them with others.

After speaking at a Christmas banquet in Spartanburg, South Carolina, Fred and I were invited to the home of a woman named Louise "to see her house." We didn't know what was so special about it, but we were willing to go even though it was late in the evening. We arrived at what appeared to be a one-story ranch-style brick home with a breezeway and garage. The outside was framed in Christmas lights and we could see a big Santa in an old sleigh in the breezeway. As we entered the foyer we faced a large sparkling Christmas tree and a circular staircase banked with poinsettias. The initial view was overwhelming, but only a taste of what was to come. The dining room table was set with Christmas mats and pewter plates ready for a company dinner at any time. The kitchen had bubbling hot cider in Christmas mugs and trays of special cookies. On the counter was a collection of about fifty cheese graters, each one with a candle inside shedding light out through the little holes. Each room had a totally different theme and its own

Christmas tree decorated to fit its own space. The laundry room tree had ornaments of clip clothes pins, tiny sockstretchers, and miniature flatirons. The breezeway had Santa plus a huge tree and a hidden door heading into Santa's workshop, complete with animated elves in the rafters and at the workbench. Louise and her husband are in the lumber business, and their forty-two grandchildren love to come to the secret shop where "Bebop" has a wooden barrel full of all kinds of wood scraps. The children can choose their own pieces of wood, take any size hammer they want from the selection at hand, grab any kind of nail from open cans, and make themselves anything they want to build. Examples of past masterpieces are nailed to the wall as eternal memories of childhood creativity. I could hardly resist picking up a hammer and getting to work.

In the basement was a childhood heaven, a huge gingerbread house covered with candy glued to the walls. Lifesavers, lollipops, and candy canes were available in baskets everywhere and one room was designated as the Candy Room. In the center of the basement family room was a large rug with a Santa Claus in the middle.

The fireplace was long enough to hang all sixty stockings, each one differently decorated to represent the individual's personality and preferences. It was right out of a picture book—"The stockings were hung by the chimney with care."

By the time we emerged from the lower level I thought I'd seen more Christmas trees than I knew existed, but Grandma Louise said, "You haven't seen the upstairs yet." So up we went, stepping around the poinsettias, passing the gold-framed portraits of the eight family brides, and entering another floor of Christmas fantasy.

The largest room was the "bridal suite" with a huge canopied bed and sitting area with its own white Christmas tree trimmed with red velvet bows. The room has been prepared for the family brides and will no doubt be used in the future as forty-two grandchildren walk the aisle and come back to the homestead for their wedding night.

"Memaw" took us to the wrapping room which outdid Neiman-Marcus. Not only was there a wrapping counter equipped with scissors, tape, tags, bows, and stickers, but on one whole wall rolls of Christmas wrapping paper were ready to be used. Everyone in the family and many friends besides knew that the wrapping room was always open for their use. Even at Christmas there were some rolls of birthday paper available, and with each season the supply of paper changed. For those of us who can never find paper for an emergency birthday gift or if we find the paper we have no tape, this room would be heaven on earth. It would be worth driving across town to have the security of knowing that everything you needed to prepare a designer package would be at your fingertips. Just seeing this room inspired me to go home and organize the rolls of paper I have standing dusty in a corner of the garage.

At the far end of the hall was a long room under the rafters called the storage room. In there were all the empty boxes from the Christmas decorations and shelves of carefully marked boxes for Valentine's Day, Easter, Halloween, and Thanksgiving. Wreaths for every season were wrapped in plastic and hanging on one wall and a clothes rack with all kinds of costumes stood next to shelves full of wigs, hats, and masks. Whatever kind of party you had to attend, you could come to "Memaw's" and find a fitting costume.

As we went back to the family room, I noticed the train track that went completely around the room high over our heads. Each of the large open cars was filled with Santas, elves, toys, dolls, and presents. As I watched wide-eyed at the moving trains, one daughter told me that even the trains changed with the seasons. At Easter the cars are filled with bunnies and at Thanksgiving with pumpkins and harvest flowers.

When we finally left after two hours of museum viewing, Louise reached into a Christmas basket and pulled out two pre-wrapped gifts for Fred and me. We learned she gave a present to each guest who came through the house at Christmas and that she opened her home for every type of group from her church or social organizations that wanted to have an unforgettable Christmas experience. As I left with my present, Louise gave me a fluffy angel doll with a halo and said, "Put it by your tree and remember that we wish you a blessed Christmas."

I will remember Louise and her unbelievable home. I will remember a woman who cares enough to spend a month decorating her home for Christmas for the benefit of others, a woman who makes available wrappings and costumes for those who don't have them, a woman who gives gifts to those who have already accepted her hospitality, a woman who is willing to spend the time and effort it takes to share her dream with others.

I can't buy a big house like Louise's or find a spot for costumes and a wrapping room, but I can think ahead of how I can share my holidays with others. I'm grateful as I raised my children that I did have different placemats, centerpieces, and napkin rings for each holiday and that I kept them in labeled boxes for the children to pull out each season and that I encouraged celebrations for every possible occasion—including Ground Hog Day.

Probably few of us could begin to compete with Grandma Louise, but we can see the value of sharing with others whatever we do have, of making holidays memorable even if we live alone, of putting up a wreath or a tiny tree, of giving out an Easter basket to a shut-in, of sending a Valentine to a friend. We may never get so much as a postcard in return, but it doesn't matter. Of the hundreds of people that will pass through Louise's home at Christmas, few will write thank-you notes, although they should, and fewer will bring gifts. Some will drop a dish or break a figurine, but "Memaw" won't be upset. She'll just stand at the door looking like Mrs. Santa Claus, smiling and hugging and lov-ing and sharing all she has with others.

Ron and I Share the Dream

A few years ago when I was speaking in Dallas, the committee asked my brother Ron to introduce me. I had no idea what he would say as he makes humor out of every situation. I assumed he'd come up with funny stories about some of my old boyfriends or about how terrible I was at sports. Everyone in the audience was expecting Ron to make them laugh and we were all surprised when he seemed serious.

He told us all that everyone at KVIL had taken personal psychologi-cal profiles. When he met with the counselor for his evaluation the man stated, "This shows that you had a very strong mother who had a consistent influence upon your life and who instilled in you moral and social values."

Ron shared with us that he told the man he must be wrong because his mother was a very low-key, passive person who never tried to control him in any way.

The counselor affirmed that all the tests showed a remarkable female influence from birth through his teen years and into his adult life.

"Could it be my sister?" Ron had asked. He then began a tribute to what I'd taught him throughout his life: speaking, writing, poetry, humor, manners, style, ambition, and excitement.

As I sat amazed at his complimentary comments, he concluded, "And so I present to you the woman who made me what I am today!"

I burst into tears at this unexpected tribute and could hardly make my way to the platform. People in the audience were touched by his sincerity and his humility and many of them had tears in their eyes.

I will never forget that introduction. Everything I'd ever done for him had been because I loved him and felt I had to protect him. I couldn't let anything happen to him. I'd enjoyed every moment of our relationship and I'd always been his number one fan and encourager. I'd never looked for thanks because it had all been so much fun, but to receive his praise and know he'd noticed was the reward of my lifetime.

I know Ron Chapman would have made it to the top if I hadn't been his sister, but I'm so grateful I've been able to share in his dream.

I hope I can also be part of your dream. I hope if you've been discouraged by living a routine existence that you'll dare to dream that there is more to life than this.

I hope that if you've been waiting for something exciting to happen to you that you'll begin to move for yourself, that you'll read and think and listen. I hope you'll prepare your dream.

I hope you'll continue to work, to keep yourself above reproach, to understand your personality, to function in your strengths, and to have a passion for your product. I hope you'll wear your dream with confidence.

I hope that you have no need to start over again, but if you've failed frequently, have an uncomfortable feeling about your identity, or have lived in a world of denial, be willing to repair your dream.

I hope that you won't hug your successes to yourself and make money a mini-god. I hope you'll be willing to give of yourself to others that they may be able to share in your dream.

Dare to dream—and may all your dreams come true!

> "If you have a dream, follow it. If you
> catch a dream, nurture it.
> And if your dream comes
> true . . . celebrate it!

NOTES

1. *People*, 2 May 1988.

2. *D*, December 1989.

3. Neil Lawrence and Steven Bunk, *Stumpjumpers* (Hale & Iremonger Pty., Ltd, 1985)

4. Arthur Willliam Edgar O'Shaughnessy, "Ode."

5. *Parade*, 23 December 1990, pp. 20–22.

6. *New Zealand Herald*, 29 September 1990.

7. Ibid.

8. Ibid.

9. Ibid.

10. Oswald Chambers, *My Utmost for His Highest* (New York: Dodd, Mead & Co., 1979), p. 347

11. John Leo and Elizabeth Taylor, "Exploring the Traits of Twins," *Time*, 12 January 1987.

12. Melvin Konner, "Who Am I?" *Omni*, January 1990.

13. *My Utmost for His Highest*, p. 347

14. *Omni*, January 1990, p. 64

15. *New York Times*, 7 May 1990.

16. *Options*, October 1990.

17. *New Yorker*, 7 May 1990.

18. *USA Today*, 15 March 1990.

19. *Los Angeles Times*, 28 August 1987.

20. Ibid.

21. Steven H. Wildstrom, "Decoding the Life of Spymaster Casey," *Business Week*, 22 October 1990.

22. Steven Kanfer, "The Man Who Mumbled," *Time*, 5 November 1990.

23. *Los Angeles Times*, 28 August 1987.

24. *Time*, 1 October 1990.

25. Ibid.

26. "The Corporate Bully," *Golden Wing*, June 1989.

27. *Time*, 10 September 1990.

28. *Newsweek*, 25 September 1989.

29. Ibid.

30. *New York Times*, 9 September 1990.

31. Ibid.

32. Eric Felten, "Too Early for Judgment on Souter," *Insight*, 13 August 1990.

33. *USA Today*, 9 September 1990.

34. *New York Times*, 9 September 1990.

35. *USA Today*, 9 September 1990.

36. "Our Loss, Her Dream," *Life*, December 1989.

37. Ibid.
38. *Psychology Today*, December 1988.
39. *Psychology Today*, May 1988.
40. Ibid.
41. *USA Today*, 5 December 1990.
42. Ibid.
43. *My Utmost for His Highest.*
44. Dr. Seuss, *Green Eggs and Ham* (New York: Beginner Books, 1960).
45. Tom Peters, *Thriving on Chaos* (New York: Harper & Row, 1988), pp. 120, 172.
46. *Powerline*, Winter 1987.
47. *Fortune*, 9 October 1989, p. 79.
48. *Entreprenuer*, October 1989, p. 20.
49. Perry W. Buffington, "What a Bore!" *Sky*, January 1990.
50. *Churchill: His Wit and Wisdom*, p. 47.
51. Alexandra Long, "Page Proof," *Vogue Australia*, August 1989, p. 48.
52. Richard Lederer, *Crazy English* (New York: Simon & Schuster, 1989).
53. *America West*, January 1990.
54. *Orange County Register*, 22 October 1990.
55. Ibid
56. *Fort Worth Star Telegram*, 17 May 1989.
57. *Dallas Times-Herald*, 16 April 1989.
58. Ibid.
59. *Fort Worth Star Telegram*, 17 May 1989.
60. Ibid
61. Ibid
62. *Dallas Morning News*, 4 May 1986.
63. Ibid
64. Ibid
65. *Dallas Morning News*, 5 February 1989.
66. *D*, December 1989.
67. *Dallas Times-Herald*, 16 April 1989.
68. *D*, December 1989.
69. *Dallas Morning News*, 4 May 1986.
70. *Houston Chronicle*, 15 April 1988.
71. Gretchen Morgenson, "Are You a Born Sucker?" *Forbes*, 27 June 1988.
72. *Baptist Message*, 12 January 1989.
73. *Dallas Morning News*, 5 February 1989.
74. *Dallas Times-Herald*, 16 April 1989.
75. Ibid.
76. *D*, December 1989.
77. *USA Today*, 29 November 1990.
78. Ibid.
79. *Time*, 16 January 1989.
80. *Options*, October 1990.

81. *Vanity Fair*, August 1989.

82. William Manchester, *The Last Lion*.

83. Florence Littauer, *Personalities in Power*.

84. *Newsweek*, 25 September 1989.

85. From *Time*, 9 November 1989, and *Wall Street Journal*, 29 September 1989.

86. From *Insight*, 8 October 1990, and *Newsweek*, 21 August 1989.

87. From *Newsweek*, 31 August 1989; *Time*, 11 September 1989; and *National Enquirer*, 25 October 1989.

88. *Personalities in Power*.

89. *Redbook*, January 1991.

90. *Newsweek*, 25 September 1989.

91. Cathleen McGuigan, "The Perfectionist," *Newsweek*, 25 September 1989, p. 63.

92. Richard Zoglin, "Let's Get Busy!!" *Time*, 13 November 1989, p. 92.

93. Ibid.

94. Review of *An American Life* (*Time*, 5 November 1990).

95. Ibid.

96. *Time*, 3 December 1990.

97. *New York Times*, 28 November 1990.

98. *Time*, 3 December 1990.

99. Review of *Trudeau and Our Times: The Magnificient Obsession*, (*South China Morning Post*, 10 November 1990.

100. Ibid.

101. *The Australian*, 9 November 1990.

102. *Time*, 12 November 1990.

103. *The Greenville News*, 2 December 1990.

104. *Los Angeles Times*, 22 November 1990.

105. Ibid.

106. *Dallas Morning News*, 4 May 1986.

107. Ibid.

108. Robert Forst, "The Road Not Taken," 1916.

109. Ann Trebbe, "Oprah: Weight Gain No Failure," *People*, 7 January 1991.

110. John Schwartz, Dody Tsiantar, Karen Springen, "Escape from the Office," *Newsweek*, 24 April 1989.

111. Jimmy and Rosalyn Carter, *Everything to Gain*, (New York: Random House, 1987).

112. *Newsweek*, 8 May 1989.

113. Daniel L. Brick, M.D. "Matching Dreams to Reality," *Marriage Partnership*, Spring 1988, pp.81-2.

114. Ibid.

115. Patti Jones, "Always Look on the Light Side," *Redbook*, January 1991.

116. Ibid.

117 Norman Cousins, "Proving the Power of Laughter," *Psychology Today*, October 1989.

118. *Dallas Times Herald*

119. Stuart Warner, "That's a Tough Act to Follow, Brother," *Akron Beacon Journal*, 22 April 1988.

120. *D*, December 1989.

121. Alan W. Petrucelli, "Dolly's Spiritual Side: Believe in Your Dreams," *Redbook*, January 1991.

122. Ibid.

123. *USA Today*, 4 Decembver 1990.

124. Ibid.

125. *American Way*, 15 November 1990.

126. Ibid

127. Ibid

128. Ibid

129. Alexandra Tuttle, "Making a Blessed Connspiracy, *Time*, 5 November 1990.

130. Ibid

131. Ibid

132. *Chicago Tribune*, 15 November 1990.

RECOMMENDED RESOURCE ORDER FORM

NUMBER ORDERED		$	TOTAL
_____	1. *Your Personality Tree*, Florence Littauer, Word Books	9.00	_____
_____	2. *Hope for Hurting Women*, Florence Littauer, Word Books	9.00	
_____	3. *Raising Christians—Not Just Children,* Florence Littauer, Word Books	9.00	_____
_____	4. *Silver Boxes: the Gift of Encouragement,* Florence Littauer, Word Books	13.00	_____
_____	5. *Make the Tough Times Count:* *How to Rise Above Adveristy,* Florence Littauer, Here's Life Publishers	9.00	_____
_____	6. *Freeing Your Mind from Memories that Bind,* Fred and Florence Littauer, Here's Life Publishers	9.00	_____
_____	6. *The Promise of Restoration,* Fred Littauer, Here's Life Publishers	9.00	_____

Shipping & Handling (Please add $2.00 per book) _____

Sub Total _____

Calif. Residents Please Add 7% Sales Tax _____

Total Amount Enclosed _____
(Check or Money Order)

Charge: Master Card/Visa # _____

Name on Card _____ Exp. Date _____

Make Checks Payable and Mail to:

> Class Book Service
> 1645 S. Ranch Sante Fe Road #102
> San Marcos, CA 92069
> 1-800-433-6633